Zhang Yingli

MY IMPRESSION OF CHINA

– China's Image in the Eyes of Foreign Officers

Translated by Wang Fangfang etc.

CHINA
INTERCONTINENTAL
PRESS

图书在版编目（CIP）数据

我的中国印象——外国军官看中国（英语篇）：英文/ 张英利主编；王方芳等译．—北京：五洲传播出版社，2011.1（外国人看中国）

ISBN 978-7-5085-1974-6

I．①我 ... II．①张 ...②王 ... III．①中国－概况－文集－英文

IV．①K92-53

中国版本图书馆CIP数据核字(2010)第 197203 号

主　　编/张英利
副 主 编/贺从念　徐　辉
编　　译/陈　锐　王方芳　韩晓峰　檀生兰
　　　　　王　斌　沈志雄　康建武

我的中国印象
——外国军官看中国（英语篇）

编　　著/张英利
配　　图/陈　锐　李业茂
责任编辑/高　磊
设计制作/张　红
出版发行/五洲传播出版社
　　　　　（北京市海淀区北三环中路31号生产力大楼B座7层）
电　　话/8610-82005927　82007837（发行部）
网　　址/www.cicc.org.cn
承 印 者/北京外文印务有限公司
版　　次/ 2011年1月第1版第1次印刷
开　　本/ 787mm×1092mm　1/16
印　　张/ 17
字　　数/ 100千
印　　数/ 1-3500册
定　　价/ 78.00元

Contents

Forward   1

Harmounious China and Harmonious World   3

Building Harmonious Society in China: Challenges and Countermeasures   4
Is Modernized Chinese Military a Threat to International Peace and
    Stability?   14
China's Harmonious Society: Towards a Sustainable Social and Economic
    Development   25
China in Lebanese Eyes: Excellent Model of Development, Promoting a
    "Harmonious World"   32
Understanding PRC's Status on Rights, Freedoms and Civil Liberties   46
Harmonious China: Its Challenges and the Way Forward   56
The Building of the Law System in China   66
China's One-Child Policy: Impact of Demographic Changes and Future
    Imperatives   77
Towards a Peaceful Resolution of the Taiwan Question   88

China's Reform and Opening-up & Social and Economic Development   97

China's Critical Path to Success in 60 Years   98
China's Reform and Opening-up Policy towards a Sustainable Economic
    Development   106
The "Middle Kingdom" has Waded Across the River: The Reform and
    Opening-up Policy in Perspective   114
Understanding China's Theory and Practice of Reform and Opening-up   130
Achievements and Challenges of China's Reform and Opening-up   139
Perception Management—a New Challenge for China   147
The Problems Facing China Today and Tomorrow   158
Challenges Facing China in Her Economic Development   164

Foreign Policy of the People's Republic of China   171

China's Foreign Policy—Successes and Challenges   172
China's Foreign Policy Featuring Peace, Development and Cooperation   183
View on China's Foreign Policy   192
China's Foreign Policy Featuring Harmony   200
Understanding of China's Independent Foreign Policy of Peace   206
China's Rise as Soft Power and Challenges   215
The Role of the Chinese Media in China's Foreign Policy   229

Life in China   237

Culture of China   238
China Knew and China Seen: An Overview   247
How is the Chinese Culture Seen in Some Latin American Countries?   259

Forward

As a country with an ancient civilization of five thousand years, China has experienced numerous frustrations, ups and downs amid its development. Today the world has moved into a new era featuring the rapid development of science, technology and globalization. Under the leadership of Communist Party of China, through six decades of hardworking and three decades of reform and opening-up, China has achieved tremendous success, which is attracting growing worldwide attention. People of different cultures, colors and countries all wish to get a deep insight into China, a country rich in appeal, attraction and power to influence. This book, from the unique perspective of foreign officers, aims to open the third eye to watch China.

Writers of the articles of the book are all foreign officers from twenty countries in Asia, Africa, South America and Oceania. They had gained some knowledge of China through various channels and media before their arrival here, which, however, might not be accurate and objective. During their one-year stay in China, besides classroom study, they also had extensive and profound exchanges with Chinese governmental officials, experts and scholars. They went to other regions at different levels of development for visit and investigation. Such experiences of extensive and close contacts with Chinese society enabled them to develop more comprehensive, systematic and deeper understanding of China. So it's fair to say that their perspectives are different not only from foreign media but also from those foreign people who have had a short stay in China. And as senior officers, they have both theoretical attainments and more in-depth, rational reflections with regard to issues such as social development and national security, which enrich the book with unique value of reference.

The book comprises four parts, viz. Harmonious China and Harmonious World, China's Reform & Opening-up and Social and

Economic Development, China's Foreign Policy and Life in China, describing from different perspectives, and in a true and comprehensive way, various aspects of Chinese society such as the politics, economy, culture and life. Writers of the twenty-seven articles are all senior foreign officers attending the Defense and Strategic Studies Course (English) 2009-2010 at the College of Defense Studies, National Defense University. Most of them talked about their understanding of and reflections on China's development, not only expressing their sincere compliments to the rapid development of China but also analyzing the problems China is facing or will face, putting forth many pertinent and valuable suggestions. All these are of high reference value not only to foreigners to understand China, but also to domestic readers to correctly view the development of China. Anyway, since those officers have stayed in China for a limited period and in economically developed regions, they did not get a thorough understanding of the relatively backward parts of China. And for many friends it was their first time to come to China, so it is natural that there exist some limitations in their views which thereby require a dialectical approach from the readers.

Due to the inadequate level of the editors the book is liable to some inaccurate expressions or translations. Valuable opinions from the readers will be warmly welcomed and highly appreciated.

Once again I'd like to express my heartfelt gratitude and pay high tribute to every foreign officer, relevant staffs and units for making unremitting efforts to the publication of the book.

Major General Zhang Yingli,
Commandant of CDS, NDU
November 2010, Beijing

1 Harmounious China and Harmonious World

Building Harmonious Society in China: Challenges and Countermeasures

Sundar Pudasaini
Brig. Gen., Nepalese Army

Introduction

China, now, has been perceived as a major power on the basis of its global economic and increasing political importance. It is even considered as an emerging superpower. China plans to quadruple national economic output again between 2000 and 2020. In almost 31 years since the reform and opening up policy was implemented, China has seen tremendous changes in both the economic system and social structure. However, in such a large territory with such a big population, along with the great achievements made in a short period of time unavoidably trigger some problems that ultimately hinder in the attainment of social harmony. These include the growing income disparity (between rich and poor, city and countryside, and coastal and inland regions), the urban and rural development imbalance, environmental degradation and inadequate social guarantees. These enormous domestic problems represent a danger to stability in China, and have international repercussions too, in the form of transnational pollution and climate change.

Former president Jiang Zemin's generation of leaders concentrated on binding the new business elite to the party (knowingly accepting the resulting income disparities), whereas the new leadership under Hu Jintao, who took over the power in Nov. 2002, initiated a turn to social partnership and a fairer distribution of resources. This policy shift was accompanied by the preparation of two new concepts that together basically outline the Chinese version of sustainability. In Oct. 2004, at the fourth Plenum of the Central Committee elected by the Sixteenth

Party Congress the "Scientific Development Concept" and "Harmonious (socialist) Society" concepts were adopted as the official slogans of China's modified course. The "Harmonious Society" stands in the first place for improved provision of education, health care etc and greater social justice in general, and for sustainable economic growth taking environmental costs in to account. In other words, it is a sustainability strategy concentrating on reducing social inequality and environmental harm. President and party leader Hu Jintao outlined the aims of the concept in Feb. 2005: "democracy and rule of law, fairness and justice, trust and comradeship, vitality, stability and order, and harmonious coexistence of man and nature." In all these respects people should come first. At the Seventeenth Congress of the Chinese Communist Party in Oct. 2007, Hu Jintao's "Scientific Development Concept" which includes the "Harmonious Society" was adopted as part of the Constitution of the Communist Party of China and as such entered its official ideological canon.

Ideological Bases of Concept of Harmonious Society

The concept of harmonious society had been the part of ideology in Marxism theories, Mao Zedong's thoughts, Deng Xiaoping theories and Confucius philosophy, which is briefly explained in the following sub-headings.

(a) **Theories of Marxism.** The dimension of values: both Marx and Engels stressed that the supreme values of human development is the freedom and comprehensive development of the human beings. In order to realize such ideal values, the human society should develop in this direction and the society should be the association of free men, "the free development of each individual is the condition of free development of all the people." In such society, the human beings can be liberated from various confrontations and conflicts of the nature and society. So we can draw the inference that the solution of basic social contradiction and confrontation and the promotion of free and comprehensive development of human beings mean the harmonious development of the human beings.

(b) **Mao Zedong's Thoughts.** Many Chinese researchers believe, there is no concept of harmonious society in Mao Zedong Thought, but there is basic meaning of "harmonious society" in it. The fundamental aim of the Mao's theory of correctly dealing with the internal contradictions is to realize the harmony among various social strata within the society. In the field of ethnic relations, he directed the "regional autonomy of ethnic minorities" system, and tried to establish a kind of equal, harmonious and united relations among various ethnic groups.

(c) **Deng Xiaoping Theories.** Deng's contribution to the formation of the concept of harmonious society should not be neglected. In 1986, Deng said: "the basic principles of socialism are two: one is economic development; another one is common prosperity. We allow some people and some regions to get rich first, the fundamental aim is to realize common prosperity as soon as possible." In 1990, Deng said: "Common prosperity which we had talked about since the beginning of reform and opening up will definitely become central topic one day." "The polarization will cause the conflicts among different ethnic groups, regions, social strata, and even the conflicts between the central government and local governments, the country will go into trouble." In 1992, Deng made a complete explanation of the nature of socialism: "both planning and market are the means of economic development. The nature of socialism is to liberate and develop productive force, abolish exploitation and polarization and realize the common prosperity in the end." Soon after that, Deng believed that the issue of common prosperity in China would be put on agenda at the end of last century.

(d) **Confucius Philosophy.** Confucius ideology has dealt a lot about the importance of "Harmonious Society." Indeed the term itself is often explained and justified by one of the philosopher's sayings, namely "the gentleman values harmony with difference." This statement expresses the idea that there can be plurality and diversity of opinions without social conflict necessarily having to break out. Basically Confucius and his philosophy were criticized as the ideological superstructure that was responsible for the national humiliation of the "century of shame" during which China degenerated from one of the most powerful empires in

Participants visiting Xiaotangshan Biopark in Beijing suburb

history to a backward "semi-colonial and semi-feudal" country. During the Cultural Revolution of the mid-1960s to mid-1970s Confucianism again came under sharp attack. Only after 1980s Confucianism experience something of renaissance.

Whatever had been the position of philosophy in Chinese politics earlier, now the Communist Party attempts to get the support for its legitimacy by adopting elements of the national philosophical heritage and giving them a positive view, but without throwing the Marxist and Maoist tradition. The Chinese leadership is propagating the concept of harmony, in the sense of living together peacefully.

Problems affecting Social Harmony

Environmental Degradation

Three decades after the reforms were launched, China's one-sided focus on rapid economic growth has led to palpable structural environmental deterioration. One direct result of the dynamic economic growth is air pollution and emissions of greenhouse gases. Of the world's twenty cities with worst air pollution sixteen are in China. Almost 70 percent of China's energy needs are met by coal-burning, and is responsible for 70 percent of air pollution and 90 percent of its emissions of sulfur dioxide. Another threat to air pollution is increasing urbanization driven by massive migration and the expansion of the middle classes. Everyday about fourteen thousand new cars are registered in China, which is contributing to air pollution.

The second great problem for China's environment is the enormous waste and increasing contamination of water supplies. Seventy percent of China's rivers are polluted, and for urban water bodies the figure rises to more than ninety percent.

The third complex of environmental problem to China is desertification, soil erosion, and large-scale deforestation. More than one quarter of China's land is desert, and the area is growing at a rate of about 2,100 square kilometers annually.

Income Disparities

Coastal and Inland Provinces. Geographical location has always given China's coastal regions a comparative competitive advantage over the inland provinces. However, the central government started its opening up policy by initiating four special economy zones in the two coastal provinces of Guangdong and Fujian, and subsequently fourteen more coastal cities in nine provinces were also given this status. Provinces having this status enjoyed tax exemption, which enabled the coastal provinces to attract foreign direct investment (FDI). Experts see regional inequality is the distribution of foreign direct investment as the main reason for the coast/inland disparity. One consequence of this disparate development was that by 2006 the per capita GDP of the richest coastal region was ten times that of the poorest region in western China.

Urban/Rural Income Gap. In addition to the wealth gap between the coastal and inland regions, there is also one between urban and rural areas. In 2005 the cities nationwide were on average 3.22 times wealthier than the countryside. Not only are average incomes in the cities higher than in the countryside, but city-dwellers also enjoy a range of other rights and privileges, such as unemployment benefits, better access to health care and schooling that are denied to the rural population and the unregistered migrants who move to the cities in search of work.

Gap between Rich and Poor. The economic reforms since 1978 have massively widened the divide between rich and poor. Within a couple of decades China has gone from being one of the world's most egalitarian societies to a country marked by great inequality. Today the top 10 percent of the urban population commands 45 percent of the total urban wealth, while the bottom 10 percent owns just 2 percent. According to the Chinese Academy of Social Sciences 85 percent of Chinese citizens are devoid of basic housing facility. The Gini coefficient, used to measure social inequality, has risen from 0.31 at the beginning of the reforms (1979) to 0.496 in 2006. The share of GDP going to wages and salaries has fallen from 15 percent in the mid-1990s to 11 percent in 2006. Although wages have risen at an annual rate of about 15 percent since 1993, state revenues and the profits of state-owned and private businesses has even risen faster.

Social Security System

China's cities and countryside must still be regarded separately as far as social security is concerned, not least because the household registration system is still in force. A distinction must also be made between benefits to which the working population contributes, such as unemployment insurance and pension schemes, and assistance fully granted by the state. Social insurance schemes (pension, accident, health, unemployment, and maternity) that require an individual personal contribution are less successful even where they are actually mandatory, at least for the urban population. Therefore, social security system in China is not very effective to date and needs a lot of attention.

Corruption

It is another factor which prevents any society from being harmonious and China is also not spared by this social evil. In China, corruption cases were rampant especially during the social transition period. The procuratorial organs in China filed major corruption cases against 35,255 officials in last five year alone. Of them 13,929 officials involved were of county and above the provincial and ministerial levels.

Approaches and Counter Measures

The government can no longer ignore the health-related, economic, social and political consequences of these economic developments. In order to counter the conflicts and problems affecting the attainment of the harmonious society concept, the Government of People's Republic of China has adopted a number of approaches and counter measures as mentioned below.

(a) **Environmental Protection.** The government has integrated a response to the harmful environmental trends in the harmonious society concept, as can be seen in the following statement from the Chinese State Environmental Protection Administration (SEPA) website: "bluer skies, greener earth, purer water, cleaner air—a more harmonious relationship between people and the environment." The important lesson the government draws from the environmental crisis is the necessity to link the economic growth with sustainability factors and thus to move away from the purely expansive growth strategy. Quantitative energy saving and environmental targets were included for the first time in the 2006-2010 national five-year plan, which provides for reliance on coal to be cut from 74 to less than 60 percent, air pollution to be reduced by 10 percent by 2010, and energy efficiency to be increased by 20 percent.

Since 2007 question of environmental protection and energy have been dealt with at the highest political level in a "leadership group" of representatives of the relevant ministries and agencies chaired by Premier Wen Jiabao. Realizing the important role the NGOs can play in the field of environmental protection; by 2005 the government granted permission for the registration of 2,768 environmental NGOs in China. Still, in Jan. 2008 the State Council published a plan for cleaning up China's lakes, with the goal of completely eliminating pollution by 2030.

(b) **Regional Balance and Bridging the Gap between Rich and Poor.** The Chinese government is aware that a policy that is focused one-sidedly on macro-economic growth rates cannot guarantee social peace in the long term. On the one hand, it must ensure that the inland regions also participate in the economic boom, on the other; it must balance out social inequalities through transfer payments and by setting up a viable

Participants visiting Shanghai logistics base of China's navy

social security and health system. Since the mid-1990s the government of China has been placing increasing emphasis on developing neglected regions and rural areas. Special programs have been set up, such as "The Great Opening Of the west" and later "The Revival of North-East China" initiated under Hu Jintao's leadership. Huge railroad from central China to Tibet has been implemented under this agenda. The government adopted measures designed to reduce the social divide between city and countryside. In 2004 it resumed subsidies to agricultural production, for example for seed and agricultural machinery, and above all for grain production. The important step to date was the abolition on Jan. 1, 2006, of the agricultural tax, whose history in China goes back 2,600 years. The same year a start was also made with abolishing school fees in all rural areas and making teaching materials free of charge.

(c) **Improvement in Social Security System.** Very big country with world's largest population, of course, faces difficulties to have better social security system. Despite numerous constraints the government under President Hu Jintao seems to be determined to tackle the country's social problems and rising state revenues increasingly make it possible to fund for such social programs.

Recommendations

China has, after achieving phenomenal achievement in economic field, been striving for building a harmonious society by paying enough attentions on environment, income disparities, and regional imbalance and social security aspects. However, the following few recommendations are deemed necessary for building a real harmonious society in China.

(a) China already has relatively good laws and regulations in environment sector, but is inadequately enforced in the provinces; therefore, the implementation of these laws and regulations must be made effective.

(b) Energy generated from coal should be replaced by green energy. And the targets set in achieving energy efficiency and emission reduction must be met on time.

(c) The central government must play a greater role in counter-acting income disparities and regional imbalance in development. The government must make full use of economic leverage, such as, budget, taxation and welfare, to coordinate distribution and redistribution for the reduction of income disparity and regional imbalance.

(d) Regional development attention needs to focus on geographical, ethnic and religious factors and the issue of difference in productive force among regions.

(e) China must develop immediately policies to help bridge the gap between the rich and the poor which continue to widen.

(f) In order to uplift the living standard of 150 million people who are still under poverty line, government urgently needs to fully cover them under social security umbrella.

(g) Government must find a way to compensate the workers whose rights and interests are neglected, through not having their rights to collectively negotiate (Trade Unions) over payment, social security rights which are common in developing countries.

(h) Government of PRC has been working very hard to uproot the social evil like corruption from the country, however appropriate measures for combating corruption should still be high on government agenda.

Conclusion

By and large China is a harmonious society, however, with the rapid economic development, the environment got degraded, the gap between the rich and the poor widened along with the regional imbalances in developments, which ultimately might upset the attainment of harmony in society. Therefore, the government of President Hu Jintao, soon after taking over the office, put forward the "harmonious society concept" drawing on both the Marxist and Maoist tradition and elements of Confucian philosophy. The rehabilitation of tradition takes up popular currents in the society and co-opts them for the harmonious society project. The most urgent need to act is in the field of environment and energy (air and water pollution, deforestation), which is causing health hazards to population and climate change. A threefold social divide (rich/poor, urban/rural, coastal/inland) leads to social tensions. The urban/rural gap is the most serious, in particular because of the systematic discrimination of millions of migrant workers, where the government must pay greater attention. This very important concept of building harmonious society in China has been taking up its shape gradually and needs unremitting nationwide effort for another decade or more.

Is Modernized Chinese Military a Threat to International Peace and Stability?

Md. Zahidur Rahman

Brig. Gen., Bangladesh Army

"Chinese people are the most peace loving people in the history of mankind."—Leo Tolstoy

Introduction

China has a comprehensive concept of national security that includes not only defending its sovereignty and territorial integrity, but continuing its economic and social development and maintaining its international stature. Chinese perceptions about its national security are more diverse and complicated than ever before. Its security paradigm includes an over-dependence on foreign resources, the US's disregard for multilateralism, and China's own population's hatred for Japan and wide ranging of non-traditional security threats.

Military modernization being an important element in China's national security strategy generated western speculations on its intent and motivations, despite amplified reasons stated in the Chinese Defence Policy. Enormous amount of information is available openly to understand the motivations of China's leadership. ..."Chinese sources—namely, scholarly journals, the news media, official policy pronouncements, and personal interviews—demonstrate that Chinese intentions and motivations are not a secret." This paper is an encapsulated analysis on the justifications of Chinese military modernization efforts at the back drop of the propagated fear by the western powers.

Why does China Need to Modernize Its Military Forces?

Former Secretary Rumsfeld questioned China's military build-up as it really does not face any threats that justify its military modernization. But the Chinese perspective is very different from the West and they need to have an insight into the Chinese perception of comprehensive of national security. Western thought, descended from the ancient Greek philosophers, through rational thought, logic, and debate leads to one right answer. On the other hand, Chinese see the world in a more holistic way—an influence of Taoism, Confucianism, and Buddhism. Chinese strategic thought founded on dialecticism, does not seek one answer rather seeks more than one answer.

China is surrounded by a complex and brittle peripheral security milieu from Kashmir and Afghanistan in the west to the Korean Pninsula in the east, and then to the South China Sea and Taiwan Strait. All these are closely connected to China's ational security and "the American factor" acts as a catalyst to all these problems.

The US: The Hegemonic Threat: The core content of US global strategy since the 20th century has been to contend for and maintain its world hegemony status. The US pursuit of its unipolar strategy has become a constraint on the modern international order. Instead of the UN-centred system, the US is pursuing a new security structure with itself at its centre. Thus, the US national security doctrine threatens the international balance of power on which China's continued stability, growth, and rising international stature depends.

China Threat Theory: "China threat theory" is propagated to breed fear and mistrust about China's intentions which leads the US to enact more policies of containment and less of engagement. The report to Congress in 2005 and 2006 questioned motivations and the desired end states of Chinese military expansion. The US publicly published reports on the military power of China. Japan for the first time agreed with the US to treat the defence of Taiwan as their "common strategic objective." The US has troops stationed all over the globe with hundreds overseas military bases, while China does not have soldiers stationed overseas. The US involvement in dissuading the EU from lifting its arms embargo and discouraging Israel and Ukraine from selling weapons to China is the US efforts to contain China. Even after President Obama's visit who assured engagement with China, the US planned to go ahead with the arms deal with Taiwan. "…The spread of the China threat theory in itself is a threat

Participants visiting rural areas in Beijing suburb of Changping

to China."

Threat from Japan: Japan's military strategy and the US-Japan alliance are currently forming a new challenge and strategic threat to China. The build-up of theatre missile defence—a military cooperation with Japan is seen as an effort to contain China. A series of changes in Japan's defence policies and efforts to amend its constitution in favour of greater operational latitude by its military forces, all exemplify Japan's capability to move beyond its strictly defensive posture. The possibility of revising the three non-nuclear principles and the Peace Constitution would allow Japan to pursue nuclear weapons. In 2005, Japan named China as a threat in its *National Defence Program Guidelines* for the first time. Japan's *2005 Defence White Paper* publicly questioned China's military modernization and would pay close attention to China's navy. Anti-Japanese sentiment by Chinese, East China Sea issue and Japan's involvement in Taiwan affairs provide the possible likelihood for military engagement.

Threat from India: Chinese and Indian leaders made frequent declarations of good neighbourliness, friendship, and mutually beneficial cooperation. But the mutual suspicion still exists as the border dispute is yet to be resolved. India poses a conventional threat with its stronger navy, sophisticated arms acquisitions, and growing nuclear arsenal. Civilian nuclear cooperation with India confirmed the extent to which the US would go in maintaining regional strategic balance. Sanctuary to Dalai Lama and splittist activities of Tibetans in India are directly endangering China's security. There are competitions between India and China for resources, market share, and international influence and in the arena of foreign relations in South and East Asia, India's attempts to gain membership in the UN Security Council and the Nuclear Suppliers Group. While India is not considered as much of a threat as either the US or Japan, it does pose a threat to China's territorial integrity, economic development and international stature.

China's traditional security paradigm is far more concerned about any containment by the US, Japan, and/or India than any military confrontation with anyone. The threat of containment is less of a military nature and more of a diplomatic, political, and economic one. Nevertheless, aforesaid three states have significant ideological, historical or territorial disagreements with China and possess the military, economic, and/or international diplomatic means to go to battle over such differences.

Non-Traditional Threats: Vulnerability of China to extremely wide-ranging non-traditional threats is fairly high. Terrorism and transnational crimes have already affected China. Risks of diseases and environmental problems have extremely increased. Here only energy security is highlighted to present how severely China is vulnerable. 85 percent of China's oil passes through the Indian Ocean, Malacca Strait, and the South China Sea. While 18 percent of the US oil comes from the Gulf, 60 percent of China's imported oil comes from there. Any meddling in Malacca Strait could halt nearly all of China's energy supply. Most vulnerability is the dependence is confined to the Middle East. China is not only competing with the US but also comes into conflict with US containment policies against Iran and Sudan. When the US and the Western powers have alternative means of transporting oil through pipelines from central/ South America, and from Central Asia and Russia respectively, China depends highly on sea lines of communication over which it has little control. When secure energy supply justifies modernization of Chinese navy but also raises a great concern to its neighbours.

There are many non-traditional threats which are common to the US and China. If the US and China pursue these common objectives together instead of focusing on the potential threat, energy and resources could be better spent against such threats affecting the globe.

To a country surrounded by fledgling states, historical invaders, nuclear powers, and grappling with issues of terrorism, proliferation and so on, justifies modernization of its military. But this is surely being a concern of the SE Asian nations including Japan and India and hence China needs to be engaged deeply with these countries on its security concern to build mutual trust. How it behaves in securing its national interests in international and regional settings in future may be debated.

Is Modernized Chinese Military a Threat to International Peace and Stability?

Mearsheimer—in his book, *The Tragedy of Great Power Politics*, argued that "the ultimate goal of every great power is to maximize its share of world power and eventually dominate the system"—in other words, to become a hegemon. He said, "China and the US are destined to be adversaries as China's power grows." Thus, the US should not act to engage China, but act to contain and weaken China. "A wealthy China would not be a status quo power but an aggressive state determined to achieve regional hegemony…so it is not too late for the US to reverse course and do what it can to slow the rise of China." On the other hand, Joseph Nye warned that "If we see China as an enemy, China actually may become one." Nye, an advocate for engagement, suggested that when assessing China the economic and political arenas should be taken into consideration, not only the military.

Does China's peaceful development mean more threats or opportunities to surrounding countries and international order? Will modernization of Chinese military affect the peace and stability in international milieu? Will modernization of Chinese military generate arms race in the region? The following paragraphs would hopefully shed some light in contrarily to the School of "offensive realism," propagated by Mearsheimer and other realists.

The Premise of Chinese Exceptionalism: Chinese see their country as unlike any other, given their long history, pursuit of peace, and inherently defensive rather than offensive approach to international relations. Despite frequent invasions, China maintained its pursuit of peace. The story of explorer Zheng He has come to symbolize this uniquely peaceful disposition to the Chinese. Western explorers conquered the land they discovered, but Zheng's fleet did not subdue the newly discovered lands by force. Chinese writings are all based on the idea of Chinese exceptionalism. For 2 millennia, China considered itself the hub of civilization. China is the only uninterrupted civilization in world history. Professor Qu Xing summarized China's "no offensive" posture in this way:

"Traditional Chinese culture pays attention to 'broad love' and 'nonattacking,' advocates the 'kingly way' of convincing people by reasoning, despises the 'domineering way' of overwhelming others by force. The Chinese invented gunpowder, but they do not use it [with] guns to invade others, the Chinese invented the compass, but they do not use it to [guide] warships to prowl about the four seas."

"Comprehensive national power" is another unique Chinese concept that takes all political, economic, military, scientific, historical and societal factors into consideration. The Western concept of national power emphasizes influence and force, contrarily Chinese one emphasizes survival, development, and international influence.

Influence of Confucianism: Confucian principles of benevolence and righteousness maintained the concept of "no offense," infused military strategy in the past and has the same reflection today. Military strategists influenced by Confucianism advocated cautious war and "opposed rashly beginning war." Mao Zedong directed military intervention in Korean Peninsula at the last moment when China's security was threatened. Chinese strategic culture places great emphasis on just cause: *"When war cannot be avoided, the issues of right and wrong in the war are of primary importance."*

Philosophical Trends in the Security Paradigm: There is a unique emphasis in Chinese writings on morality and justice in warfare. As early as the 5th century BC, Chinese military strategists stipulated that wars must have a just cause, the enemy should be notified of pending attacks, and innocents should be protected. The concepts of defence and justness in China's national security can be traced back to the famous writings of Sun Tzu and other military theorists. China is unique in its emphasis on defence rather than offense. Mo Zi, a Chinese thinker, is credited with the concept of "no offense." The Chinese elite commonly refer to the Great Wall as a symbol of this concept. Their ideas permeated the writings by Mao Zedong and Deng Xiaoping, and today they are reflected in the language the government uses to describe its new security concept.

"Active defence," "peaceful development," "win-win," and "mutual security through cooperation" all reflect its long-standing culture of nonaggression, benevolence and peace.

Window of Strategic Opportunity for China: The concept of strategic opportunity is the most important idea to understand Chinese threat perceptions. Deng Xiaoping proclaimed in the 1980s that "peace and development are the main themes of the era." The 16th Party Congress declared that the first 20 years of the 21st century are "a period of important strategic opportunity which China must tightly grasp and in which a lot can be achieved." In current international order China has relative stability and space to pursue both its economic modernization and an increasing role in the international arena. Hence, China must make use of it, while it will not seek any venture that will threaten to peace and stability.

Will Modernization of Chinese Military Generate Arms Race?

For last 19 years China had two digit defence budget. From 2000 to 2009, it raised from $14.6 billion to $70.27 billion. In 2009, the US published estimates that showed China's military spending as high as $150 billion. This is a point of contention between the US-China relations. Some observers have responded to the accusation by the US negatively in light of the US's own military expenditures which are 12 times larger than China's, and nearly 5 times larger than even the highest estimate, with the US having no major external threats since the end of the Cold War. The US is the most powerful country in the world. Then, is the US the biggest threat to the world?

The US is more cautious on the development of cyber capabilities of China and space programme. Modernization of China's self defence nuclear power might compel Japan to go for nuclear option and India to intensify its nuclear programme. Japan will also be more concerned on acquisition of aircraft carrier(s) by China. South Korea's military initiatives are more in response to a possible conflict with a nuclear North

Korea. India plans to spend more than $30 billion to upgrade its navy. It will add 40 warships and new fighter jets. It's attempt to acquire nuclear submarine, more aircraft carriers and first unmanned moon mission, analysts see as a race with China.

Rapid rise in defence budget in every year indicates that China also imbued with western Realistic School of Thought—power will bring the lasting peace. Economic and power cycle shows that every hegemony or super power had certain period of time to enjoy its power, and then declined. This is because the pursuit of military greatness leads to economic stress and decline of power. Then why should China follow the same philosophy when it has its own historical values. China can make a difference in international system, but certainly not through military power. Chinese "comprehensive national power" is the answer, by not giving undue emphasis on military power. China should develop its military in graduated scale only to ensure security to its core interests so as to prevent any arms race in the region. Its comprehensive power generated more from socio-politico, economic, science and technological strength than military power will ensure lasting peace and stability both domestically and externally.

China Does Not Constitute a Threat to International Peace and Stability

Realistic view prevails that China would unavoidably follow the same historical track of Germany in its rise. The history of Germany's rise would not be repeated in China. Such a historical comparison itself is defective as China has its own unique experience of development and rise. On Taiwan issue China should wait like West German instead of settling it through military means. Once China becomes a strong state and power, this problem has the all possibility of being resolved through peaceful way as it happened in German. Should the situation leads to military intervention, China will surely get a hostile Taiwanese people which will not unite them as a single nation—a dream far away.

Prof. Joseph Nye said in online interview:

"I don't think that China is a big power pursuing expansion militarily. My main worry lies on the Taiwan issue. It's best for the Chinese mainland to use soft strength to attract Taiwan, because 'honey can glue more flies than vinegar.'"

China's development has provided many opportunities for the development of its neighbours. It has not achieved at the cost of the interests of the US or its neighbouring countries. Japan though economically benefited, psychologically regards China as a threat. Most Asian countries can accept China's development, can coexist peacefully with China and can benefit from China's development. Prof. Joseph Nye said that *"As long as China's development is peaceful development, the development will not be achieved at the cost of neighbouring countries or the US. Other countries around the world can benefit themselves from China's economic growth."*

Rise of China will be unlike that of any other country in history. China will be able to develop without resorting to violence or conflict for two reasons. First, it does not seek hegemony like other rising powers, or to challenge the current international system. Second, China's rise can occur peacefully because of the globalized economy and China's importance within it.

In cold war era, developing nations had reasonable manoeuvring space in international system. In today's unilateral order, isn't the state of developing countries worse than before? The US's aggressive foreign policy affected their honour and dignity severely and hoped to be better in trending multi-polar or even in US-China bipolar structure. At a forum of China-Africa Cooperation, African foreign ministers admitted that they are immensely benefitted from the cooperation with China.

Despite sceptical questions by the outside world, China still endorses the idea of creating harmonious world. Equality and peaceful coexistence are the foundation of engagement between different countries. Chinese should focus on building political mutual trust, rather than being distracted by the western exaggerated media stories. China should learn to work with Western media, helping them get more knowledge about China to improve China's image. The most important thing is that the Chinese government should be very prudent in handling internal and external affairs, so as to show to the outsiders that China does not constitute a threat.

Conclusion

China's new security concept has evolved in response to its increasingly complex, interconnected security environment. The US is a prevalent force in China's security considerations. The most enduring regional threats are emanating from Japan and India. China is more concerned on threat of economic and diplomatic containment than the military containment. China threat theory affects America's China policy, blending of containment and engagement, having more weight on containment. The inclusion of Taiwan is the most disturbing aspect of the expanded US-Japan alliance from the perspective of China. Despite western concerns of Chinese military modernization, external and internal imperatives justify the modernisation of its military. However, expansion with modernized military might raise arms race in the region. It is the degree of modernization that will concern the US and the other regional countries.

Rise of China as a new big power will produce fears and suspicions among the major powers. China must be prudent in avoiding the hyperbole of such worries. It is very important to emphasize China's peaceful development, and that's why it is very important to vigorously develop China's soft power to draw other countries.

The opportunities fetched by China outweigh the threat it constitutes. China's economic growth has become a main factor in the global economy and China has helped in bringing about global political stability. Only ill motivated forces purposely incite the "China threat theory" aiming to contain China's development and the growth of its international influence. China's foreign policy, efforts to strengthen the authoritativeness of the UN, contribution to fair and multi-polar international order, observing the principles of peaceful coexistence and the norms of international law—all these prove that China adopt a realistic and responsible attitude to China's development and its global role. At the UN, Chinese leaders once promised to the world that *"China will never seek hegemony."*

China's Harmonious Society: Towards a Sustainable Social and Economic Development

Sabri Bin Adam
Brig. Gen., Royal Malaysian Air Force

"The essential motivating force of socialism is to advance the forces of production, freed from the fetters of backward relations of production, eliminate exploitation, end social inequality, and achieve the ultimate goal of a common prosperity for all people." —Deng Xiaoping

Introduction

The People's Republic of China (PRC) celebrated the 60th anniversary of its founding on 1st October 2009. The event which Mao Zedong famously characterized by declaring that the "Chinese people have stood up" was celebrated in the biggest and most impressive way. It was jubilantly celebrated by all of its multi ethnic, multi cultural and multi religious societies. This year celebration, themed "I march forward with my motherland," saw the military, as the guardian of PRC's interests which include its sovereignty and territorial integrity,

Participants visiting the Classical Gardens of Suzhou

paraded the latest hardware and weaponry in the People Liberation Army's (PLA) inventory. It demonstrated that the PLA possesses the necessary power and might, which includes nuclear powered missile to fulfill the role of its existence. It also gave a message that with the state's interests well guarded by the PLA, the nation can now focus their effort toward developing its economic and social well being which include safeguarding the environment. The PRC under the leadership of Hu Jintao and the current top team had, during the Political Bureau of the Communist Party of China (CPC) Central Committee meeting on 23rd January 2009, renewed their commitment "to continue promote economic growth, social stability, and the governance capacity of the CPC through the application of the scientific outlook on development."

The Scientific Development Concept is the current official guiding socio-economic ideology of the CPC incorporating sustainable development, social welfare, a person-centered society, increased democracy, and, ultimately, the creation of a Harmonious Society. The

Chinese government top priority in the application of the scientific outlook on development had always been to maintain fast and steady economic development, to adjust the country's industrial structure and to safeguard and improve the livelihood of the Chinese people. Nevertheless China is still facing with a number of challenges and problems during its social and economic development which entail issues of vital interest to the Chinese public, such as corruption, huge unemployment, absent social services, and environmental decay, to be addressed with stepped-up efforts. These include narrowing the income gap between the rural and urban dwellers, closing the development gap between the western and eastern regions of China as well as to achieve "green" growth through technology upgrade, increased industrial efficiency, renewable fuels, and control of pollutant emission. The outcome of this strategic effort is envisaged to provide the necessary setting towards the full realization of socialism with Chinese Characteristics that is the "Harmonious Society."

Reason for the Inception of Harmonious Society's Concept

The social lives in China that I knew, through the input of international media, before arriving China are in great disagreement to the real China that I see and experienced right now. What I saw is that changes are affecting every aspect of the population's lives. There are visible changes in the social, economic, military as well as the political life of the PRC. These changes are partly "the outputs of a process of a relatively unbroken period of economic reform" that began at the 3rd Plenary Session of the 11th Central Committee of the Communist Party of China (CCCPC) in December of 1978. It was then reaffirmed at both the 3rd Plenary Session of the 12th CCCPC in October of 1984 and the 14th National Congress of the CPC in October of 1992. It was at these meetings that the majority of the realistic modernists within the CPC clearly affirm the reform agenda. The adoption, clarification, and reaffirmation of a new economic development strategy based upon decentralization of control over the state owned enterprise sector, dismantling of the rural commune system, increased use of material incentive in workplaces, and ultimately, the "modernization" of the Chinese economic infrastructure (as well as the military) was its outcome.

Deng's economic growth-oriented policies which were resolutely acknowledged by the Chinese society since its affirmation by the CCCPC in 1978 had relentlessly detracted from the overall societal development due to unstated focus on GDP growth. Although there are great gains, the development opportunities were seen by the majority of the population as though not benefitting them. What they saw was huge unemployment, corruption, ruthless and unacceptable competition, absent social services as well as environmental decay which directly impede their progression towards achieving prosperity. The policies had perpetually left a large portion of the Chinese population behind while those at the coastal regions were prospering. The affected populations are obviously bewildered, confused and infuriated at the outcome of the policy. Whilst the policies were supposed to benefit them, it had actually impinged on their lives because of disparity in economic and social development as well as the degradation of environment due to apparent consequence of development. Deng's economic growth-oriented policies seem to backfire and these negative developments if allowed to deteriorate could affect stability and harmony. The government of the day thus needs to find a remedy to right what had gone wrong.

The leadership of President (also CPC General Secretary) Hu Jintao and his team has since 2002 steered the country's policy towards a more balanced and sustainable development, under the title of building a "harmonious society." This ideological campaign is said to be the latest creation added to the idea of Socialism with Chinese characteristics.

Concept of "Harmonious Society" Defined

Based on the reason for its inception, this paper defined "Harmonious Society" as an official agenda whose primary goals include narrowing the income gap between the rural and urban dwellers as well as closing the development gap between the western and eastern regions of China. Its other goal is to achieve "green" growth through technology upgrade, increased industrial efficiency, renewable fuels, and control of pollutant emission.

Realization of a Harmonious Society

The idea of building a "harmonious society" was first embraced by the Third Plenary Session of the 16th Central Committee, which convened in Beijing on October 11 to 14, 2003. It was brought to agenda during the 6th Plenary Session of the 16th CCCPC from October 8 to 11, 2006 and was ratified into the CPC's constitution at the 17th Party Congress in October 15 to 21, 2007.

The Chinese government, as part of its strategy to promote the "harmonious society," is reviving Confucianism. Although a large population of the Chinese does not believe in religion, they however do subscribe to the traditional Confucianism morals values and beliefs. The tradeoff for material gains had in due course eroded those traditional Confucianism morals values and beliefs which led to spiritual loss hence creating a "spiritual vacuum." The PRC's leadership saw the erosion of these traditional values and belief if not properly mitigated and compensated by worthy values, would obviously create a callous society which deem to be detrimental to the concept of socialism as aspired by the current PRC's leadership. This was clearly demonstrated by those unscrupulous and greedy populations, who in their search for material gain had unwittingly disregard moral values which led to the social ills that were mentioned earlier. The situation, if left unchecked would obviously affect China's economic growth and hence retard the development of a united and prosperous China. Therefore there was a need to thrash out an approach to the "country's increasingly serious social problems and general instability." The conclusion was the need for a new ideological campaign to shift the focus of the official agenda from "economic growth" to "social harmony" which includes the development of "democracy, the rule of law, justice, sincerity, amity and vitality" as well as a better relationship between the people and the government and "between man and nature," meaning environmental harmony.

One of the serious negative consequences of the PRC's rapid industrial development has been the degradation of the environment such as increased pollution which includes water and air pollution. Hence efforts to control China's pollution problem have become a top priority of the Chinese leadership. To reflect the growing importance the PRC Government places on environmental protection, it upgraded the State Environmental Protection Administration (SEPA) to a ministry level agency in March 1998. In 2004, the central government instituted the Green Gross Domestic Product project, in order to determine the true gross domestic product, adjusted to compensate for negative environmental effects. Beginning of 2006 also saw the government greatly expanded expenses into environmental protection, and a series of new laws have been passed. Enforcement of these laws is also being expanded. The PRC has strengthened its environmental legislation and made some progress in stemming environmental deterioration. During the 11th Five-Year Plan (2006-2010), the PRC plans to reduce total emissions by 10% and bring China's energy efficiency up by 20%.

For the many things that the government is trying to do, some have already shown results. For instance, energy intensity (energy use per unit GDP) drops around 4.8% in 2008 in addition to 3% drop in 2007. The emission of sulfur dioxide in 2008 dropped 11% compared with 2007. Industrial deaths/accidents have reduced by about 75% due to forced closures of 12,555 small mines across the country since 2005 and improved scrutiny. China is one of a few countries in the world that have been rapidly increasing their forest cover. It is also managing to reduce air and water pollution. This was clearly demonstrated in the government plans to enhance sewage and rubbish treatment facilities and prevent water pollution, accelerate green belt and natural forest planting programs, and increase energy conservation initiatives and pollution control project utilizing part of the US$498 billion economic stimulus package of November 2008.

The government measures to reverse the widening income gap includes supporting the rural economy by setting price floors for agricultural products, subsidies and/or preferred loans for machineries, fertilizers and so on. Specific examples include the increased effort in providing social insurance for vulnerable groups, or the recent announcement of an intention to build a rural pension system. Whilst the primary government response to lagging development in the western regions were to sufficiently build up the infrastructure first before attracting investors. This is because logistics is a main issue in the rugged west.

The CPC is also showing its determination to fight corruption "by urging officials to declare personal assets" such as houses and investments. The government also displays its grit in combating mafia style organized crime. It had done its job well and had managed to put on trial both the gang members and the enforcement officials who served as gang protectors; officials who concealed the proceeds of crimes and accepted bribes.

Conclusion

The outcome of rapid and uneven development environmental degradation, income disparity, characteristic of present-day PRC society, such as greater corruption and higher crime levels caused tensions within society and therefore need mitigation. The proposed solutions by President Hu Jintao and his team to shift the focus of the official agenda from "economic growth" to "social harmony" through the concept of Harmonious Society is timely and appropriate. It is envisaged that the concept will mitigate the growing wealth disparity which will reduce imbalances and inequalities, and hence a happier nation.

The concept, if literally translated is about the CPC's ability to adapt itself to the reality of contemporary China, China that seek to be a developed country. The consequences of that aspiration are many but the CPC need to face those challenges to remain relevant as a "responsible stakeholder." The mechanisms to address issues that arise are in place and clearly laid out as stated government policies. Its successful implementations signify CPC's governance capacity in stewarding contemporary China toward a sustainable social and economic development whilst ensuring its environmental health. The government and its machineries had so far done its job well by ensuring appropriate action were taken between fulfilling the need for state control and freedom of people which requires continuous re-adjustments during implementation.

China in Lebanese Eyes: Excellent Model of Development, Promoting a "Harmonious World"

Roland Abou Jaoude
Col., Lebanese Army

Introduction

In the summer of 2007, having just finished the Nahr el Bared battle in which the Lebanese Army and the Engineering Regiment that I've commanded for seven years achieved total victory, I was extremely satisfied as a commander, and the army's Headquarters gave priority for training abroad to those who participated in the battles. Two places were offered for me to choose from but my response was negative for both and I insisted on going to China. Two years later my request was approved and I was assigned to a year of study in the National Defense University. I was ecstatic to finally get to see the China I had read and heard about.

This eminent country characterized by its ancient authentic culture and its medley of historical sites such as The Great Wall, Terracotta

Warriors and the Horses of qin shi huang as well as world famous ancient philosophers like Confucius and strategists like the author of Art of War, Sun Wu, reflected 5000 years of civilizations and history. The founding of the People's Republic of China occurred in 1949. Although the new China has shown its resolute vitality, 30 years of opening up and reform helped China's economy realize steady and rapid growth which has attracted the world's attention toward the present and the future of China. All my understanding of China was certainly basic historical facts and general information, that I have read, about its geography, politics, economy, socioculture, legislation and environmental issues, in addition to some theses and studies concerning the political system, state structure as well as environmental protection, and human rights.

However, after having spent several weeks in NDU_CDS_PLA and having visited a lot of places, historical sites, military and civilian institutions, cities, and having had direct contact with Chinese civilians and military, in addition to the lectures, I can say that I acquired a better, wider and deeper knowledge of China.

General Background

The People's Republic of China is the third largest country in the world; it has a land area of 9.6million km². Located in the eastern part of the Asian continent, and on the western shore of the Pacific, with land boundaries totaling about 22,800 km, China has 14 neighboring nations by land and 7 neighbors by sea and has a coast line that measures approximately 18,000 km by sea. Moreover, 5,400 islands dot China's territorial waters. Many territorial disputes have arisen: Even though some were resolved, many remain undetermined.

China's population is 1.33 Billion, which is approximately one fifth of the world's total population. As for the natural increase of China's population, it should be kept under 8 per 1,000 (government policy) so the population will not exceed 1.36 billion by 2010.

China is a unitary multiethnic nation made up of 56 different ethnics. Because the Han accounts for 91.65% of the population, the other 55 are customarily referred to as "ethnic minorities."

In China, at present, there are 23 provinces, 5 autonomous regions, 4 municipalities directly under the central government, and 2 special administrative regions.

China is an ancient country and has one of the world's oldest civilizations. It features unity, continuity, inclusiveness and diversity, and consists of states and cultures dating back more than five millennia.

The most famous Chinese philosophies are Confucianism and Taoism. The Confucianism, with Confucius as the founder, is a word affirming thought with (ren) humanity and (yi) being righteous as the core. "Ren" means that a friendly relation should be established among people and the way to establish such a relation is to put oneself into the other's shoes. Taoism is opposite to Confucianism in many aspects, and it emphasizes the non-action principle as well as the nature, and advocates spiritual freedom.

China's policies are derived from the cultural spirit of the Chinese people that spread Happiness whether you are successful with the Confucianism or you are unsuccessful with the naturalism of Tao.

The constitution stipulates that all citizens are equal, and the state respects and safeguards human rights. It guarantees the basic rights and interests of citizens, freedom of religious belief, residence and legitimate private property, the right to criticize and suggestions to any state organ or functionary, and exercise supervision, the right to material assistance from the state and society when old, ill, or disable, as well as the right to receive education.

The basic structure of China's political system consists of the leadership of the CPC, the people congress system, the multiparty cooperation and political consultation system, and the regional ethnic autonomy system.

Development of China's Policies

Phase One (1949-1955): China was up against a number of difficult problems for instance post-war national construction, the Korean war, preparation to liberate Taiwan and international standing. China's policy was based on three mainstays. As chairmen Mao pointed out: "Clean the House," "Start Afresh," and "Lean to One Side."

Phase Two (1955-1970): The interference of the Soviet Union in internal affairs, and the "two China" strategy by the US, constituted threats to China in need of help from as many friendly countries as possible, China launched an all round diplomacy campaign so that it can go against Imperialism, Revisionism and all the reactionaries and to keep the momentum of domestic development.

Phase Three (1970-1978): China was up against the most awful domestic disorder because of the "cultural revolution" and the most horrible international circumstances, the country was also surrounded by all types of hostile forces, China's policy stood on the "One-line strategy" and "Three World Theory." Mao Zedong, China's leader during the three phases mentioned above, presented the following policy layout: "Clean the House, Start Afresh, Independence and Self-reliance, Leaning to One Side, Three-World Strategy and One Line Strategy."

Phase Four (1978-1999): China encountered the demanding duty to save the economy from complete fall down and to enlarge its diplomatic scope so as to pull alongside the wagon of globalization.

China's policy solely focused on the reform. China attempted to preserve balanced relations with superpowers and engage comprehensively with neighboring and developing countries.

Deng Xiaoping, China's leader (1978-1989) had a policy layout based on Themes of the Times, Peace and Development, New Global Order, Global Security, Civilization, Independence and Self-reliance, "One Country, Two Systems," Put aside Differences and Joint Development.

Deng examined China's recent historical experience, concentrating on one main thought: that we ought to incorporate the universal truth of Marxism with the concrete realities of China, blaze a trail of our own and build socialism with Chinese characteristics. This idea turned out to be the general guiding principle for modernizing China.

The following policy layout was that of Jiang Zemin (1989-end phase): Multi-Polar Theory, Create a Better Surrounding Environment, Reform of the Global Order, New security initiatives, Diversity of cultures, Coexistence and Harmonious Development.

Phase Five (1999 onwards): Since the turn of the 21st century, China has been up against the changing world. At home, it faced some difficult problems such as sustainability of development, social coherence, disproportions in revenue distribution, economic structural modification, and the harmony among social groups. Thus, the country has to deal with these issues straight on, with the aim of constructing a "well-to-do society."

Simultaneously, China has been faced with a chaotic post cold war international environment. Together globalization and the international financial crisis have placed China at a crossroad. China has additional duties to accomplish, more complicated problems to adjust to, and more rough battles to fight in order to project its image and to preserve the peaceful environment for its domestic economic development and social progress.

Participants visiting Yonghegong Lama Temple in Beijing

In the area of foreign policy, China aims to be a liable stake holder at the bilateral level. China tries to be a responsible cooperative partner at the multilateral level.

China has undergone a reform which presented with the occasion for many countries to advance their economic development through trade and investment, and through China's experience.

Throughout this phase, the Chinese had two leaders Jiang Zemin, and Hu Jintao (2003 onward). The later had the following policy layout: Effective Head-of-State Diplomacy, Principle of People First, scientific development perspective, multilateral diplomacy, Reform International Institutions, Reform of the Global Order, Regionalism, and Theory of Harmonious World.

China's Achievements: Pestle Analysis

Politics and Legislation

Political System and Legislation

In relation to government matters, China practices a political reform targeted at developing "socialist political democracy." It has performed the Supervision Law, providing judicial control system at all levels. Simultaneously, it has taken actions to put a stop to corruption in the public sector and check the increasing commercial bribery scandals. China has also handled some local concerns regarding ethnic minorities with sound ethnic policies. This provides the Chinese people with greater freedom of thought, self-reliance, and independence; it also contributes to social harmony.

Foreign and National Defense Policies

Although there were radical changes in the international situation over the past twenty years, China has abided by Deng's ideas on diplomacy and accomplished huge success in diplomacy, China-Gulf Cooperation Council, and China-New Zealand, China-Chile, China-Australia and China-Pakistan, and signed important agreements with its partners.

It has suffered the results of the tremendous modifications in Eastern

Europe and the breakdown of the former Soviet Union, and the pressure and sanctions forced on China by some Western countries and it has successfully shielded its sovereignty and national dignity.

In 2005, China adopted the concept of building a harmonious world. In 2009, the country has vigorously developed economic and trade relations with African nations on the basis of equality and mutual benefit, never forcing its own development model on others. The principles of more lively and self-motivated strategy of opening up to the outside world, "promoting economy through diplomatic means" and "diplomacy for the peoples" denote China's diplomacy in a new era.

Any nation that intends to have diplomatic relations with China must recognize the PRC government as the sole legitimate government of China, and be willing to observe the principles of mutual respect for territorial integrity and soverenty, mutual non aggression, noninterference in each other's internal affairs, equality and mutual benefit, and peaceful coexistence.

In line with these principles China has established diplomatic relations with 171 countries. The theory of regional integration is highlighted by a multi layer framework around China with a good, rich, and comfortable neighborhood.

Dedicated to the upgrading of its national defense, China has manufactured several nontraditional modern weapons and munitions which have been demonstrated in the 60th anniversary of China. Additionally, experiments were carried out in outer space in accordance with related international conventions, a restricted quantity of weapons was exported and joint military exercises with other countries were executed (professional military performance during the exercise in Queshan Training Base). Nevertheless, China will not pose a military threat to others.

The basic grounds for the formulation of China's defense policy:

"Six never" refers to never seek aggression, never seek expansion, never interfere in the internal affairs of other countries, never ally with any country, never establish a single military base on foreign soil, and never station a single soldier abroad.

"One insistence" refers to the insistence on resolving the international quarrels in peaceful ways.

Economy

Reform and Opening-up

After the "cultural revolution," China's national economy was a wreck. Deng Xiaoping, in a firm approach, adopted the notion of opening up. He believed that "the world is an open one." The concept of reform and opening up, also known as "Dengism" does not refuse Marxism or Mao Zedong Thought but instead tries to project them to the existing socio-economic status of China. The resolution to initiate reform and opening up was taken by the CCCPC in December 1978.

China has established a market economy and the market has replaced the government to play a decisive role in resource allocation and social development.

China is encouraging the improvement of its administrative system and distribution system. It has implemented a crisis management system for public emergencies and enhanced the social credit system and the notary system. When it comes to controlling online publishing activities, campaigns against copyright violations on the Internet were launched. Moreover, attempts in protecting intellectual property rights for trademarks and safeguarding intangible cultural heritage were intensified.

Several attempts to pay tribute to China's WTO commitments were instituted in order to open up to the world even more, to support cultural exchanges, and to send young volunteers abroad. By the end of 2006, China had become totally open to foreign banks. Furthermore, the Chinese Government encouraged them to integrate locally and has spent up the financial restructuring in rural areas. China has also established systems against money laundering.

With an annual growth rate of 8-10 percent, early 2007 highlighted China's continuing "sound and rapid" economic growth. To promote just competition, China has put in place an Anti-Monopoly Law. Moreover, China is a large energy producer and it is proactive in developing renewable resources and building nuclear power plants.

China has gone into a novel stage in its reform, the stage of all-round reform, since the shift from the orthodox planned economy to a modern market economy and from a closed or semi-closed state to the decision to open up the country in all-round way, by the following modernizations fields: agriculture, industry, science, technology and defense. The all-round reform in the new stage involves the following aspects: the market-oriented reform targeted at encouraging a sound and fast development of the national economy, the political, social, restructuring and dynamic strategy of opening up.

The process of reform was up against difficult matters, the country has found that the key to face those difficulties and to rise high is to promote the reform in all-round way in the new stage. As a matter of fact, opening up and modernizing were obvious in our visit to Shanghai (Jinmao Tower and Urban Planning Exhibition Hall) and Beijing Olympic City.

Agriculture

The development of modern agriculture in the New Countryside Construction Program is on top of China's priorities. Increasing investment in education in rural areas and vigorously encouraging wide-ranging rural reforms were among the measures taken. The social security system and the new type of Medicare system created for farmers can essentially meet farmers' demands. Additionally, concerning the farmers' problem of lack of potable water, China has tried its best to resolve it.

Socioculture

China is learning from the experiences of countries with high urbanization levels, and marching forward in a pattern of high concentration in urban development. Furthermore, it is trying its best to decrease the harm caused by weather-related disasters. The government is preparing for a peaking of the elderly population, and is working towards a social restructuring targeted at offering fundamental and secure public services. It is planning on creating a sound social security system that includes all Chinese citizens.

China was successful in reducing poverty rate to 1.3% of the total population and is still trying to decrease the number of poor Chinese people.

Education and Health

On one hand, Chinese leader Deng Xiaoping said "I support sending more students to study abroad, not a dozen but thousands, tens of thousands and more." As a matter of fact, more than 1.2 million Chinese students studied abroad since 1978.

On the other hand, the establishment of overseas Confucius Institutes is working towards the encouragement of Chinese language teaching, and this put China on the map as one of the leading destinations for foreign students.

China's continuing progress in healthcare aims to cover all residents, peasants and urbanites in order for them to be free of any medical costs. Concerning the state policy of family planning, which has been implemented for decades, it will basically remain unchanged by 2050. Nonetheless, China now plans to regulate the sex ratio imbalance of infants, and create a conversion from the most populous country to a nation of a more capable population.

Human Rights

According to the law and the constitution, the Chinese Government respects its citizens' right to freedom of religious belief and protects human rights. The international recognition of the country's progress in human rights was demonstrated in China's election as one of the members of the United Nations Human Rights Council by a large majority.

Technology and science

China's lunar investigation projects, the Compass satellite navigation system, and the government's efforts in cracking down on academic corruption in R&D, demonstrate its motivation in the field of science and technology.

Environment

In a proposal to diminish negative impacts to the natural environment caused by economic development and to shelter itself from poisonous garbage dumps, China will take a more proactive approach in managing its environmental problems.

Reason for Success and Challenges—Swot Analysis

Reasons for the success of China's policies

Strengths (internal):
- Collective leadership
- Pragmatic approach
- Scientific outlooks
- Stability and flexibility
- Independence and self-reliance.

Opportunities (external implications):
- Two front goals
- Widespread diplomacy
- Peaceful development
- Open door strategy
- Harmonious world
- Non interference.

Challenges to China

Weaknesses (internal):

- Protocol of development when it comes to efficiency, equity and wealth distribution.

- Momentum of economic development investment regarding consumption

- Over population jobs for the youth, and social security for the elderly

- Weak leadership in some local government especially in the rural areas

- Severe pollution crisis as a result of the widespread development of the economy.

Threats (external implications):

- Local and global competitiveness

- Technology: China is still far beyond high-tech countries

- Energy and resources, alternative energy, renewable energy, energy efficiency

- Hypothetical innovation in foreign affairs

- Worldwide image and status

- External privileges and duties.

At present, China is still a developing country striving to achieve its ambitions of peaceful and sustainable development.

A pain in the hearts of people is that China's unity is still incomplete.

Intricate issues on regional security are rising. There are disagreements on territorial and maritime interests between China and some countries.

Recommendations

Building on Strengths, Removing Weaknesses, Exploiting Opportunities, Minimizing Threats, and taking into consideration main China's Stakeholder "Peoples" expectations, I tried to develop some ideas as follows:

At present, the new leadership had arranged to make domestic concerns such as economic expansion and constricting the gap between the well-off coast and deprived inland regions their number one priorities, however regional development attention should concentrate on geographical, ethnic and religious factors and the concern of diversity in productive force between region and ameliorate the quality of local government direction so as to offer solutions to the local problems or to suggest to the central government suitable propositions on what should be done.

China ought to institute a quality control system to guarantee products quality and safety.

China should genuinely study its environmental setback with a view to tackling the intricate structures of issues including nature, economy, society, institution and industrialization damaging it.

The process of industrialization with computerization should be extended to small and medium companies principally exporters of low end products.

China ought to preserve its position regarding "one China" principle or unified China. Nonetheless, the domestic and surrounding countries' problems have to be resolved by negotiations even if it lasted decades (Taiwan issue, major problem) and by taking into consideration reciprocated profit (win-win strategy).

China has to balance domestic factors and foreign policy goals and move up its agenda in order to meet directly the new challenge of a division becoming more and more blurred, between domestic and foreign affairs.

In order to market China, serious and deliberate endeavors are needed from China's foreign policy and other public relations agencies.

China must work with all prospective major powers and be of importance in international institutions and in the world order, since the world cannot develop without China and China cannot develop without the world.

President Obama's administration in the United States grew increasingly supple towards joint venture regarding international issues. Additionally, the financial crisis may perhaps assist in encouraging the proposal of multilateral world system and integrated global economy.

The United Nations, the organization that has the largest number of member nations should play a dominant role in international affairs. The common desire is for the establishment of a just and sensible new political and economic order in the world, which assists in generating a long-term peaceful environment for the development of all countries in the world.

The theories mentioned above imply that in China, opening up, reform, modernization and change (policies and strategies), can't be transformational but incremental and long term, and must go along with a communication system at all levels (people and organizations), in addition to a continuous reviewing (assessment) process. Therefore, while keeping to a "gradual" approach, the reform in the new stage will also need "relatively obvious breakthroughs."

Conclusion

China has always, observed the strategic thinking initiated by former Chinese leaders Mao Zedong, Deng Xiaoping, Jiang Zemin, and Hu Jintao. Thus, the nation has recorded monumental achievements in unswervingly implementing its independent policy of peace and Harmony.

The key of success remains "people's interests and expectations," best resources management, just wealth distribution, in addition to an appropriate health care system, education, housing, and basic needs for all citizen. In this regard, the Chinese model of development has proven

Participants visiting green ecological village in Beijing suburb——Zhenggezhuang Village in Changping District

its success especially for developing countries especially third world countries.

The Chinese believe that the following ideas, leadership of CPC, peaceful development, construction of a harmonious world, status of China as a developing country, China's development is favorable to the world and the development model of China, must remain unchanged

Furthermore, China is continuously growing to be in the future a harmonious country and a significant participant, in a multi-polarized world as the nation's international status and prestige rise steadily, however, in the long term, the harmonious world remains the strategic vision for China and the Chinese people.

Understanding PRC's Status on Rights, Freedoms and Civil Liberties

Pushkar N. Regmi
Deputy Inspector General, Nepalese Police

During past 4 months of my stay in China, I came across massive contacts with the Chinese citizens of various class/creed/professions/ regions etc, travelled places & carried out close observations in line with the people's freedoms, read the news media most regularly, studied books & publications related to this issue, and most importantly after deciding to prepare the module paper in the topic mentioned above, I went through numerous resources, which upshot me in developing a better understanding on this subject which I never had before. On the basis of these activities, the paper is prepared.

General Introduction

China's history of being a nation state dates back to 5000 years. With the declaration of the People's Republic of China on Oct. 1st, 1949, the country has stood and gained popular recognition around the globe.

Ethnicity, Language and Culture

With 56 different ethnic groups (mostly with their own dialects), the population of China is 1.32 billion. 22 of them have their own scripts. The Han nationality is in majority. The official language is Mandarin. *Han Zi* is the most commonly used writing language.

Chinese culture flourished around Yellow River (now central & the Valley of north China) between 2500-2000 BC. Despite the ravages of time and war, there are still a lot to see architecturally, e.g. imperial structures of Beijing, the colonial buildings of Shanghai and Buddhist/Confucian/ Taoist temples etc. Calligraphy has been China's highest form of visual art. Funerary art was already a feature ranging from ritual vessels & weapons to pottery figures, jade and sacrificial vessels.

Religion and practice

PRC's law has guaranteed the non intervention of religious performances. So the people are free to worship, pray & consecration as monks & nuns unless their activities hamper social harmony and national integrity.

The nation has over 100 million cohorts of different beliefs, more than 100,000 religious sites and about 300,000 religious hermits.

Economy

With the inception of "Reform and Opening up" Policy in 1978, China's GDP grew at an average annual rate of nearly 10%, that exceeded to 13% in 2007. In the year 2008, China became the world's second largest merchandise exporter and the third largest importer.

Poverty Reduction: 490 million people who were below the line of poverty in 1979 have been reduced to 10% of the population till 2004. The rate of unemployment now seems to be around 4.3%. The percentages of total workforce that are engaged in economic activities fall as 43% in agriculture, 25% in industry, and 32% in various service sectors.

Education

After the Cultural Revolution, China realized that rising of education level and development of science/technology & intellectual resources are necessary to meet the goals of modernization. Then, plans for nine-year compulsory education & good quality higher education in 1985, and "Law on Promotion of Private Education" in September 2003 were reinforced simultaneously. As a result, over 70,000 private schools and 1,279 private institutes of higher learning are spread all over the country with a total enrollment of more than 14.16 million and over 1.81 million respectively. Similarly, the statistics (of MoE) reveals that more than 1.2 million students studied abroad between 1978 and 2008. People's desire of education has been officially supported. Leader Deng Xiaoping once said that *"I support sending more students to study abroad, not a dozen but thousands, tens of thousands and more."*

Political Paradigm

China's Socialist form of Political entity is successful in maintaining good governance and embarking the roads of development. A brief understanding of some of its major components are presented below:

The Constitution of PRC

Constitution is the Supreme law of the land and is the source of all laws. The constitution clearly defines the structure of the nation, country's guiding principles, Rights & Duties of the citizens as well as procedure of forming all constitutional & major state organs. Since 1949, four constitutions have been formed in China; in the years 1954, 1975, 1978, and the current constitution was formed on 4th Dec. 1982. The periodical amendments of this will be discussed in later part.

People's Courts

There are 4 levels of courts in China. The lowest is "Grass Root People's Court" which is established in the counties, the "Intermediate People's Court" at prefectures & cities; and the "Higher People's Court" in provinces are the second and third level of courts.

The "Supreme People's Court is the highest judiciary organ" (**Article 127** of the constitution). This court presents its periodical reports to the NPC and its standing committee. This has been authorized to examine the functions of other level people's courts, special courts and military courts.

People's Procuratorates

"The people's procuratorates of the PRC are state organs for legal supervision." - **Article 129**. The "Supreme People's Procuratorate" is the highest level legal entity and serves as the "Legal Adviser" of the government. In addition to monitoring & advising the low level procuratorates; this also works in defending cases that arise against the government (e.g., Cases endangering state and public security, creating economic disorder and violating citizen's rights etc.).

National People's Congress

"The NPC of PRC is the highest organ of state power" - **Article 57.** Its deputies are elected from all provinces, autonomous regions, municipalities, special administrative regions and the armed forces. The administrative, judicial, procuratorial, military & state's other organs are formed by NPC.

Standing Committee of NPC is the permanent body. NPC's main functions are to: Supervise the enforcement of the Constitution, Elect President & Vice-President and choose the leadership of the highest organs of the state (e.g. members of the Standing Committee of NPC, President, Premier of the State Council, Chairman of the Central Military Commission etc), Decide on questions of War and Peace, Examine & approve the plan for national economic and social development etc.

Some Important Features

PRC's political organogram contains following additional features:

i. Leadership of the CPC: PRC under the leadership of CPC has been successful in winning the trust of citizens in maintaining harmonious societies and stability in the country through exemplary statesmanship.

ii. Multi party cooperation and political consultative system: The basic ideology of this system is to uphold the representative participation of entire ethnic groups and political parties in the nation building process.

iii. Regional ethnic autonomy system: Ethnic minorities are granted to establish local government under the central leadership. They are exempted of sharing their income & taxes to the center which further supports their development activities with all necessary resources.

National Defense and Security

China's defense policy refers three basic features:

- An independent national defense which is not dependent on others.

- Is self-defensive in nature, constitutes no threats to anyone and is never intended for invading others.

- Is never intended for attacking others first.

China, in its defense system has developed "Three in One" armed forces, namely: The Chinese People's Liberation Army (The Army, Navy, Air Force, Second Artillery Force & the Reserve Force), the Armed Police Force, and the People's Militia respectively.

These three components are responsible for national defense and domestic security. The jobs of China's defense forces' are not merely limited within the national territory but they also involve in peace building activities (abroad) by participating with the United Nations missions.

Freedoms/Rights: A Summary of State's Systems in Its Promotion

Constitution, as already stated, is the Supreme law of the land. This clearly states the Rights & duties of the citizens and ascertains to govern the country by rule of law. With concise prologue of people's freedoms & rights, a brief outline of the subject will be presented in this section.

Definition of Rights

i. The rights that are considered by most societies to belong automatically to everyone, e.g. the rights to freedom, justice, and equality. - **Encarta Dictionary.**

ii. Recognition of the inherent dignity and of the equal and inalienable rights of all members of the human family is the foundation of freedom, justice and peace in the world. - **United Nation's Universal Declaration of Human Rights, 1948.**

iii. All citizens of the People's Republic of China are equal before the law. Every citizen enjoys the rights and at the same time must perform the duties prescribed by the Constitution and the law. - **Article 33 of PRC's Constitution.**

In order to spell out the minimum conditions for human life and dignity; the basic freedoms & rights include free from discrimination on the basis of age/sex/race/religion etc, access to basic education/employment/property, freedom of movement & assembly, Speech & expression, religion, to participate in voting etc.

PRC on Citizen's Freedoms and Rights

The constitution has undergone four times periodical amendments which took place in 1988, 1993, 1999 and 2004 respectively. The prominent features of these amendments are:

1988 Amendments: The State protects the lawful rights & interests of the private sector of the economy…, the right to the use of land may be transferred according to law.

1993 Amendments: The state practices a form of socialist market economy. Collective economic organizations have autonomy to elect/remove their managerial staffs & decide on major issues as per the law.

1999 Amendments: China practices ruling the country in accordance with the law …, The State protects the lawful rights & interests of individual & private economies and guides/supervises/administers such activities.

2004 Amendments: The State protects the interests and rights of … the individual and private sectors of the economy, Citizens' lawful private property is inviolable and the State protects the rights of citizens to private property & its genetic transfer.

Synopsis of the Freedoms/Rights Guaranteed by the Constitution

Rights to survival and Progress

A right to live and sustain progress is the congenital rights of the citizen. PRC's citizens have access to all sectors of economies like government jobs, business/trades/industries, academics, technical arena, agriculture etc. Government has also introduced policies for social security, e.g., supporting the family having minimum or no sources of income but suffering by prolonged illness and/or seriously handicapped. Health services are stretched all over China and additional supports are kept ready to respond any emergencies. The policy complies with the people's right to live & progress.

Participants visiting Beijing Prison

Civil and Political rights

Article 34 states that "All citizens of the People's Republic of China who have reached the age of 18 have the right to vote and stand for election, regardless of nationality, race, sex, ..."

Article 35 states that "Citizens of the PRC enjoy freedom of speech, of the press, of assembly, of association, of procession and of demonstration." Thus, Constitution allows freedoms of speech, press & forming association.

"Citizens of China have the right to criticize and make suggestions to any state organ..." - **Article 41**. They may lodge their complaints, or criticism even against the government authority for the violation of law; and the authority must deal it responsibly. Law permits the rights to claim if they suffer losses through infringement of their liberties by any state agency.

Religious & cultural beliefs are the integral values of the societies. "Citizens of the PRC enjoy freedom of religious belief" - **Article 36.** Thus, citizens are free to enjoy the freedom of adhering to religious belief, organizing religious programs and carrying out their activities.

The system of ethnic autonomy is another feature of people's freedom. They may carry out their cultural and economic activities uninterruptedly. "All nationalities in the PRC are equal" - **Article 4.**

Economic and Socio-Cultural Rights

Economically, all private or state employees enjoy social insurance facilities. The cultural freedom cannot be interfered until they violate laws.

The right to receive education is secured by constitution. **Article 46** states that "Citizens of the PRC have the duty as well as the right to receive education. The state promotes the all-round moral, intellectual and physical development of children and young people."

Women are put into priority in terms of caring their rights. "Women in the PRC enjoy equal rights with men in all spheres of life, ... The state protects the rights & interests of women, applies the principle of equal pay for equal work for men & women alike ..." - **Article 48.**

Besides, with the approval of the government, over 2700 "Legal Aid Centre for Women" (by All China Women Federation) and "The China Disabled Person's Federation" are working in protecting women's, physically handicapped & weaker section of people's rights all over the country.

Judicial Provisions for People's Freedoms and Rights

"The freedom of person of citizens of the PRC is inviolable ..." - **Article 37**. Citizen cannot be apprehended unless approved or decided by a people's procuratorate or a people's court. Similarly, unlawful search of citizens is also prohibited. "The personal dignity of citizens of PRC is inviolable" - **Article 38**. Likewise, intruding one's private residence without the owner's permission is a crime and nuisance. "The home of citizens of the PRC is inviolable. Unlawful search of, or intrusion into, a citizen's home is prohibited" - **Article 39**.

One of the major rights of a citizen is personal privacy. The privacy of the citizen is protected by the constitution. "The freedom and privacy of correspondence of citizens of the PRC are protected by law" - **Article 40**.

China's has expressed its commitment for the protection of people's liberties and rights in its White Paper too; such as, People's Right to Existence and Development, Civil and Political rights, Judicial work in safeguarding Human rights, Protecting the legitimate rights and interests of women, Guarantee of rights and interest of Minorities, Guarantee of rights and interest of disabled etc.

Apart from these, China has also signed the "International Covenant on Economic, Social, and Cultural Rights" in October 1997 (ratified in March 2001) and the "International Covenant on Civil and Political Rights" in October 1998 (yet to be ratified).

Recommendations and Conclusion

China believes that non-interference in internal affairs is universally recognized principles of international law, and is applicable to all fields of mutual relations and particularly to the field of people's freedoms &

rights. Here, it would be relevant to have a look on the "Inadmissibility of Intervention in the Domestic Affairs of States and the Protection of Their Independence & Sovereignty" **(Charter of the UN)** which stipulates that *"No State or group of States has the right to intervene, directly or indirectly, for any reason whatsoever, in the internal or external affairs of any other State,...."* Thus a nation's internal situation is never "a conducive environment" for others to exert influence in the name of the violation of people's liberties/rights/freedoms.

Although conditions of freedom & rights in China need improvements; much progress has been made since last twenty years. Lionel Vairon, a senior French diplomat, underlines this fact in his newly published book "Threat of China?" He states that *"... among the Western criticisms toward China, regarding its human rights are full of word choice and game. Regardless of those lengthy speeches and articles, Western human rights organizations and their allies claim that the Chinese political system violates human rights, but their claims are results of their biased theoretical thinking, because they have been refusing to face up to the substantial progress that China has made."*

Keeping in view of the allegations, some recommendations are laid down as:

i. Regional disparities cause growing agitations. Effective policies and strategies would work in preventing further agitation and instability.

ii. Develop mechanisms to monitor and correction if the "Equity and Justice" to people is denied by any governmental or social elements.

iii. Active involvement towards Resources security, Environment Protection, Health security of pandemic diseases, addressing economic recession etc helps China in winning the confidence of Global society.

iv. Set-up worldwide Media network that helps to communicate the policies and actions of PRC on freedoms and rights.

v. Enhance access to external media, since the censorship of i-net cannot stop information exchanges in today's era.

vi. Massive untranslatability of Chinese books/publications in major int'l scripts is main factor in letting people know about PRC's activities.

Despite the differences between China and western world, the US now seems to have been realized the progress China has made over the issues of freedoms & rights. The US State Department, Bureau of East Asian and Pacific Affairs, in its October 2009 report has mentioned that "... *China's economic growth and reform since 1978 has dramatically improved...,* *increased social mobility, and expanded the scope of personal freedom. ... meant* *substantially greater freedom of travel, employment opportunity, educational and* *cultural pursuits, job and housing choices, and access to information. ... China* *has also passed new criminal and civil laws that provide additional safeguards* *to citizens. Village elections, ... have been carried out in over 90% of China's* *approximately one million villages."*

Finally, in fact, China and western world have differences over citizen's freedoms & rights, which are due to differences in their own histories, cultures, religions, social systems, levels of economic development and ideologies etc. However, the primary goal, ideal, and substance of people's freedom & rights are same. Thus, it is advisable that China has to move all out to propagate its national perception, initiatives & policies on people's rights & freedom in a greater degree, but that must always be backed with reality and rational logics.

Harmonious China: Its Challenges and the Way Forward

Dato'Nasaruddin Othman
First Admiral, Royal Malaysian Navy

Introduction

National harmony plays an important role in the development of a country considering the multi-ethnicity of its population. Hence, a harmonious society in a nation is paramount towards national political, economic and social stability. Undoubtedly the journey towards achieving a unified and harmonious society is not an easy task, all the more, related to a country like China with 56 multiethnic groups, with different cultures, traditions, religious beliefs and social background is a major responsibility that China has to shoulder.

Creating a harmonious society out of various ethnics groups could be a challenge, though not an impossible task. The difficulty varies depending on the degree of pluralism, structure and characteristic of the communal groups. These obvious challenges are critical and have to be addressed to ensure the sustainable growth of China's development through its reform and opening-up is not affected.

In this regard China among others in its development strategy focused significantly towards social and human development. In ensuring these, the Chinese President, His Excellency Mr. Hu Jintao in 2006, asserted

Participants' group photo taken on their visit to Xiamen

the principle of Harmonious China which among others expounded democracy and rule of law, stability and orderliness and harmonious coexistence between man and nature as a path to facilitate and enhance the development and prosperity of China. Similarly, his vision was expressed in his speech in the United Nations Assembly in 2009 for a harmonious world seeking peace, building harmony and peaceful coexistence amongst nations.

Society in Harmony

A country with multiethnic, multicultural, and multi-religious society has the obvious chances or the ingredient for social instability. In such an environment, unity and harmony is the key factor in achieving social stability, a condition necessary for economic growth and wealth generation. As such, forging strong cohesion to attain a sustainable harmonious environment is vital and China cannot afford to ignore it. Therefore, conscious efforts regarding strengthening family ties, neighborliness, and all other important social values must be given paramount importance continuously and consistently in line with China's vision for the future and its national interests. In order to ensure cohesiveness in building a harmonious society, what path China has to focus? Generally, there are varying factors to be considered relative to China's development programs and its priorities. Nonetheless, China as members of the United Nations has fundamentally understood the guiding principles in attaining a harmonious society as declared in the United Nations Millennium Development Compact 2000. Among others are the eradication of poverty, improve health and education, human rights, cultural development, economy and political structure. Having these in mind but non-exhaustive, where and what are the challenges faced by China in her process of building a harmonious society? Let's view some of these contributing factors which will affect China's harmonious development process.

Educational Development: Harmonious China is closely related to social construction for the people's well-being. As such, there is a need to look into social development, to improve living standards, social reforms, improve social management and promote social equity and justice. This is reflected in China's Social Development Goals 2020. The strategy of this Social Development Goals among others is focusing on education given to China's vast resources on potential quality of human capital. In this regard, China adopted the approach of compulsory education for the benefit of all but more so towards the rural poor. Balanced development on educational infrastructure and provisions of funds has strengthened the educational system in China where the government had spent RMB 2.43 trillion in the period of 2003 to 2007. Under the guidance of unified principles and policies for education, the central government gives the power to the local authority in the autonomous regions to independently plan and develop their educational system. Having said that, whilst giving independent planning and development of educational system to the autonomous region is a positive approach towards unity, however, the tendency of inconsistencies and not adhering to the national education guiding principles cannot be ignored that may well affect national integration.

In comparing with developed nations in relation to China's education system and training methods there are rooms for improvements where in developed nation's educational environment, it encourages innovation and character cultivation. Apart from this, distant learning is encouraged and recognized. In ensuring the rural or the interior area is within reach of good education and closing the educational gap, distant learning through satellite data transmission technology leading to an open training network for all levels of education should be made available.

Medical and Healthcare System: Harmonious family with healthy environment contributes to the development of a nation. Much focus has been given to the medical and healthcare services bringing about social contentment and a healthy community at large. Various health and medical institution has been established ranging from hospitals to Medical Research Institutes. Managing these hospitals and institutions requires certified medical doctors and nurses where currently a ratio of

1.52 doctors per 1000 people with facilities of 2.45 hospitals' beds per 1,000 people exists. Additionally various campaigns and programs especially to improve rural health services, such as sending experienced doctors to work in rural areas, upgrading of water supply, sewages and toilets' facilities were undertaken by the government. Urban health services have been strengthened with the establishment of various community health centers, better insurance system and medical aid improved. These achievements are reflections of China's efforts and progress in health and medical care enjoyed by the people.

Despite all these improvements in medical and health services, due to China's huge population and the imbalanced of development between urban and rural areas, and between eastern and western regions, not all areas are covered in medical and health services including further development of its medical proficiency. The rising cost of medical and health services to an extent imposes on the people and there is a need for government control, and the overemphasis of commercializing the medical services would compound the situation. In the past China has showed serious vulnerabilities to epidemics such as SARS, and the importance of medical efficiency and proficiency cannot be overemphasized.

Labour Force and Employment: Employment places an important role in ones livelihood which directly impact on the social and political stability of a country. China being the most populous nation in the world with an estimated population of 1.3 billion needs to plan an employment strategy both for medium and long-term period. This is being so with the acceleration of urbanization and industrialization of the country where migration of workers from rural to urban area has increased. The trend of population growth, high rate of unemployment coupled with the vast majority with low qualification will remain for some time and is putting pressure on employment requirement. Added to these, the information age and technological advances, has posed more challenges in term of job skills relative to available labor forces. Another area of concern is the high dependency of the Chinese economy on the foreign direct investments

Participants' wives celebrating Children's Day together with Chinese children

and trade relating with employment issues. Recessions and decline in these areas would have a significant impact on China's growth and contribute to China's social problems. In general along with insufficient of new job added with the migration of agricultural labor forces into industrial and service sector, structurally, a visible living void is created between availability of quantitative and qualitative labor forces.

As such, promoting various tertiary and technical educations base on market demands has to be considered. For the rural population, the government has to adjust the structure of agricultural and rural economy, expanding the rural employment capacity and measures taken to transfer the surplus of rural workforce from agricultural base to non-agricultural field.

Social Cultures: Cultural development in accordance to UNESCO's 1982 Conference on Cultural Policies, defines culture as "the whole complex of distinctive spiritual, material, intellectual and emotional features that characterize a society or group. It includes not only the arts and letters, but also modes of life, the fundamental rights of human beings, value systems, traditions and beliefs." Thus, culture constitutes a fundamental dimension of the development process interwoven with economic and political development objectives such as political culture, economic culture and religious moral culture which in turns have linkages between them. With these guiding principles, coupled with the interest and priorities of nation building, culture could be referred in two perspectives, ideally, the national level cultures which refer to those institutions, ideologist, pattern of behavior, and values which are shared by all citizens of the country. Whilst, subset to this national culture, it is referred as the traditional culture which is the "way of life" of the various ethnics groups which formed the nation.

Drawing within these dimensions, Chinese culture which has been preserved until modern time encompasses from Chinese characters, taboos, mythical animals, food and costumes to name a few. It was observed, some of these Chinese traditional cultures have been eroded by time in passing which may result in one form or another, the deterioration of the harmonious environment of family and society at large in China. To discuss a few, it was noted that the Chinese people have always been accustom to dining together since in the olden days. The etiquette of dining is of no exception with sitting order, arranging of dishes and how to propose a toast.

Current trend due to rapid development such as trend-setting lifestyle, patronizing fast-food outlets coupled with the one-child policy, to an extent has virtually eroded family cohesiveness and the society tends to be very individualistic. This is a phenomenon facing most developing nations.

Political Culture: Understanding the tiers in culture behavior, on the national front of the Chinese political culture, it has gone through the mills from foreign invasion, capitalism, and socialist democratic form of government with the inception of the People's Republic of China since 1949. By constitution, the President is the Head of State who promulgates statues and major decisions adopted by the National People's Congress and serving the States for two consecutive terms of ten years. The administrative structure of the State is divided into provinces, autonomous regions and municipalities who are directly managed by the central government. To assist the administrative system, the State established a local government namely the provincial, prefecture, county and township government. The National People's Congress (NPC) elects the President, Vice President and members of other committees were elected during the Congress. Point to note, is the power of the Standing Committee where when the Congress is not in session, they are empowered to elect or dismiss within their authority. The peculiarity in the system is at the Local's People Congress, where those below the county level will only act and observe regulation based on higher authority direction. The absence of a voting right at this level would reflect that democracy is not far reaching and it may expose the system to abuse and corruption. Currently with China's effort towards eradication

Participants visiting a textile mill

of corruption in due course would contribute to good governance and the people's confidence of the government.

Under the premise of socialist democratic with Chinese character formed of government, it is well reflected through the development and economic progress of China, and the huge sentiment of the public support to the government. Opportunity for the public to vote from those serving below the county administrative level should be considered to pave the way for greater transparency and a democratic system of the government in China.

Economic Culture: China's economic reform has been implemented since 1978 when past system implemented were not successful. This reform is characterized by opening to the outside world inclusive of reforms in foreign exchange control and foreign investment. Understandably, rural China than, was operating under the people's commune system. Realizing the opportunities in these reforms, in 1984, about 99% of China's countryside farming was done by contracting land to individual farmers producing positive results. Furtherance to these successful reforms in the agriculture sector, the industry sector followed suit led by the state-owned enterprises through the delegation of power diminishing some of the interest enjoyed by the enterprises and localities. In return, these enterprises were allowed to share profit made with the state and allowing free trade based on market price. Undoubtedly, China has succeeded in its economic reforms where its GDP has been sustaining its growth annually. These success stories were due to good governance and practices by the Chinese government which among others are the planning and marketing strategy being implemented concurrently and relaxing regulation to the newly emerging industrial non-state-owned enterprises to enter the free market. In adopting the economic development policy of opening up, the Chinese government started to develop region by region as the main line of implementation. China's Open Door Policy placed its focus on the coastal region with the implementation of the special economic zone such as Shenzhen and other coastal cities. Further to this, the focus moved towards the border region and inland areas to boost the economy of inland China.

In such a trend, it is obvious that imbalanced development will occur coupled with unequal wealth distribution and the sentiment of discontentment and unhappiness between the developed and underdeveloped areas will arise. China has made great efforts and inroads towards a balanced development of the country. While there is a need to prioritize its development program based on its national capacity and strategic considerations, equal emphasis should be given towards alleviating the quality of life of the less developed regions in terms basic needs and amenities so as to mitigate the imbalanced development that China is not able to avoid.

Conclusion

Building a harmonious society as advocated by His Excellency President Hu Jintao is paramount to China's development. China in its infancy stage of development could not afford to witness a major social unrest and instability that may critically affect its growth towards prosperity. As such great efforts have been made to sustain its growth and taking significant steps in improving the quality of life of its people. It is fair to say that China's approach in transforming its society through its education system will in turn change the society to become more cultured. And a cultured society will lead the people to be more disciplined and adhere to the universal rule of law in social interactions. Politically, China has made tremendous reforms in its system of government adapting to the reality of contemporary China. The restructuring of the administrative system featuring checks and balances measures would make it more transparent and strengthened the people's confidence in the system.

On the economic front, the sustainability of China's GDP for the past years is a reflection of good governance and sound strategic foresight of the government. It is optimistic to say with China's market-oriented reform, will promote a continuous rapid development of the national economy. This growth will undoubtedly contribute to the wealth of the nation and the society at large. However, China is still faced with the unequal distributions of wealth and the imbalanced development between the provinces. This disparity is a grave challenge to China's goal towards a harmonious society and if not well address may lead to social unrest and instability. Nonetheless the various strategies, policies and cooperation in placed between the public, organization and the government of China is the ingredients in directing the nation to a common goal towards realizing a harmonious society.

The Building of the Law System in China

E. M. Nakapipi
Col., Namibian Army

Preface

The socialist system has been introduced and practiced in China for only decades, which is a short period compare with other socialist system adopted in the history of mankind. To keep improving and developing socialist political democracy and to enable the people to fully enjoy and exercise their rights as the master of the country has always being the firm goal of all the endeavor of the Communist Party of China (CPC) and the Chinese people.

At present and for a period to come, the CPC and the Chinese government is actively and steadily push forward the reform of the political system, stick to and improve the socialist democracy system, strengthen and improve the socialist legal system, reform and improve the methods of leadership and rule of the CPC, reform and improve the government's decision-making mechanism, promote the reform of the system of Administrative management, boast reform of the Judicial system, and promote economic development and social progress in an all round way.

Introduction

The Chinese Law is one of the oldest legal traditions in the world. In the 20th and 21st century, law in China has been a complex mix of traditional Chinese approaches and Western influences.

For most of the history of China, its legal system has been based on the Confucian philosophy of social control through moral education, as well as the legalist emphasis on codified law and criminal sanction. Following the Revolution of 1911, the Republic of China adopted a largely Western-style legal code in the civil law tradition (specifically German-influenced). The establishment of the People's Republic of China in 1949 brought it with more Soviet-influenced system of the socialist law. However, earlier traditions from Chinese history have retained their influence, even to the present.

China's legal system has come a long way in just over twenty years. Two decades of reform produced remarkable changes in institutions, law, and practices, to mention just a few of the more significant development: The Ministry of Justice, dismantled in 1959, was re-established in 1979. Law schools were reopened and have trained great numbers of professional lawyers.

But elements outside the People's Republic of China, in particular the western media coverage of China's legal system is overwhelmingly negative, in specific emphasis, the need to strengthen the rule of law in China, and international trade and globalization spur transformations in various areas of Chinese domestic law.

Of course, western media tends to report what is newsworthy rather than important and positive developments, which in practice too often mean the unusual or sensational. We cannot expect much reporting on what is routine and usual, and news report does not necessarily tell the story of China's legal system.

Historical Course of Building a Socialist Country under the Rule of Law

China has a 5,000-years history of civilization. And the Chinese legal system goes back to ancient times. As early as 21st century BC, consuetudinary law appeared in China's slave society. In the Spring and Autumn and Warring States period (770-221 BC), written laws were promulgated in China, and systematic written code of law appeared. In the Tang Dynasty (618-907 AD), China had fairly completed feudal laws, which was passed on and developed in the following feudal dynasties. The Chinese system of law emerged as a unique one in the world. Ancient China made significant contributions to the legal civilization of mankind.

After the Opium War broke out in 1840, China was reduced to semi-colonial and semi-feudal society. To obliterate the sufferings of the country and rejuvenate the Chinese nation, people with lofty ideals tried to transplant to China modes of the rules of law from modern Western countries, but failed for various historical reasons. Under the leadership of the Communist Party of China (CPC) the Chinese people, after revolution, construction, reform and development, gradually took the road of building a socialist country under the rule of law.

The founding of the People's Republic of China in 1949 ushered in a new era for China's promotion the rule of law. The period from 1949 to mid 1950 was the period when China's socialist legal system was first set up. In September 1954, the first session of the First National People's Congress (NPC) was held, which marked the system officially established in the country, and the central People's Government led by Chairman Mao Zedong drafted the Constitution to be discussed on the first meeting of the First National People's Congress.

It was the fundamental law and the cornerstone for further development of democracy and the rule of law and provided a powerful weapon for the implementation of people's democracy and made it clear that the NPC was the political system of the country.

The Rule of Law has been Established as a Fundamental Principle

It is a fundamental principle as well as the common understanding of all sectors of society to govern the country according to law and build a socialist country under the rule of law. Moreover, the socialist idea of the rule of law has been gradually established, with the rule of law at the core, law enforcement for the people as an essential requirement, fairness and justice as a value to be pursued, serving the overall interest as an important mission, and with the leadership of the CPC as a fundamental guarantee.

The CPC's Improvement of Its Governance Capability

The party has constantly enhanced its consciousness and firmness in governing the country in a scientific and democratic way, and by law. It has led the people in making the constitution and laws. Meanwhile, it has carried out activities within the scope prescribed by the constitution and the law, with the constitution as the fundamental criteria by leading the people in making and abiding by laws and guaranteeing law enforcement to consolidate its ruling position.

Legislation and Legal System with Chinese Characteristics

The People's Republic of China is a united, multi-ethnic and unitary socialist country. To guarantee the uniformity of the legal system of the state and reflect the common will and overall interest of the people, China exercise uniform yet multitier legislation.

The Constitution

The Constitution is the supreme of fundamental law of the People's Republic of China (PRC). The current Constitution created in 1982 centered socialist legal system with Chinese characteristics has basically taken shape. It provides that the NPC is the supreme organ of the state power over a structure of other People's Congress at various levels. It has states that no organization or individual is above the law and makes the people's congress and state administration responsible to the people. It also provides that leadership is through the working class, which in turn is led by the Communist Party. It contains more extensive rights than any of the previous constitutions.

Legislative Law

In accordance with the legislative law of the PRC, laws on the following affairs have to be made exclusively by the NPC and its Standing Committee: Affairs involving state sovereignty, the formation, organization as well as the functions and power of the state organs, the system of regional ethnic autonomy, the system of special administrative regions, the system of self-government of people at the grassroots level, criminal offense and their punishment, deprivation of citizens' political rights, mandatory measures, and penalties involving restriction of the freedom of the person, expropriation of non state owned property, basic civil system, basic economic system and basic system of finance, taxation, customs, banking and foreign trade, and system of litigation and arbitration.

China's socialist legal system with Chinese characteristics is open and developing. As China is at the stage of social transformation, its legal system is phased and forward-looking. It will continue to promulgate new laws and revised present ones, so as to develop and improve the legal system.

Legal System of Respecting and Safeguarding Human Rights

China takes as its constant goal the elimination of poverty, enjoyment of the human rights to the full by everyone and building of a prosperous, strong, democratic, culturally advanced and harmonious modern socialist country.

China's basic stand on the development of human rights is: placing top priority on people's rights to subsistence and development, making the development the principle task, and promoting citizens' political economic, social and cultural rights to achieve their all-round development. Based on its constitution, China has formulated and improved a series of legal system to codify and institutionalize the safe guarding of human rights.

Rights to life

China attached great importance to safeguarding its citizens' rights to life. The constitution, criminal law and general principles of the civil law all included fundamental stipulations on protecting citizens' right to life. The Production safety Law, the law on the Prevention and Treatment of Occupational Diseases, and Laws of Protecting working people's life and health.

China still retains the death penalty in the law, but exercises strict and cautious control over the use of death penalty to ensure that it applied only in the most serious crimes. In fact, the death penalty only applies to persons of the age of 18 years and above and nor even affects pregnant women. The law also prescribes the two years probation of execution, which is conducive to rigorously controlling the death penalty and possible reducing the actual number being executed.

Rights to Personal Freedom and Dignity

The Constitution rules that freedom of the citizens of the PRC is inviolable.

No citizen may be arrested without the approval or decision of the People's Procuratorates or People's Court, and any arrest must be made by a public security organ. Unlawful detention and deprivation or restriction of citizens' freedom of the person by other means is prohibited. The residences of citizens are inviolable, and unlawful search of, or instruction into, a citizen's residence is prohibited. The freedom and privacy of correspondence of citizens are protected by law, and unlawful censorship of citizens' correspondence is prohibited.

The Criminal Procedure Law expressly outlaws extortion of confession by torture, and prescribes strict legal procedure for compulsory measures and means, including detention, execution of arrests, investigation and gathering of evidence, related to personal freedom and safety.

Rights to Equality

The constitution establishes the principle that all citizens of the PRC are equal before the law. Every citizen is entitled to the rights and, at the same time, must perform the duties prescribed by the constitution and the law. Protection or punishment is applied equally to everyone regardless of personal differences. No individual or organization is privileged to be beyond the constitution or the law, and all acts in violation of the Constitution or the law must be investigated.

Then law prescribes that all ethnic groups in the PRC are equal, and that the state protects the lawful rights and interests of the ethnic minorities, and discrimination against and oppression of any ethnic group are prohibited. All ethnic groups have the freedom to use and develop their own spoken and written languages, as well as the freedom to preserve or reform their own folkways and customs. The law protecting woman rights stipulates that woman enjoys equal rights with man in all spheres of life, political, economical, cultural, social and family.

Political Rights

It is stated that all power in the PRC belongs to the people. The legislation law prescribes that deprivation of any citizen's political rights can only be done in accordance with the law. The right to election is an important political right for citizens. The law stipulates that all citizens of the PRC who have reached the age of 18 have the right to vote and stand for election, regardless of ethnic status, race, sex, occupation, family background, religious belief, education, property status or length of residence, except for persons deprived of political rights in accordance with the law.

Freedom of Religious Belief

The PRC Constitution stipulates that, citizens enjoy freedom of religious belief. No state organ, public organization or individual may compel citizens to believe or not believe in any religion; nor may they discriminate against citizens who may believe in or not believe in any religion.

The state protects normal religious activities. No one may use religion to engage in activities that may disrupt public order, impair the health of citizens or interfere with the education system of the state. Religious bodies and religious affairs are not subjected to any foreign domination.

Rights and Interests of the Working People

The law on labor contracts, law on labor disputes mediation and arbitration, the promotion of employment, paid annual leave of employees, labor security supervision and law regulate and promote employment, rationally defined the rights and obligations of employers and employees, and protect the lawful rights of employees. The regulations on work-related injury insurance, unemployment insurance, collection and payment of social premiums, interim measures on maternity insurance for enterprise employees' rules guarantee necessary material assistance to the working people in regard to old age, unemployment, illness, work-related injury and childbearing. The regulation on the employment of the disabled, provision on the labor protection of female, prohibit of child labor and other regulations and rules provide special protection for physical health and lawful rights of all underprivileged groups.

Rights of Economic, Social and Culture

The Constitution rules that the lawful private property of citizens is inviolable. It stipulates that, the property rights of the state, collective, individual and any other holder of such rights shall be protected by law, and may not be encroached upon by any entity or individual. Law protecting elderly, maternal and infant healthcare, minors, and disabled and other laws reinforced the protection of special groups.

Judicial System and Fair Administration of Justice

The People's Court is the judicial organ in China, and the People's

Procuratorates is the supervisory organ for law enforcement. The People's Court and People's Procuratorates, in accordance with the constitution, organic law of the People's Court, organic law of the People's Procuratorates, civil procedure law, administrative law and criminal procedure law, independently exercise their adjudicative organs, public organizations and individuals.

The System of Public Trial

The People's Court follows the principles of openness according to law and timely openness in adjudication of cases. Some civil cases such as divorce or cases involving commercial secrets maybe heard in private sessions if the parties concerned so request. Except for cases involving state secrets, individual privacy and minors, all other cases are heard and decided by the People's Court in an open manner, a public notice is always issued about a forthcoming public trial, allowing citizens and media to observe the trial.

The System of Challenge

Any party concerned in a case is entitled to apply to the court to remove any one from the adjudication personnel whom he/she believes had an interest in the case or is otherwise related to the party concerned in the case and may endanger the defendant's right to a fair trial. If any of the adjudication personnel is a party concerned in the case, he/she must withdraw from the case.

The System of Defense

In order to guarantee the human rights of criminal suspects and defendants, and ensure the fairness of the criminal proceedings, criminal suspects and the defendant has right to defense according to the law and the people's court has the obligation to ensure that all defendants are entitled to defense. Criminal suspects and defendants may defend themselves or ask one of two people to serve as their counsels. Based on fact and the law, the counsels provide the court with their own materials and give their views. They may plead that the criminal suspect or the defendant is not guilty, or has committed a lighter crime than he/she is accused of, or ask the court to lessen or relieve criminal liabilities in a bid to safe guard the legitimate rights and interests of the criminal suspects or the defendant.

The System of Reviewing of Death Sentence

Reviewing of death sentences is independent of the system whereby the judgment of the second instance is final. This is important because it requires that all death sentences be reexamined and approved. Apart from the death sentences given by the Supreme People's Court according to law, all death sentences must be reported to the Supreme People's Court for review and approval.

Progress made in respecting and guaranteeing human rights through the improvement of the criminal justice system

The procedures for handling capital punishment have been further improved. The judicial system with respect to minors has also been improved, with the gradual adoption of the methods of investigations, arresting, charging and trial suitable to the situation of minors. There has been an obvious drop in the number of overdue detainees. Legal supervision of the execution of punishment has become more standard.

Pilot programs in the reform of the prison system are proceeding smoothly. The quality of education in prison has been improved, and the legitimate rights and interests of those incarcerated protected according to law.

Conclusions

1. The immense achievements of the construction of the socialism with Chinese characteristic has basically taken shape, and produced remarkable significant development changes in China's legal system, and have made the Communist Party of China and the Chinese people full of confidence in the road of political development chosen by themselves.

Participants visiting Palace Museum in Beijing

2. The socialist political democracy has enabled the Chinese people to become master of their own country and society, and enjoy extensive democratic rights.

3. China's socialist political democracy accords with the nation conditions ensure that the people give full play to their enthusiasm, initiative and creativity in building and managing the state as master of the country and society, and promote economic development and social progress in an all-round way.

4. Along with economic developments and social progress, China's socialist political democracy will be further perfect and with its great advantages and strong vitality, full demonstrated.

5. In the future, the Chinese people will surely enjoy more and more substantial fruits of their political civilization.

China's One-Child Policy: Impact of Demographic Changes and Future Imperatives

Anil Kumar
Capt., Indian Navy

Introduction

China implemented its "One-Child Policy" in 1979. This was done to control the population growth being faced by the country at that time, in order to ensure that economic growth is not stifled by a rising population. The program has been very successful in controlling the overall population of China, which is expected to peak at 1.46 billion in 2033 and decline thereafter. However, the demographic changes brought about by the policy also caused some adverse side effects, which may require to be addressed immediately to avoid detrimental consequences.

China's One-Child Policy

Genesis of the One-Child Policy

China's one-child policy was conceived and implemented in response to concerns about the social and economic consequences of rapid population growth in the 1950s and 1960s. There were two main issues that were meant to be addressed by this population control policy: Firstly, to ensure that rapid population growth does not jeopardise economic development. And secondly, to ensure that there is no food shortage due to a very large population.

Although government family planning services became available to the people of China in 1953, falling death rates resulted in an overall population growth of 2.8%. This eventually resulted in adding almost

250 million people between 1953 and 1970. Compared to the meagre 0.3% population growth that existed before 1953, this kind of growth was unprecedented and relatively very large. Rapid growth rate put considerable strain on the government's efforts to meet the day to day requirements of the people and this eventually resulted in the government's serious consideration of an effective population control mechanism.

The fourth Five-Year Plan in 1970 therefore included measures to control the rising population. This was done by means of provision of contraceptive and abortion services in both rural and urban areas, and promotion of later marriages, smaller families and larger interval between children. These measures resulted in the population growth dropping to 1.8% in the next five years, by 1975. The target set thereafter for 1980 was to attain an overall growth rate of 1%.

One important figure in the study of demographics is the Total Fertility Rate (TFR). The Total Fertility Rate is defined as the average number of children that are born per woman. The Total Fertility Rates in China declined from 5.7 births per woman in 1970 to 2.8 births per woman in 1979. Nonetheless, campaigns and policies implemented thus far could not achieve the target of 1% overall population growth set by the government. This led to the government's formulation of its "One-Child Policy" in 1979.

The "One-Child Policy"

Details of what the one-child policy involved and how it was to be implemented varied at different times. The aim was to curtail the population to 1.1 billion and certainly to 1.2 billion by the year 2000. The initial policy, implemented in 1979, limited each couple to one child. Violation of this norm resulted in substantial monetary fines and loss of certain societal privileges, and this was strictly enforced in urban areas. Important policy changes took place in 1984 and 1988 that allowed couples in most of rural China to have two children. Minority ethnic groups received the rights to first two and then three children, and now even urban couples have the option of having a second child without penalty if they are from one-child families.

In addition, based on their location, 53.6% of the country lives in "1.5-Child Regions" where a couple is allowed to have a second child if the first one is a daughter. By 1990, the percentage of population who were allowed to have only one child comprised 63.1%, those that could have two children stood at 35.6% and the ones that could have three children, at 1.3%.

Implementation of the One-Child Policy

In urban areas, implementation of the programme was simple enough. In some of the advanced cities like Shanghai, most couples were already having only one child because of the pressures of work. So it was relatively easy to achieve a compliance rate of 90% in the urban areas, within a few years.

On the other hand, the situation was different in rural areas. With no government pension to support them in their old age, peasants and others in rural areas required the support of their children to look after them in their old age. Added to this was the cynical outlook of the rural populace towards the government's policies at that time, because they could simply not comprehend the need for such a policy. The social structure prevailing in villages also resulted in family planning workers compromising to needs of their friends and relatives. Gradually, villagers developed a process of negotiation and compromise which allowed a degree of flexibility within the policy. As a result, the proportion of women who had only one child fell only by 10% till 1990.

Demographic Changes Brought about by the Policy

Population Growth

The rate of population growth reduced to 1.46% per year in the 1980s and to only 1.02% in the 1990s. In the 1990s, the population reporting system became very unreliable because of false reports and underreporting of births, especially from the rural areas. For example, in 1991-92, perhaps a quarter of all births were missed by official reporters. The most recent input available is the 2000 Census, which put the Total Fertility Rate (TFR) at 1.22, a dismally low figure by all standards. Much confusion and embarrassment has been caused by the figures reported in 2000, reaffirming the fact that severe under-reporting is prevalent with respect to birth figures. Results from carefully analysed studies by experts put the total fertility rate at 1.6, while the UN Population Division estimates a TFR of 1.71%. The current and projected figures for TFR are shown in Fig 1.

Fig 1. China's TFR per Woman (1990-2050)

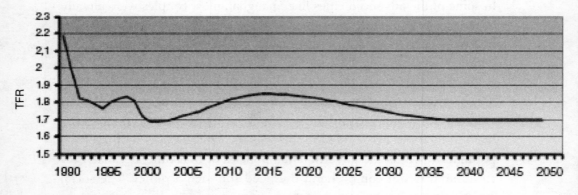

Source: *Age-Specific Fertility Rates and Selected Derived Measures*. US Census Bureau International Database 2002.

It can be observed that the TFR is expected to decline from 2015 onwards and stabilize at a figure of 1.7 by 2038. The "replacement level" TFR for maintaining a constant population is between 2.1 (for most industrialized countries) and 3.0 (for developing countries). In other words, China's population should decline almost indefinitely at the current and projected TFR figures. In spite of this, the growth rate of population is currently estimated to be 1.07% per year, based on the 2000 census. The actual and predicted total mid-year population figures of China from 1950 to 2050 are shown in Fig 2.

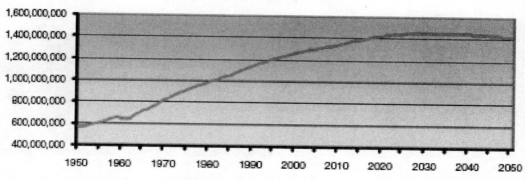

Fig 2. China: Total Midyear Population

Source: US Census Bureau International Database 2002

The graph indicates that the population of China is still growing. This continued growth despite TFR below replacement levels is due to the growth driven by past trends in the 1950s and 1960s when mortality rates reduced significantly, while fertility rates remained high. The population of China is expected to reach a peak figure of 1.46 billion in 2033, and decline almost indefinitely thereafter, based on current predictions by the US Census Bureau. By 2050, the population is expected to reduce by 43 million people, compared to that in 2033.

Age Structure

China's population age pyramid is shown in Fig 3 based on the 1982 and 2000 census, and projected for the year 2030 based on current estimates by the UN Experts Group on Demographics.

It can be seen that in 1982, at the start of the one-child policy, China's age structure was bottom heavy, characteristic of a young and growing population, as is normally seen in the case of developing countries. Nevertheless, the impact of the one-child policy and reducing fertility rates can be noted in the lower percentage of children below 10 years. The 2000 census reaffirms the trend and shows a mature age structure, with the largest percentage of the population in the working age group. Projected only 30 years ahead, with assumptions of moderate further improvement

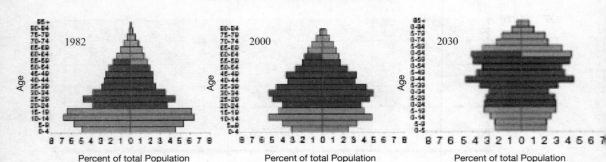

Fig 3. Population Age Pyramid of China

Source: *Demographic Dividend and Economic Prospects for Economic Development in China*. UN Experts Group Meeting on Social and Economic Implications of Changing Population Age Structures. Mexico City, 2nd Sep. 2005.

in life expectancy and continuation of the current fertility level, China's population will be a very old one. In other words, during a brief span of only half a century, China's age structure would have moved from one that is characteristic of a young and growing one, to that of an old and declining one.

Gender Imbalance

The natural biological sex ratio for the human species is 105 baby boys for every 100 baby girls. The ratio in China remained near this figure till the 1980s, when the implementation of the one-child policy caused drastic changes. By the year 2000, the boy to girl ratio at birth stood at 117 and it is estimated that 123 boys are born today for every 100 girls. Based on current trends, this is only expected to become worse in future.

The primary reason for this skewed ratio has been due to the gender inequality that has been carried forward from the Confucian culture. In the long history of Chinese feudal society, the ethical principals set the tone of inequality between people; women were inferior and subordinated to men by regulation. Although women have acquired many rights since 1949, old ideas deeply rooted in traditional practices still influence the society at large in China. Moreover, male children are preferred in rural areas as they can be utilized for farming and other rigorous jobs, besides being expected to look after parents in their old age. All these reasons have eventually resulted in the severe gender ratio imbalance that is prevalent in childbirths today.

It has reached consensus that the rising gender ratio imbalance in China is attributed directly to sex-selective induced abortion (mainly eliminating female foetuses) based on accessible Type-B ultrasound devices. Underreporting of female births has been another factor, with unwanted girl children being left with relatives, abandoned or left at orphanages. The reduced health care available for girl children especially in rural households has also led to a spate of infantile deaths.

Furthermore, the one-child policy allows couples living in the 1.5-child regions to have a second child if the first one is a girl. As almost half the population is allowed to have a second child conditionally if the first child is not a boy, this naturally contributes to the imbalance in gender ratio. More couples have also been noted to undertake selective abortion, to ensure that their second child is a boy.

Impact of Demographic Changes

Economy and Development—Shrinking Workforce

Looking at the Population Age Pyramid in Fig 3, it can be observed that the size of the mainland workforce is already peaking, both as a share of population and in absolute numbers. By 2020, the number of people retiring will be in excess to those entering the workforce. This change is better depicted in Fig 4 where the changing demographic structure is plotted against time.

The working age population comprising people of the 15-59 age group is increasing as of now and this increase will continue till 2015, when it peaks at a figure of 923 million people. Thereafter, it shrinks rather quickly from 2025 onwards. By 2050, the working age population would have shrunk to 750 million. This would seriously impact the development process due to reduced availability of workforce, with consequent effect on the economy.

Fig 4. China: Absolute Age Structure

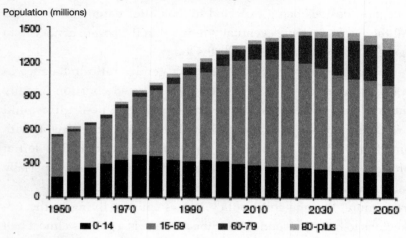

Source: Nations Population Division

Fig 5. China: Dependency Ratio

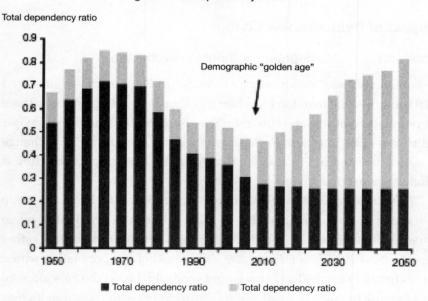

Source: United Nations Population Division

Dependency Ratio

A simple way to measure the relative sizes of important age groups is to use the Dependency Ratio, which defines the number of people who are "dependent" on the working age population. The Total Dependency Ratio is defined as the ratio of the total number of dependents (children and elderly) to the working age population.

$$\textbf{Total Dependency Ratio} = \frac{\textbf{Total Non-Working Population}}{\textbf{Working Population}}$$

Fig 5 depicts the dependency ratio of China projected into the future based on UN estimates. It can be noted that the dependency ratio is currently at its best, at a figure of 0.47. Nevertheless, from now onwards the dependency ratio is going to rise, and by 2050, it would have reached a figure of 0.8 per worker. In other words, the number of dependents per worker would fall from the present 2.3 to a much lower figure of 1.2 by 2050. Such a situation essentially means that the earnings from the workers would be distributed to more number of people, with a lesser amount available per person, thus affecting the spending capacity and consequently, the overall standard of living.

Increased Public Liability

Looking deeper, the elderly dependency ratio would increase from the present 0.16 to 0.56 by 2050. In other words, from the situation today when six workers support one pensioner, less than two workers would be supporting one pensioner in 2050. This would naturally introduce a heavy burden on the government in terms of pension expenditure. Moreover, healthcare needs in case of the elderly are also much higher than in case of the young, which would incur additional public sector expenditure.

Social Implications

The severe gender ratio imbalance in China has led to a situation where 40 million single men would not be able to find brides by the year 2020. This could lead to problems such as abduction of women and other associated social issues. The severe shortage of marriageable women could also result in prospective grooms looking for brides from neighbouring countries, with consequent effects on the social and cultural aspects of the society, besides permanently altering the demographic structure of the country itself.

In many developed cities of the country such as Shanghai and Beijing, couples have been having single children for over one generation now. If this continues for another generation, a new norm of "4-2-1 family" would evolve: composed of four grandparents, only two children and only one grandchild. The children in these families will have no brothers or sisters, no uncles or aunts and no cousins: Their only blood relatives will be their ancestors! This is of serious significance for a country that has strong cultural roots.

Future Imperatives

The above observations clearly indicate that it is time that China takes a relook at the one-child policy. Some of the economic, social and cultural effects of this policy are quite detrimental and therefore, need to be addressed in all earnest. Some suggestions are included in this section.

The current fertility policy that permits couples to have a second child based on the sex of the first child is not a good one to help promote women's status but is instead a compromise to son-preference common in the society. This implies that sons and daughters are not equivalent, girls are inferior to boys and daughter-only couples need to be sympathized. As a result, it may pose serious social consequences by intensifying the gender ratio imbalances being observed now and may even lead to raising the female mortality in some way. This therefore requires to be reviewed at the earliest, to prevent the unnatural gender ratio from becoming worse.

Although it may not be prudent to completely abolish the policy abruptly because of the unknown effects that it would have on female TFR, it is recommended that a step-wise approach could be adopted while addressing the issue. The urban population is already finding it difficult to have more than one child because of the pressures of work and lack of time. In the big cities of China, many people are leading the sort of lives that have brought down fertility in richer countries. In fact, even if the restrictions were loosened immediately, the birth rate might not tick up very much. It is therefore possible that even if the one-child policy is completely abolished, the spurt in fertility rate may not be similar to that of the 1960s.

One recommendation is to change the one-child policy to a two-child policy. Notwithstanding the enforcement of the one-child policy, the TFR of women has not reduced below 1.6. This is because of the fact that the policy has only been strictly enforced in urban areas. In rural areas, the 1.5-child policy and non-reporting of births during census have resulted in most couples having more than one child. If the policy is changed to a two-child policy, it would mostly impact the urban people, who make up less than 30% of the total population. Even if such a policy results in a larger overall population, the proportionate increase in the workforce would help offset dependency costs. Furthermore, the increased workforce would reduce the elderly dependency ratio and allow the government to transfer to families (and the private sector) more of the financial responsibilities of looking after elderly dependents. A larger working population would also promote China's GDP and continued economic growth. In addition, the greater individual freedom would positively impact societal well being and gender ratio.

Conclusion

China's one-child policy which was implemented three decades ago was meant to be a temporary measure to control the explosive population growth prevalent at that time. The programme has been instrumental in arresting the population growth of China, and it has avoided the addition of 250 million people during the last 30 years. The population figures are expected to decline from 2033, after reaching a peak figure of 1.46 billion. In these terms therefore, the policy can be termed as very successful.

Some of the adverse effects of this policy are however being felt now, in terms of workforce availability, social issues and gender ratio imbalance, with no ready solutions available at hand. These adverse effects can be mitigated by addressing each specific issue carefully, and incorporating necessary changes in the policy. The one-child policy itself requires to be seriously reconsidered and should be either abolished or modified sufficiently, to obviate its ill effects on the Chinese society as a whole.

Towards a Peaceful Resolution of the Taiwan Question

A. Mohammed
Col., Nigerian Army

Introduction

After many centuries of Chinese sovereignty over it, Taiwan was seized by Japan during the war it fought with China in 1894-95, and reverted to China in 1945 after Japan had been defeated in World War II. The status of Taiwan and its adjoining islands as an integral part of China is accepted in many international documents. In particular, the three super powers— the US, Great Britain and China proclaimed in their Cairo declaration of 1 December, 1943, that their aim was to stop and punish Japan's aggression, deprive her of all the islands that she had seized or occupied after the second world war, and also restore to Republic of China all territories taken by Japan from the Chinese such as Manchuria, Formosa and the Pescadores Islands (Penghu Islands).

On October 25, 1945, the Chinese government recovered Taiwan and Penghu Archipelago, resuming the exercise of sovereignty over Taiwan.

The Central People's Government of the PRC was proclaimed, replacing the government of the Republic of China to become the only legitimate government of the whole of China and its sole legal representative in the international arena, thereby bringing the historical status of the Republic of China to an end. This is the replacement of the old regime with a new one in a situation where the main bodies of the same international laws have not changed and China's sovereignty and inherent territory have not changed there from, and so the government of the PRC naturally should fully enjoy and exercise China's sovereignty over Taiwan.

The Taiwan question ought to have been resolved except for the interference of the US whom prevented the unification so that she can serve her strategic interest very well in South East Asia and the Pacific. The purpose of this paper is to examine the lingering Taiwan question and in doing so will cover the strategic significance of Taiwan, policies on Taiwan, the current situation and the way forward.

Strategic Significance of Taiwan

Taiwan's geo-strategic significance arises from its location astride the Western Pacific sea lanes of communication which runs from the Strait of Malacca to Japan, South Korea and east wards. Taiwan lies adjacent to both the Taiwan Strait and the Luzon Strait. The Taiwan Strait separates Taiwan from the Mainland and connects the South China Sea to East China Sea in the northeast. Taiwan also commands the East Asia waterways and also the Chinese domestic waterways. These waterways are some of the most strategic waterways in the world today. Taiwan, Japan and the Philippines act as the outer shield of defense of the US. Its location half way between Japan and the Philippines, adds to its significance in the Pacific Ocean. Japan's major shipping is through Taiwan Strait. The Taiwan Strait is one of the most strategic waterways in the world and it witnesses competing strategic interest of US, China, Japan and Russia. The strategic significance of Taiwan is the main reason the US is so reluctant to see a unified Taiwan because the position she occupies will have to be relinquished and hence, her strong hold on

Southeast Asia will no longer be effective.

US Policies on Taiwan

It has been the intention of the US right from the beginning for Taiwan and Mainland not to re-unite, as a follow up all the policies of US have tended to make the re-unification impossible. It is on record that a forceful re-unification would have taken place because mainland had concluded preparation to do so except that before it actually took place the Korean War broke out. The active role China played in that war is partly the reason why US holds very deep resentment against her till today. It was clearly stated on June 27, 1950, when US President Harry Truman said that "occupation of Formosa by Communist forces will be a direct threat to security in East Asia and to US forces fulfilling their legitimate and essential functions there." Thereafter, US Seventh Fleet entered the Taiwan Straits to prevent any attack on Formosa. This singular act marked the beginning of strained relationship between China and the US which lasted for several decades. Following the normalization of China-US relationship in 1979 there was a slight shift in US policies in relation to the Taiwan issue. The US terminated its security treaty with Taiwan, but nonetheless declared that "it continues to have interest in the peaceful resolution of the Taiwan issue." To bolster this declaration, congress adopted the Taiwan's Relation Act, which stated that " it is the policy of the United States" to resist the coercion of Taiwan, both through sales of defensive arms to Taiwan and by possible direct American involvement in any military crisis in the Taiwan Strait. The US was willing to accept the eventual reunification of Taiwan under mainland Chinese rule if that came to pass, but it continued to insist that this or any other outcome be achieved by peaceful means and backed up this insistence with the implicit threat of military action.

From the signing of the 1972 Shanghai Communiqué until the mid 1990s, American policy was that the United States would be satisfied with any resolution of the status of Taiwan that is acceptable to the people on both sides of the Taiwan Strait, so long as the resolution was achieved peacefully. American policy sought to deter each side from taking actions to resolve the situation in a way not acceptable to the other. To understand the recent shift in American policy requires a careful decoding of texts and slogans that were encoded purposely in order to avoid clarity, achieving what came to be known as "strategic ambiguity." The 1972 Shanghai Communique set down the essence what was then a new policy:

The United States acknowledges that all the Chinese on either side of the Taiwan Strait maintain that there is but one China and that Taiwan is a part of China. The US Government does not challenge that position. It reaffirms its interest in a peaceful settlement...

Here the US put in place both end and means that was to serve it well for years to follow. So the insistence on peaceful resolution was aimed essentially at deterring mainland attack. Strategic ambiguity lay in the fact that US never explicitly stated that what it would do to enforce this requirement. It did, however, conspicuously maintain in and around Taiwan the means for a military response adequate to any PRC action.

In 1982, the United States signed another communique with China, promising to reduce arms sales to Taiwan. But the agreement also reemphasized the importance of peaceful solution and left room for continued arms sales as long as peaceful resolution was not achieved. The US at the same time gave "six assurances" to Taiwan, the main idea being that Washington would not push Taipei into talks with Beijing. These agreements did little to change American policy. So by 1995-96, the US was still insisting on peaceful resolution and deterring aggression by strategic ambiguity. It is obvious from the contents of all US's policies on Taiwan that they are strategically aimed at keeping Mainland separated from Taiwan how else can it be reconciled that on one hand America is calling for a peaceful reunification and on the other it is providing incentive to Taiwan to resist.

Taiwan's Position on Unification

The position the Taiwanese are taking on the unification with Mainland is greatly influenced by the deep resentment they are nursing against the Mainland that agreed to hand over Taiwan to Japan following the defeat of China in 1894-95. The Taiwanese argue that since they were left to their fate the improvement in the security environment is no justification for reuniting. The incentive being provided by America has embolden Taiwan to the extent that she says that if there is to be any formal association between the two sides of the Taiwan Strait she must be treated a sovereign state and further asserted that she is willing to cooperate provided China embraces democracy a move she is sure China will not accept. Taiwan is employing this delaying tactics so that she can continue to remain autonomous based on the present status quo. The interesting aspect is the fact that Taiwan is not in any form of doubt that she is a part of China.

In order to guarantee her survivability Taiwan has continued to provide herself with elaborate security against a probable attack by China. As a matter of fact despite the emphasis on developing domestic defense industries, one additional strategy that has broad agreement among Taiwan elites is strengthening political and military ties to the US, including buying US military hardware. In addition to the strictly military capabilities they provide, US arms sales to Taiwan obviously imply a political relationship-not only a willingness by America to support Taiwan against the PRC military threat, but also the package of consultation and training that accompanies the transfer of a modern weapons system. In Beijing's eyes, this brings America and Taiwan closer to reviving their defunct military alliance. In mid December 2009 the issue of arms sale to Taiwan by US came up a move China vehemently condemned. As long as the US continues to back Taiwan the possibility of a peaceful unification seems distant for now and most improbable.

China's Policies on Taiwan

The "One China Principle" is the basis on which Beijing drew her policy on Taiwan. On this basis, China establishes the basic principle of "peaceful reunification, and one country two systems." The key points of this basic principle and relevant policies are: China will do its best to achieve peaceful reunification, but will not commit itself to rule out the use of force; will actively promote people-to-people contacts and economic and cultural exchanges between the two sides of the Taiwan Straits, and start direct trade, postal, air and shipping services as soon as possible; achieve reunification through peaceful negotiations and on the premise of the One China Principle, any matter can be negotiated. After reunification, the policy of one country two systems will be practiced, with the main body of China continuing with its socialist system, and Taiwan maintaining its capitalist system for a long period of time to come. After reunification, Taiwan will enjoy a high degree of autonomy, and the Central Government will not send troops or administrative personnel to be stationed in Taiwan. The contents of the one China policy show that all points have been reasonably covered to allow for a peaceful reunification. China had been most reasonable and generous especially in the areas of allowing Taiwan to remain democratic and not inserting any military in Taiwan. The failure of Taiwan to accept these conditions might force Beijing to reconsider its threat to use force because Taiwan has not been able to provide a credible commitment not to pursue independence.

Current Situation on the Taiwan Question

Following the defeat of DPP in the 2008 elections, and the reemergence of KMT, there appears to be a more favorable atmosphere that portends likely peaceful resolution of the Taiwan question. During his inaugural speech on 20 May 2008 President Ma Ying-jeou reiterated that the goal of his administration was neither to seek unification nor independence but to maintain the status quo. The choice of retaining status quo is a lesser evil than seeking independence. The choice of independence would have closed all likely windows of negotiations. Although the choice of status quo is considered better yet it has some ambiguity in it that will serve the strategic interest of Taiwan because it allows her to remain autonomous. The big question is for how long China will be ready to continue to tolerate the stalemate.

By facilitating cross straits interactions Taiwan has achieved two aims being the enhancement of her economy and gaining respite from China by making her believe that the unification is on course. Taiwan also uses this advantage to continue to develop her armed forces without hindrance. Although China seeks peaceful resolution to the problem, there is the need to set a bench mark on when the status quo is to end otherwise it will linger for too long and might possibly remain unresolved because Taiwan stands at an advantageous position.

The Way Forward

Several solutions have been proffered towards the reunification of Taiwan with the Mainland; so far the progress has been very slow because the intention by the US and Taiwan is for it not to take place. This is mainly so that US can conveniently serve her strategic interest in Southeast Asia and the Pacific. Bearing this in mind China's main thrust is to compel the US to review her policies on Taiwan. China can do so by addressing the very reason why the US wants to perpetually retain a presence in Southeast Asia and the Pacific.

An improvement in the security environment in Southeast Asia and the Pacific will nullify any pretext of maintaining a peace in the region. China has in the past made several concessions in addressing the differences she has had with her neighbors the position of leadership is currently enjoying should encourage her to be more forthcoming in the resolution of existing border problems with her neighbors. The issue of South China Sea is to be pragmatically approached in such a manner that the totality of the problem is addressed. China should also address her problems with Japan and India. Thereafter the need to exert a lot of influence over North Korea to abandon her nuclear programme is made imperative. The essence of doing so is to stabilize the region thereby making the presence of US irrelevant.

Having stabilized the region it is expected that all members will be left in no doubt in the commitments of China towards peaceful coexistence with others. Thereafter she will seek the cooperation of members of the region as she exerts diplomatic pressure over the United Sates particularly in the UN when she tables the problem of Taiwan. China will then seek for a time table to be set towards her reunification with Taiwan. A further request could be made to compel US, on its part, to publicly pledge, unambiguously, submit that it would not support or defend a Taiwan that declares formal independence and to also provide the incentive towards the reunification by compelling Taiwan to reunite with Mainland. To guarantee the commitment of US, the UN and other regional organizations are to be drawn into the paper work that will isolate Taiwan if she defaults rather than relying on the words of the US who has in the past reneged on similar issues.

The remarkable achievements China has made in the area of her achievements and peaceful coexistence with the people of Hong Kong and Macao could be showcased as an incentive to the Taiwanese.

Conclusion

History has shown that Taiwan was a part of Mainland but

Discussion between the participants and the Chinese officers

circumstances of war with Japan led to their separation. At the end of the Second World War Japan was compelled to return Taiwan to China. Due to the policies of the United States the unification has not taken place up till now what is rather obtainable is a situation where Taiwan is neither independent nor re-united with the Mainland. The existing situation favors Taiwan and she would want to retain it, bearing this in mind the need to set the time for the re-unification thus becomes paramount. Although cross strait interactions have commenced earnestly, they are measures that can only douse tension but not lead to unification what is rather required is a commitment from US that can lead to the re-unification.

Recommendations

It is recommended that:

a. China should adopt a more pragmatic approach in addressing the security situation in Southeast Asia and the Pacific to create a stable situation that will make the presence of US in the region irrelevant.

b. China should use diplomatic muscle both at regional and international forum to extract a commitment from the US towards her re-unification with Taiwan.

c. At whatever cost a time table should be made towards the reunification.

$\mathscr{2}$ China's Reform and Opening-up & Social and Economic Development

China's Critical Path to Success in 60 Years

R. N. Nguuku
Col., Kenyan Army

Introduction

The People's Republic of China was founded on 1 Oct. 1949. The country was founded immediately after the end of the Second World War. Before and after the war, China had two competing political parties, the Communist Party of China headed by Chairman Mao Zedong and the Kuomintang headed by Chiang Kai Shek. After the Second World War the Kuomintang attempted to destroy the Communist Party. A civil war broke out in the country in 1946. The CPC seized the military initiative leading to strategically decisive battle and defeated the Kuomintang. Its leadership retreated to the island of Taiwan.

On 21 Sep. 1949, the first Chinese People's Political Consultative congress was held in Beijing chaired by Mao Zedong. During this meeting, Mao Zedong announced that "The Chinese people who account for one fourth of the world population have raised themselves up on their feet, the days when the Chinese people were considered uncivilized are over." On 1 Oct. 1949, Mao announced on the Tiananmen Rostrum the founding of the New China and the central Government of the People's Republic of China.

The Early Years 1949-1956

China was established on an old foundation of economy, culture and backwardness. The government introduced the policy of the great leap forward. This was an economic model focusing on heavy industry and large agricultural production; the small agricultural lands were merged into larger people's communes, massive infrastructure development commenced. This was followed by nationalization of the private capitalist economy and individual agricultural collectivization. The country went through a reconstruction period of 3 years up to 1953; the CPC then realized that it was going to take a long time to achieve the socialism status. This transition was going to take between 10-15 years. The main task of the transition was to complete national industrialization and the socialist transformation of agriculture, the handcraft industry, capitalism industry and commerce. The national industrialization was the dream of every Chinese.

By 1956, the socialist transformation of the private ownership as the means of production had been completed. The socialist economy was thus established. The PRC then entered a new era of socialist construction but there was one principle contradiction between the requirement to establish an advanced industrial country and the reality of backward agricultural development of the economy, culture and an existing system unable to meet these needs. The CPC therefore embarked on the arduous and torturous task of resolving these contradictions.

The Exploration for Development 1957-1965

The CPC during the 1950s was in the exploration stage. In 1957, the CPC launched a national campaign against what was called the "Rightists." This proved to be a bad mistake to allow national construction to be guided by the class struggle theory.

From 1959-1962, the CPC embarked on correcting the errors made earlier and adjusted the economy. By 1965, the domestic economic situation considerably improved with the national industrial and agricultural output value increasing to 59.9% over that of the 1957.

The Cultural Revolution 1966-1976

In 1966, when the economy was showing good signs of momentum of development after years of adjustment, the outbreak of the Cultural Revolution made the economy to take a major downturn. Mao sought to ensure that China hewed its own road of socialist construction based on the long standing political ideals but political ideals and practices were divorced from the reality of the actual situation prevailing in China. The desired end state of strengthening the nation could not be achieved. The Cultural Revolution was hijacked by some people to further their own political ambitions which were totally against what Mao had desired. There was a great lose to the Chinese society.

The Reform and Opening-up

The decision to begin reform and opening up was made at the Third Plenary Session of the 11th Central Committee of the Communist Party of China (CCCPC) in December 1978. Before the reforms China's economy was very underdeveloped. The policy commenced with four modernizations in the sectors of:

a. Agriculture
b. Industry
c. Science and Technology
d. Military

The Four Modernizations were designed to make China a great economic power by the early 21st century. These reforms stressed economic self-reliance. The modernization process was accelerated by stepping up the volume of foreign trade by opening up its markets, especially the purchase of machinery from Overseas.

Economic History

From 1949 to 1978 the economy was a centrally planned one. Private businesses and capitalism were non-existent. To propel the country towards a modern industrialized communist society, Mao Zedong instituted the "Great Leap Forward" which was observed both within and outside as a major economic failure. Mao was succeeded by Deng Xiaoping. The new Leadership began the policy of reform and opening up. Collectivization in agriculture was dismantled and farmlands were privatized to increase productivity. A wide variety of small-scale enterprises were encouraged while the government relaxed price controls and promoted foreign investment. Foreign trade was focused upon as a major vehicle of growth, which led to the creation of Special Economic Zones (SEZs) first in Shenzhen (near Hong Kong) and then in other cities. Inefficient state-owned enterprises were restructured and the unprofitable ones were closed, resulting in massive job losses.

The reform and opening-up policy became a success story in the last 30 years. The country has world's third largest nominal GDP at 30 trillion Yuan (US$4.4 trillion). The economy is second to the US at US$7.9 trillion corresponding to US$6,000 per capita. It's the fourth most visited country in the world with 49.6 million inbound international visitors in 2006. Member of the WTO and is the world's third largest trading power behind the US and Germany with a total international trade of US$2.56 trillion—US$1.43 trillion in exports and US$1.13 trillion in imports. Its foreign exchange reserves is US$2.1 trillion, the world's largest. It owns an estimated $1.6 trillion of US securities. It is among the world's favourite destination for FDI, attracting more than US$80 billion in 2007 alone.

The Leadership

The Country has seen four generations of leaders as follows:

a. First generation. This was led by the founding father of the nation, Chairman Mao Zedong from 1949 to 1976.

b. The second generation led by Deng Xiaoping who brought economic prosperity and put China on the world map.

c. Third generation led by Jiang Zemin who worked to establish a fairly ideal socialist market economy.

d. The fourth generation led by Hu Jintao who are working to modernize the economy and the environment and to create a harmonious country and world.

Science and Technology

The Chinese government realized very early that the crux of the Four Modernizations was in the mastery of modern science and technology.

Without the high-speed development of science and technology, it is impossible to develop the national economy at a high speed. A National Science Conference was held in March 1978 in Beijing to draw a science policy. The conference was attended by China's top leaders, and 6,000 scientists and science administrators. Science and technology was assigned a key role in China's "New Long March" toward the creation of a modern socialist society by the year 2000. This was achieved and together with the policy of reform and opening up, they have brought China to be a mighty world economy.

Achievements

The country in the past 60 years has made major achievements as listed below:

a. China's economic and comprehensive national strengths have been continuously enhanced and the living standards as well as the people's welfare have been improved.

b. The mindset of the people—the opening up has brought a new vitality to the people's tedious and uniform lifestyle and way of thinking, which was dominated by the personality cult of political leaders for years, which was against humanity.

c. The people's spiritual and cultural life has been enriched to promote diversified thinking.

d. Concepts like competition, efficiency, democracy and rule of law had never been encouraged before reform and opening up, the Chinese people are today enjoying greater freedom in thinking, making choices on their own and deciding their own fate.

e. Revolutions in spiritual and intellectual life have mobilized hundreds of millions of people who devoted themselves with creativity and enthusiasm to China's socio-economic development.

f. China has established a market economy which has replaced the government in playing a decisive role in resource allocation and social development.

g. China has been gradually been assimilated into the global mainstream during the decades of reform and opening up.

h. The market economy and democracy have proved to be the most successful institutional creations in human civilization up to the present day. In its reform and opening-up, China has learned the merits of these creations and voluntarily observed the common rules for the development of human society so as to overcome the flaws of traditional Chinese concepts of rules and to promote augmentation of national welfare and restore wealth and power for the country.

i. China has learnt from Western countries' technologies and their experience in developing a market economy and democracy as well as Western civilization, in order to carry out institutional reforms

j. China has successfully seized the opportunities of the third wave of globalization and effectively participated in international division of work to develop its economy and also became a member of the World Trade Organization (WTO).

k. China is recognized today as a member of the global mainstream. Its commitments and credit in the capacity as a sovereign country warrant that she will adhere to the reform and opening-up policy in its future development.

l. China has followed the path of building socialism with Chinese characteristics and has formed a theoretical system of socialism with Chinese characteristics.

Challenges

China is faced with challenges as she moves to the next stage of being a developed country. These are:

a. The population of 1.3Bn exerts impact on various aspects of the economic and social development. While offering abundant labour resources for the economic and social development, it puts pressure on the economic development, social progress, consumption of resources and the environment.

b. There is a serious environment pollution problem due to the extensive development of the economy which needs to be addressed.

c. China is third largest energy producer in the world next to the US and Russia. It is the second largest energy consumer after the US. China therefore is faced with energy crisis due to the current rate of development.

d. The gap between the rich and the poor is widening fast. The rich account for only 20% of the total population. There is also a big imbalance in the development in the regions; the east being well developed followed by the central then trailing behind is the western region. This disparity is bound to create serious social economic problems in the country.

e. China's image in the international arena is tainted because of the wrong perception. China's foreign policy and other public relations policies have not done enough to market the right image of this country.

Recommendations

The following are recommended for continued prosperity of this beloved country:

a. The reform theories should be updated and innovated in accordance with changes in practice in order to guide further reforms.

b. The economic construction should be the central task of China's development and should remain as such under any circumstances.

c. Stick to the path of socialism, adhere to the CPC leadership and pay attention to reform innovations at the grass-roots level ordinary people while implementing the policy, which is conducive to effectively safeguarding the country's unification and social stability against the background of growing diversified interests in China.

d. Continue to cultivate a market-oriented economy and implementing the opening-up policy at a gradual pace so as to ensure China's solid assimilation into the global mainstream.

e. Continues to nurture socialism which is in the primary stage and seek understanding the essence of this theory.

f. Recognize that besides its achievements and experience, mistakes were made and these are lessons learnt and seek correct measures in order to reap the full benefits of the socialist system.

g. That economic growth was achieved at a great cost to the environment and excessive resources consumed. The environmental and resources must be restored for the future generations.

h. Develop policies to help breach the gap between the rich and the poor which continues to widen.

i. Compensate workers whose rights and interests were neglected by not having the rights to collectively negotiate over payment, social security rights which are common in developed countries.

j. That in the reform and opening-up drive in the coming years, the government should adhere to its primary experience and fundamental policies of the past 30 years and continue to focus on economic development promoting the role of the market in resource distribution and seek correct solutions to contradictions and problems that accrue in the process of socio-economic development.

k. A deliberate policy is required to market China positively in the international arena.

Conclusion

China has followed a very difficulty, long and winding path from her founding as a poor country to a country with a world class mighty economy. The success story came about through difficulty and unpopular decisions which the leadership had to make at a critical time to steer the country to the present status.

The policy of reform and opening-up which propelled the country from a near collapse to the present day success should be sustained and more done to balance these achievements so as to minimize the gap between the affluent and the poor which is growing at a very first rate. The next step which should worry the national leaders now than ever before is how to sustain the growth of the economy and achieve complete reunification of the country and maintain the elusive stability in the country's western and northern region by putting more resources in these areas in order to avoid despondency and separatist altitudes.

China's Reform and Opening-up Policy towards a Sustainable Economic Development

Hartind Asrin
Col., Indonesian Army

Introduction

In 1978, Deng Xiaoping saw China's economic progress is very slow and apprehensive, it was necessary for national reform. Sun Tzu said: Who Can see what the people cannot see is the brilliant's person and know what the people don't know is genius's person. Deng Xiaoping saw this condition and has published a national policy which can now be enjoyed by the people of China and the world was surprised to see the strongest of China's economy. China's economic development and social progress in the past period of almost 30 years have directly benefited from the reform and opening up, two great turning points of historical significance: moving from the orthodox planned economy to modern market economy and from a closed or semi-closed state to the decision to open up the country in an all-round way. Two times the economic crisis engulfing the world in 1997 and 2007 did not affect significantly to China.

This is because the four engines; Investment, Industry, Government Expenditure and Consumption of the people of China running well, after society publishing works of national reform policies of Deng Xiaoping.

China is a global actor today, but it is increasingly being called upon by other countries, notably the US and EU nations, to become a more fully engaged and "responsible" global power—as World Bank President Robert Zoellick once describe it "a responsible international stake holder." China's product flooded global markets because of the cheap price so that we can compete with the products from competing countries around the world. Otherwise, Obama visit to China from 16 to 18 November 2009 is one indication that China is calculated by the US as a global power. With the financial strength of the country, had welcome to Obama by the signing of the memorandum of understanding with the construction of Shanghai's Disney whose contract value of $3.6 billion. In 2009, China had 2.3 trillion exchange reserves and the largest reserves in the world that can support its national economy and the world economy.

Policy Analysis

"I am son of the Chinese people, and I deeply love my country and my people." This statement made Deng Xiaoping always thinking about the interests of the State and his people. The major leader and chief architect of China's reform and opening-up policies, Deng Xiaoping had launched in The Third Plenary Session of the 11th Central Committee of the CPC, held in late 1978, saw the introduction of China's reform and opening-up

Participants visiting Shanghai Urban Planning Exhibition Center

policies. The process of the new policies was from rural reform to urban reform, from reform of the economic structure to structures in all aspects, and from internal vitalization to external opening up. The huge economic strength has helped China accomplish a great number of outstanding projects such as the Three Gorges project, the Qinghai-Tibet railway, the wonderful Beijing Olympics, the successful mission of the Shenzhou-7 manned spacecraft and a successful of Special Economic Zones.

China economy growth in the last three decade average 10%. It means that China need energy to support their sustainable economic development. Otherwise, there are still some contradictions and problems in mineral resources survey and development in China, such as the contradiction between the fast economic growth and the huge consumption of some mineral resources. There is a fairly large gap between the supply and demand especially on oil. In 1982 Johnson found the key of the successful of Japan economic because of MITI (Ministry of International Trade and Industry). The successful follow by Taiwan and South Korea. To support their industry, SPC (State Planning Commission), ministry level create the strategy of energy security.

China is a developing country with a large population and relative shortage of resources. China will continue to deepen the reform, widen the opening-up, develop the socialist market economy unswervingly, take the road of sustainable economic development, and rationally use and protect its resources. China will, as usual, take an active part in international cooperation for development of resources and environment protection, and join hands with all other countries in the world in advancing boldly to achieve the sustainable economic development.With Deng Xiaoping Theory as its guidance, persisted in focusing on economic construction and engaged in an ever-deepening reform and opening up, resulting in rapid economic growth and enhancement of its overall national strength. The socialist China, instead of collapsing, has shown its great vitality. The facts have frustrated the absurd predictions of the West, and those profits are laughed at by history.

The question arises why the Chinese economy was so strong in the face of economic crisis that hit the world in 1997 and 2007? The world was shocked to see such rapid economic growth in China. The Government published a national reform policy known as reform and opening-up policy. This policy is appropriate and can be implemented through appropriate strategies including maintaining domestic market momentum, transfer from an agrarian society to industrial countries and developing infrastructure to create good quality and can absorb a lot of manpower to support these strategies. The momentum already achieved, this continuity must be maintained so that economic development is not inhibited and the energy needs to support economic development and energy reserves should be filled according to plans already made. Special economic zones are implemented should be encouraged to continue to improve the quality of SEZs in these areas and further progress of Taiwan, Macao and Hong Kong.

International Institute for Management Development (IMD) in his research concluded that there are several factors that support China could become a global economic power with strong competitiveness.

- First, China is the economic actors with economic power to the world's largest-4 visits of GDP and supported by high economic growth and fast.

- Second, China's ranking improved in the context of globalization. China ranked the best in competitiveness. This is supported by the National Protection.

- Third, achievements in the field of information technology. China is a strong competitor in the field of infrastructure construction techniques. The use of computers and telecommunications investments in fixed and ranked second in the world. Encourage greater infrastructure investment growth techniques other related industries will help China narrow the gap with developed countries of information security.

To maintenance and improve the economic sustainable, the China's government change their diplomatic strategy. Since he was elected Chinese president, Hu Jintao changes China's diplomatic strategy from "Great-Nation Diplomacy to "Oil-Nation Diplomacy." China is active to conduct diplomacy to the oil producing countries. It's implement the energy security strategy in order to support economic development desperate need of energy, especially oil.

Suetainable Economic Development Strategy

Economics' Strategies: China has released its economic strategy to support the sustainability of it's as follows. In general, there step development strategy depicts the big picture and the five year plan explains the specific method or reaching it. China's overall economic construction objectives were clearly stated there step development strategy set out in 1987 "The Three-Step Development Strategy":

Step-1: To double the 1980 GNP and ensure that the people have enough food and clothing was attained by the end of the 1980's.

Step-2: To quadruple the 1980 GDP (4 times) by the end of the 20th century was achieved in 1995 a head of schedule.

Step-3: To increase per-capita GDP to the level of the medium-developed countries by 2050 (3,400 USD) at which point, the Chinese people will be basically realized.

To realized that, China adopts the "five years plan" strategy for economic development. The 11th Five-Year Plan (2006-2010) is the currently being implemented.

Four Engines of China's Economy: Why the Chinese economy is so strong, can be seen from the four engines of China's economic development is working well. After publishing reform and opening-up policy, China's economic growth moved quickly and fast. Four engine, investment, industry, government expenditure and consumer of Chinese people support economic growth in high level. On earlier November 2009, World Bank had upgraded its 2009 growth forecast for China to 8.4 percent after recovery from global economic crisis.

FDI (Foreign Direct Investment): At present, China as over 220 trading partners around the world, and import and export volume has increased to US$ 2,173.8 billion in 2007 from US$ 20.6 billion in 1978, an increase of 104-fold. Over the same period, China's trade volume ranking has jump from the 32nd in the world to third. The utilization of foreign investment started from zero and by the end of 2007, the accumulated direct foreign investment received amounted to over US$ 750 billion. FDI come from Chinese Overseas, such as investors from Taiwan, Hongkong and all over the world. China has become attractive because of stability, cheap of labor and government guarantees for the survival of their companies.

Industry: China population is mostly farmers. In the 1980s gradually shifted to the industry and the products can meet the needs of society and the international. Electronic products and transportation and flood the world market to compete with products from other countries. Progress in the field of rapidly growing industries and encourage economic growth of China. Creativity and innovation are owned indirect of China is a positive factor in the maintenance of China economic growth and can compete globally.

Government expenditure: China has foreign exchange reserves of USD 1.6 trillion in the year 2008. With the government's foreign exchange reserves are large can freely make national economic policies, among those carrying out the development of state-owned enterprises including the development of CNPC (China National Petroleum Company), Sinopec (China Petrochemical Company) and CNOOC (National Offshore Oil Company). In addition, the government strengthens infrastructures, airports, seaport and road with quality that can support the economic activities. Government spending can attract workers with the development of large-scale infrastructure. Like veins in the human body, the infrastructure can provide blood to the entire human body, development of infrastructure to support economic activity domestically and internationally.

Consumption of the people: With 1.3 billion population of China has a very large domestic market. Consumer theory is a theory of microeconomics that relates preferences to consumer demand curves. The link between personal preferences, consumption, and the demand curve is one of the most complex relations in economics. Implicitly, economists assume that anything purchased will be consumed, unless the purchase is for a productive activity. Consumer of the people had contributed to economic growth of China extensively.

Special Economic Zones: Since the late 1970s, and especially since the 3rd Plenary Session of the 11th CPC Central Committee in 1978, the basic state policy has focused on the formulation and implementation of overall reform and opening to the outside world. In July 1979 The National People's Congress (NPC) passed "Regulation for the Special Economy Zones of Guangdong and Fujian Province" and officially designated a portion of Shenzhen as the Shenzhen Special Economic Zone (SSEZ). In 1980, there are other 4 SEZs of Shenzhen, Zhuhai, Shantou and Xiamen. In 1984, China further opened 14 coastal cities to overseas investment: Dalian, Qinhuangdao, Tianjin, Yantai, Qingdao, Lianyungang, Nantong, Shanghai, Ningbo, Wenzhou, Fuzhou, Guangzhou, Zhanjiang and Beihai. Since 1988, mainland China's opening to the outside world has been extended to its border areas, along the Yangtze River and inland areas. And the state decided to turn Hainan island into mainland China's biggest special economic zone (approved by the 11th session of the 7th NPC in 1988) and to enlarge the other four special economic zones. In June 1990, the Pudong New Area in Shanghai was opened to overseas investment, and additional cities along the Yangtze River Valley. Since 1992, a member of border cities and all the capital cities of inland provinces and autonomous regions have been opened. In addition, 15 free trade zone, and 53 new and high-tech industrial development zones have been established in large and medium sized cities.

Energy Security: The Chinese government holds that to have foreign mining companies enter China and Chinese mining enterprises enter other countries to make different countries mutually complementary in resources is of great significant for the common prosperity and healthy development of world mineral resources prospecting and exploitation. In 2004, China import 100 million barrel oil. It's the reason why the prize of world's oil increased very significant at the moment. National Petroleum Company such as CNPC (China National Petroleum Company), Sinopec (China Petrochemical Company) and CNOOC (National Offshore Oil

Company) are the state-owned enterprises. These companies have a major influence on the economic progress of China. As you know, China is the top oil consuming in Asia and the second in the world. That way, China conducted their owned strategy to cover their consuming of energy. "The Energy analyst from Washington, Roger Tissot said "The Chinese are entering Latin America without political expectations or demands....they just say, 'I'm coming here to invest,' and they can invest billions of dollar. And obviously, as a country with billions to invest, they are taken very seriously."

The government of China implemented Strategic Petroleum Reserves (SPR) in their work to their energy security. To implement SPR, China cooperates with International Energy Agency (IEA). In August 2005, China had 33 million barrel oil as SPR, its pull in Zhenhai, Zhejiang province. In 2008 China had 100 million barrel for SPR and located in Zhenhai, Daishan, Huangdao and Dalian. For long term IEA advised to China's government should have 90 days total China import today. It's would be realized in 2015. In support of the energy policy, China conducted the diplomacy to the oil-producing countries. This is done to facilitate the National Oil Companies to expand overseas.

Conclusion

To Sustainable economic development, The Chinese government through reform and opening-up policy and implemented through strategies that are innovative and creative management can increase the level of rapid economic growth, but should attempt to anticipate future developments and consider current issue of economic. It is suggested that the Government of China made the right strategies and anticipate the future, among others:

- Reduce the gaps between rural and urban areas, between eastern region and central-west areas by development the infrastructure and other public facilities.

- Realizing strategic petroleum reserves with the national oil reserves to 90 days in the year 2015, like US had 700 million barrel and Japan had

900 million barrel or 169 days for their strategic petroleum reserves.
   - Speed up the special economic zones by a series of efforts to increase GDP in close proximity to Hong Kong and Taiwan society.

The "Middle Kingdom" has Waded Across the River: The Reform and Opening-up Policy in Perspective

Joel DC Celino
Col., Philippine Army

Introduction

In the English dictionary or in the Thesaurus, REFORM as a noun is defined as the way of re-organizing and improving something such as a social or political institution or system that is considered to be faulty, ineffective or unjust. Others define reform as means beneficial change, or sometimes, more specifically, reversion to a pure original state. It was also defined as the adoption by somebody or group of a more acceptable way of life and mode of behavior. It means that it is a drastic change from the present system for a more favorable future of the majority. OPENING-UP on the other hand, is describe as commencing, initiating and launching certain things or system by way of improving something by correcting faults, removing inconsistencies and imposing modern methods or values. So in short, reform and opening up is policy that intends to change the present system of closing its doors, sticking to the beaten track and being self complacent and learn from the advanced and more develop countries.

In the later part of the 1970s, the world witnessed several phenomenons that completely change the history of the whole world. On 1 January 1979, the United States and the People's Republic of China (PRC) established full diplomatic relations after years of ignoring each other in the international arena. On that same month, the world saw the fall of the Iran Monarchy and gave rise to a different order in that part of the globe. Relatedly in May, Margaret Thatcher was elected as Britain's First Women Prime Minister after several years of male domination. Likewise, on 16 July, Iraqi President Hasan al-Bakr resigned and Vice President Saddam Hussein replaced him. Saddam Hussein assumed power that would span for more than 30 years over the country that has the biggest oil reserve in the world. On the later part of that same year, Russia invaded Afghanistan in spite of the protest howled by a lot of the nations. Such invasion would continue to haunt the world until today. And more importantly in that year, PRC under the leadership of Chinese Premier Deng Xiaoping embarked in to a pristine policy of Opening up to the Outside world. Although a perilous and precarious yet innovative policy, it will in turn not only a breakthrough in the history of PRC but will also change the complexities of the International World order in the years that followed.

Thirty years after the implementation of the policy, the effect on China's economic boom and unexpected development was enormous that would bring to the fore questions from not only throughout the Asian Region but also to the world. China has successfully sponsored the 2008 Beijing Olympics and by next year the World Exposition in Shanghai. The impact of its incredible rise has confronted the idea and issue of future dominance not only to the traditional powers in the region like India, Japan or South Korea but also to the US and to the European Community.

The Reform and Opening-up Policy in Retrospect

The 60th National Day Parade last 1 October 2009 at the fabled and legendary Tian'anmen Square at the heart of Beijing City started with the entrance of the National Flag at the center of the Parade area. It was then followed by the usual "Trooping the Line" by President Hu Jintao to all the military participants. After the "Trooping the Line," members of the Military (both male and female) started marching all in clock like precision. The soldiers marched proudly in unison that left the audience with great admiration and appreciation.

After the Marching Battalions, the Troop carriers and Tanks of different sizes started to roar towards the parading area. Next to enter were the anti tank, surface to air and ballistic missiles taking on the center stage. It was followed by the some of the Air assets of PRC—the choppers, fighter jets and supply plane. Coming from a Third World Country, the author could not help but look with envy the grandeur of the military equipment that I have seen in front of me. It was the first time in his entire life that he had seen such military might and power.

The civilian participants came in next, with their floats and made their entrance towards the center of the parade ground. The decorative floats together with the collaborative dances that go with it were such a beautiful and delightful site to look at. They were so inspiring and very colorful. The floats showed the advances and development that China has undergone and undertook in the past 60 years. They elaborately and ornately showed the growth of China in the fields of sports, education, science &technology, housing, transportation, Space travel, culture & arts, agriculture, environmental protection, medical services, cultural minorities among others and yes, the much applauded floats from Hongkong and Macao depicting further the One Country, Two Systems Concept.

The last part of the parade saw more than a thousand or so children with colorful balloons taking center stage. Immediate after reaching the center of the parading area, they released the very colorful balloons in the delight of the predominant elders and much older crowd. It was a very symbolic gesture that truly depicts—that the future of the country lies on the younger generations. As writers and soothsayers use to say, "Truly the youth is the hope of the motherland."

Participants attending seminar on the module *China Studies*

Anyone who has seen the Parade could not help but be amazed and astounded by the parade's splendor and grandeur. Media reports that more or less 180,000 people participated in the parade. It was very astonishing and remarkable. And yes it was very cinematic and colorful too. Spectators like the author were very fortunate that they seen and attended one of the most beautiful parade in the world. It was a once in a lifetime opportunity that was not for everyone to see.

The National Day Parade in a nutshell was not simply a show of force nor an extravagant undertaking by the PRC. It was story of struggle, sacrifice and strong sense of patriotism that has endured for decades. The Parade was not only the substantial and incomparable accomplishments of the PRC today. As a frequent travel to the west, the writer was genuinely amazed by the sight of the other cities like Shanghai, Guangzhou and Shenzhen. In all honesty and sincerity, one visitor cannot help but asked, how did China attained is prosperity in just small amount of time? 60 years of rapid and peaceful development? Other countries have been struggling and still developing for centuries.

The bittersweet transformation of the PRC that has withstood the blustery weather of changes through 1949 to the present was truly an astonishing and remarkable feat of the Chinese leadership. Yet it did not also come in a silver platter so to speak. In spite of its internal and external challenges, China has emerged towards prosperity, peaceful development and political strength not only on this side of the world but also in the international scene. But how could China emerge from the Cultural Revolution in 1949 to what it is today? What was the momentous event that led to its near mystical and story book peaceful revolution and development? What is the Reform and Opening-up Policy that led to this remarkable development?

After the untimely demise of Mao Zedong in September 1976, the PRC was left with no symbolical and administrative leader to look up to and emulate. China was stranded at a political crossroad and economically struggling from the chaos of the Cultural Revolution. According to Jaime Flor Cruz, CNN's Beijing Bureau Chief, "China is in an economic collapsed at that time. People were poor and isolated. A lot of them wanted to leave their provinces in order to get out of poverty. There was little international trade. There are few tourists and few cars, but there were millions of bicycles on the streets."

In August 1977, Deng Xiaoping re-emerged into the political scene and was elected as the new Central Committee Vice Chairman and the Central Military Commission (CMC) Vice Chairman. And finally in December 1978 at the Third Plenum of the Central Committee of the Eleventh National Party Congress, became the turning point and the PRC leadership under Deng Xiaoping embarked to an unprecedented and ambitious direction set towards economic development and away from the usual class struggle that was the guiding principle of previous PRC Leaders. The Reform and Opening-up Policy was envisaged.

Comrade Deng's call for reforms set off and triggered a series of expeditious changes throughout the country which commenced at the rural areas and into the cities in the years that followed. The communes that were organized after 1949 were disintegrated and disbanded. The farmers in the said rural areas retorted positively and agricultural products increased considerably. Later, Deng and the PRC leadership moved their attention and reforms to the cities by engaging with capitalism in specific "Special Economic Zones" throughout the country.

The importunate Maoist policy in the rural areas which focused for continuous socialist reforms was reversed by Deng's new policy on "Decollectivization." The people's communes were modified by a "Household Responsibility System," which surged personal initiatives and material rewards to farmers who also increased the agricultural outputs significantly. In urban centers, the industrial sector was re-arranged to concentrate power and authority in the hands of the managerial and technical experts. In order to promote and enhance economic efficiency, bonuses, good benefits and higher rates were introduced. The new policies also loosened and slacken all forms of economic controls and instigated the Special Economic Zones which became free trade areas that showed the thriving ability of a liberalized economy. Such policies alleviated millions of Chinese from poverty in the next few years. Records showed that the economic reforms that began 1978 have helped lift millions of people out of poverty, bringing the poverty rate down from 53% of the population in the Mao era to 12% in 1981. By 2001, the poverty rate was estimated by the World Bank to be at 6% of the population.

The policy further accented and emphasized the realistic goals commonly known as the "Four Modernization" and towards the improvement of relations with the West. Relatedly, under Deng's pivotal guidance, relationship with the west notably the United States and Japan expanded and improved significantly. In that same year, The US broke diplomatic relations with Republic of China (Taiwan) and established relations with the PRC. This was commonly called the One China Policy of the US.

The Reform and Opening-up Policy did not only concentrate on improving the economy and international relations with other countries. The PRC leadership was able identify other fields where modification should be given equal attention in order to be at par with the rich and more developed nations. The new policy encouraged artists, writers and journalist to espouse additional significant methods and procedures to espouse their talents but open attacks on authorities were not permitted. The regimented controls and reins on fashion, film making, music, arts, intellectual and creative fields were unfastened and slackened.

The Educational System was also reorganized especially in teaching and research establishments throughout the country with special prominence on Science and Technology was widely stressed. Local Students were also permitted and allowed to study abroad notably in Europe, US and even in Australia. At the same time, foreigners or alien students were permitted to study in China. Likewise, a more reliable and expanded Judicial System and Education was established in order to equip the lawyers with more pertinent and germane methods to practice their trade.

Also given equal importance, the PLA was modernize and restructured to be more relevant and professionalized. In maintaining with Deng's mandate to reform, the PLA has demobilized millions of men and women since 1978 and was initiated modern methods in the fields of recruitment and manpower, strategy, and education and training.

With the Reform and Opening-up Policy, the PRC is virtually a mystical tale of an economic singularity. While its neighbors were economically struggling brought about by several financial crisis, the Chinese economy grew at an average of 9.5% for the past 26 years since 1978, making the PRC the 4th largest economy in the world. A recent national economic census reported recently that growth rates were on an upturn of 10% for 2004, 9.9% for 2005 and more of the same in 2006. Now, economic strategist around the world has identified China as the third largest trading nation in the world.

China's Rapid Development: a Pandora's Box

Under the new and untested policy, the PRC achieved a dramatic transformation of unheralded growth and development instigated by the reforms and new policies. Unimaginable changes occurred since 1979 which have shamed away from uncompromising political goals of continuous revolution and the "Iron Curtain" policies that were introduced in 1949. But in spite of the rapid changes on development and virtuous relationships with the outside world that have taken place, China will still be beset with problems and challenges that needed solutions and uncompromising responses in order that the unselfish sacrifices and untiring efforts being undertaken will not go down to the drain.

The rapid economic growth resulted in an equally numerous ripple-like effects to Chinese society and system. The PRC is also confronted with some substantial and important threats and natural inequities. As a result of its rapid growth and development, China is faced with an increasing problem of inequality especially between the rich and poor in rural and urban centers. Similar problems can also be observed between the eastern and western regions of the country. Due to such disparity, unequal distribution of wealth and economic opportunities affects the lives of the population thus there is also an increase in unemployment and obviously rise in poverty. To the number of employed percentage of the population especially rural residents who work in urban centers, the living conditions of workers are also increasing. Apart from this, wage benefits such as bonuses, health care insurances among others are escalating under the present system and policy.

Another blatant issue is the implementation of intellectual property rights. Continuous disregard of such is not encouraging Research and Development among firms and companies around the country. If authorities wanted to go beyond the "assembly line" investments, this needs to be addressed in the near future.

The rapid development create a lot of changes in the Chinese society, the transformations might have an effect on the perception and acuity of the younger generations towards the present socio-political system. Undoubtedly the most effective vehicle to knowledge and the present technology, the internet if remained unabated to its easy accessed by everybody can posed a severe threat to the cultural and moral values of the Chinese youth. Similarly, a lot of members of the younger generations especially the males are attracted to western-influenced lifestyle and activities like movies and the National Basketball Association (NBA). With a population of 1.3 billion people, 300 million are playing basketball. China is the largest market outside the US. At public parks and schoolyards, teenagers play basketball—known in Chinese as "lanqiu"—dressed in baggy shorts, wearing baseball caps cocked sideways on their heads and even trash-talking in Chinese like their western counterparts.

Similar effects can be applied to foreign influenced multi-media materials could have a lasting consequence in undermining the socio-cultural up-bringing, traditions, values and lifestyle of the Youth. When the Reform and Opening-up Policy was embarked on 1979, Chinese students were allowed to study abroad. Liu Baoli, deputy director of Ministry of Education's international cooperation and exchange division, averred that an average of 130,000 Chinese have been going abroad for studies every year over the past few years, boosting exchanges in the educational fields. The US, Britain, Australia and Canada are the top choices of the students eager study abroad. The US embassies and consulates in China alone issued more than 400,000 visas, including 52,000 for students, from late 2006 to late 2007. But in spite of the large turn outs of students studying abroad, only few manage to come back to China. According to the report by the Chinese Academy of Social Sciences, it disclosed that 1.06 million Chinese had gone to study overseas since 1978, but only 275,000 had returned. The rest had taken postgraduate courses, found work, got married or changed citizenship. In short, seven out of every 10 students who enroll in an overseas universities or learning institutions never return back to live in their homeland.

Due to the fast pace economic development and opening up to the West, there might be a greater propensity and steady influence to the present system to drift towards the Western democratic political system. According to Jacques DeLisle, a professor of law at the University of Pennsylvania that there is a longstanding actuality of political science and comparative history that reveals that achieving high levels of economic development can produce social consequences, including an increase in demands for democratization and foundations for democracy. Professor DeLisle wrote that an equally venerable proposition is that rapid economic development, especially where it leaves many behind or worse off, can produce social dislocation and can produce an increase in participation that often leads to disorder and repression. The reform-era PRC in many respects seems to fit both scenarios. Written in 2004, the paper of Professor DeLisle quoted Gilbert Rozman, a professor at the Department of Sociology in Princeton University who described Chinese modernization theorists, and, later, Chinese globalization theorists that have seen the reform-era PRC heading down the path that is linked from economic development which results to social change, and eventually to a peaceful, gradual democratization (DeLisle 2004: 179-204).

On 22 November 2008, Suzanne Ogden, a professor at the Fletcher School of Law and Diplomacy in Boston argued that while the Chinese government has made a fuss about rejecting western standards for democracy and human rights, it has taken some of these standards gravely in the way people in the Party discuss reforms and have responded to criticisms that have been made. She added that while many identify democratization to be threatening the current leadership, the introduction of many rights and democratization systems have actually enhanced ability of the Party to stay in power. The author concluded articulating that it is important to acknowledge that while the PRC is not a democratic system using a western definition of the word, the country's political system is evolving and positive change is taking place peacefully.

Syed Hussein Alatas defines corruption as basically the "abuse of trust in the interest and private gain." It is an intentional violation of duty with the motive of gaining personal advantage by receiving bribes or other benefits from a party in need of a particular decision or favor affecting interests the public servant can bring about (Alatas 1999: 49-50). As such China is not accepted in the menace of corruption at all levels of Government bureaucracy. In 2008 alone, China ranked 72 out of 179 countries from least to most corrupt in the Transparency International's Corruption Perceptions Index. In the PRC, the reforms instigated by Deng Xiaoping were disparaged for reintroducing corruption in China, as the cost of the rapid development. During Mao's term, nepotism and other forms of corruption were almost non-existent. Development in any country like China, seeks to improve the conditions of living in the most comprehensive way by changing the previous conditions that deters the population, in all areas such as economic, social, political, cultural and educational. These virtuous goals of development are being undermined by corruption. It also distorts the political system, weakens the interest and welfare of the population, creates negligence, inefficiency and parasitism in the bureaucracy and prevents certain policies and honest leaders from succeeding. Corruption ha s an enduring effect of spreading throughout the total life of the society which results to political instability (Alatas 1999: 129).

In 2008, China outshined the United States as the largest global emitter of greenhouse gases by volume. (On a per capita basis, however, Americans emit five times as much greenhouse gas as Chinese.) The rise in China's emissions is primarily due to PRC's over reliance and dependence on coal, which credits for over two-thirds of its energy consumption throughout China. It adds to the sulfur dioxide emissions causing acid rain, which falls on over 30 percent of the country. Changes should be made to lessen and reduce gas emissions. Last November, China pledged to cut "carbon intensity," a measure of carbon dioxide emissions per unit of gross domestic product, by 40 to 45 percent by 2020, compared with levels in 2005. But during the historic UN climate talks in Copenhagen which ended last 19 December 2009, narrowly avoided collapse by accepting a compromise that gives billions to poor nations to deal with global warming but did not require the world's major Countries like China and the US to make deeper cuts in their greenhouse gas emissions.

Due to the rapid development in urban and rural areas throughout China, the environment is very much affected by these growths. A problem on environment degradation would erupt if the unwary abuse of the environment is not prevented or minimized. In fact estimates revealed that the cost of environmental damage was put at 2.75 trillion Yuan (401.7 billion USD) in 2005, as against the growth in GDP for the same year of 2.24 trillion yuan. A lot of more problems may arise like severe air pollution, garbage disposal problems, deforestation, poor water quality, land degradation and polluted and scarce water resources.

Aside from the usual or traditional threats to China like separatist problems, border disputes and ethnic tensions, the emergence of the more lethal and equally devastating non-traditional threats like terrorism,

Participants visiting exhibition of Chinese history

transnational crimes, natural calamities and epidemics should be given enormous attention and concern. With the new advancement in science and technology, the threat to the global community has been stateless, faceless and possesses no boundaries.

Severe Challenges and Future Prospects

In spite of the failure of the Copenhagen Accord to be Able to create nor generate tangible results and pact among the developed and developing countries on the greenhouse emission effects, China should be able to implement its own policies and system and set a good example to minimize if not prevent the emission problems. Relatedly, the PRC Leadership should seek new policies and systems that are more relevant to the changing times in order to prevent mining accidents in the future. Though the present Chinese environmental policies have made positive contributions to the overall conservation of the global environment, mining accidents are still prevalent. Not to be overlooked is the problem on logging and abuse of the forest resources. There should be initiatives to re-balance the dwindling and decreasing natural resources throughout the country due to the rapid development. Likewise, active steps should be taken in order to discover new sources of energy and lessen China's dependency on coal and other by products. China needs to study its environmental problems with a view to addressing the complex systems of issues including nature, economy, society, institution and industrialization damaging it.

More policy measures are needed to improve the employment system and strengthen and enhance better living conditions and wage benefits to all workers throughout the country. Similarly, better systems and policies should be made in order to reduce the unequal distribution of wealth and decrease inequality in economic opportunities between regions and the population. China's coastal areas have moved from the primary industrialized stage to high-grade industrialization, the western inland is still in the preliminary stages of big economic development, meanwhile, economic operation in China now face a series of challenges and problems. Structural reforms should be unleashed for more growth and stimulate the stagnant areas and regions.

The Chinese culture and traditions are deeply rooted by centuries of colorful history wedged by countless sacrifices and unparalleled efforts of its fore bearers. The rapid development and opening up to the outside world might erode the unique Chinese culture that exists today as it was for centuries. The influx of the internet and western influenced practices and lifestyle would readily affect the growing number of the populace especially the younger generations. Apart from this, the significant number of Chinese students who are not returning after having studied abroad is quite alarming. A possible brain drain and Diaspora may happen if these practices remained unabated in the following years. In order to prevent such occurrences, the Government should make policies and rewards systems to enticed or even obligate such students to return and use their acquired knowledge in China. Relatedly, equal chances and more opportunities should be made available to everyone regardless of their ethnic or cultural background.

Corruption in the global community is increasing and taking place in any legitimate organization around the world and China is not exempted in this global phenomenon. Alatas gave several measures which may mitigate if not totally abolish corruption; one, Efficient administration and proper structural adjustments of government machinery and regulations so as to avoid the sources of corruption; two, the effective functioning of an anti-corruption value system; three, the inspiring leadership of a group with high moral and intellectual standards; four, Favorable historical and sociological conditions, and five, an educated public with sufficient intelligence to appraise and follow the course of events (Alatas 1999: 33).

Due to the unclean atmosphere and unabated abuse of our natural resources, the natural world is threatened by health and epidemic diseases. During the past years we have seen the emergence of bird flu, SARS, HIV and lately the A (H1N1) viruses. The government should continue to implement measures and programs deter the spread of such viruses. Likewise, international cooperation and linkages with other countries should be made to prevent such viruses.

With its fast growing stature and growing politico-economic influence not only in the region but also in the global community, The PRC should be able to assert its role and responsibility as a non-aggressive partner in world peace and cooperation. The present system and international order demonstrates that the lone superpower—the US cannot do it all alone in maintaining world order. It's waning economic and political influence in the international arena and further restricted by its internal economic and political problems at home, China no doubt, has and must emerge as a new and most important actor in the international stage. The PRC cannot be too reluctant to assume its new role because the US-hegemonic influence is not permanent and perpetual. China must be able to be the new "steering wheel" in the global ship amidst the rough waters it is presently sailing and in the near future.

Conclusions

The Reform and Opening-up Policy that was launched in 1978 by the Vice Premier Deng Xiaoping is doubtedly the catalyst in the present development in China with close connections with the global community. In a speech at the meeting marking the Anniversary of the Reform and Opening-up Policy on December 18, 2008, President and General Secretary of the CPC Central Committee, Hu Jintao echoed the efforts and hard work of Premier Deng Xiaoping, chief architect of China's reform and opening that was declared 30 years ago. He averred that,

"Reform and opening up is the essential feature of the new era. The purpose of reform and opening up is to liberate and develop productive forces and modernize the country, which will enable the Chinese people to live better lives and rejuvenate our great Chinese nation. It is to improve and develop our socialist system, instill vitality into socialism and build Chinese-style socialism. It is to improve and strengthen the Party as it leads contemporary China in development and to preserve the advanced nature of the Party to ensure that the Party will always march at the forefront."

China's economic "miracle" and near mystical growth as a result of the reform and opening up policy since 1978, is resituating at a high cost not only in terms of the usual environmental degradation, economic inequality and erosion of some socio-cultural values but more importantly in the context of growing security threats both on the traditional and non-traditional hazards it has posed. So in order to be able to reaped the fruits of its labor, the PRC should address the challenges in due time.

In all intense and purposes, the Reform and Opening-up Policy of the PRC can be considered as one of the greatest peaceful revolutions in our lifetime because of the obvious development is has created. It brought amazing progress not only to China but also to the World in general and Asia in particular.

Whether PRC likes it or not, the "Middle Kingdom" with its astounding development and astonishing economic growth is destined to play a major role in power in Asia and in the World. Some experts even predict that by 2020, China will inescapably be the lone superpower in the World. But in spite of a date with destiny, the PRC has remained

Participants visiting Shanghai high-tech enterprises

modest in its achievements and perceived new role. Relatedly, the PRC has humbly taken the back seat in regional and international affairs. But China cannot be a reluctant superpower instead take action and assume the lead role. With more than 2,500 years of vibrant and opulent history, tampered with internal strife among states and hardened by the affliction it has suffered from Imperialist invaders culminating in the realization of freedom in 1949, the PRC will not fail in being the leader in Asia and in the world. PRC is in a better position to be able to make our world a better place to live-in under the umbrella of a genuine and authentic harmonious and peaceful world.

Understanding China's Theory and Practice of Reform and Opening-up

Bobai
Capt., Nigerian Navy

Introduction

One of the most important events in modern reforms history is the socialist countries transition from the soviet-type planned economy to the market economy started in the last two decades of the 20th century. China's experience has produced many interesting contrast to the experience of transition in Eastern Europe and former Soviet Union.

Since the beginning of the century, China has embarked on a theory and practice of reform and opening-up which centers on a transition from the subsistence type society to a development-oriented one. This is evidenced in the changes taking place in the consumption, industrial, and social structures as well as urbanization rate. Within this stage of development, the Chinese society is experiencing a gradual lessening of pressures of subsistence type while those of development are mounting in every facet. However, contradiction and problems are also becoming more prominent, particularly those relating to resources and the environment in the areas of sustainable development, balanced urban and rural improvement, fast and comprehensive growth of public needs and pressures brought about by the changes in governance and social structures. These are more in the nature of institutional contradictions rather than inevitable factors in the course of the reforms. To relieve these pressures from the reforms, it may be necessary to break through the institutional barriers impeding the maximum dividends of the reform and opening-up. The purpose of this paper is to highlight some understanding of China's theory and practice of the reform and opening-up. The paper will therefore touch on China's period of planned economy system before looking at the adopted theory and Practice of the reform and opening-up. Finally it will discuss identifiable challenges and proffer possible countermeasures.

China's Planned Economy System

The Chinese planned economy or directed economy system was an economic system in which the state or worker's council managed the economy. It was an economic system in which the central government made all decisions on the production and consumption of goods and services. In other words in its most extensive form was referred to as a command economy, centrally planned economy, or command and control economy. In that regard, the state or government controlled all major sectors of the economy and formulated all policies about their use and about the distribution of income. The planners then decided what should be produced and direct enterprises to produce those goods. The economy was in contrast to *unplanned economies*, such as market economy, where production, distribution, pricing, and investment decisions are made by private owners based on their own interests.

Foundation of the Reform and Opening-up

After the "cultural revolution," China's national economy was on the verge of total collapse. It was left in a precarious situation and the then leader Deng Xiaoping, in a resolute manner, came up with the concept of opening up. He pointed out that "the world is an opened one. China has become a country lagging behind the western nations since their industrial revolution. One of the key reasons is that China has had an economy closed within itself. Since the founding of the People's Republic of China, an embargo was imposed and we continue to be a closed economy. Such a state resulted in some difficulties for China. The lessons of the past decade have taught us that it was not workable to construct and develop our country with our doors closed." "If a country does not open up, it is very difficult to get the economy to grow. Each nation in the world must open up if it economy is to develop. The capital and technology in the west is being interrelated and exchanged."

Upon this declaration, an approach to the reform and opening-up was conceptualised in line with the conditions in China and with international experience. China has a large territory, and before opening up it was for decades operating a planned economy as earlier mentioned. It became thus a strategic issue to open up step by step and reduce the risk brought about by the transformation. Consequently, the process was to be executed in 3 phases as follows, firstly opening up special economic zones, coastal areas and then gradually the inland areas. Secondly, introducing combined operations within the country and globally, while international cooperation is conducted in a multi-layered way and in extensive sectors as well. Thirdly, the policy of one country, two systems is implemented in an innovative manner.

To this effect, the sectors that have been opened up are expanding in a gradual way and market operation likewise is becoming integrated with multilateral trade mechanism and internationally accepted best practices. Similarly, there has been a productive approach that deals with peaceful reunification of China through the process of opening-up. The smooth hand over, stability and growth of Hong Kong and Macao are successful examples of how this productive approach has been practiced.

Execution of the Reform and Opening-up

From the gamut of the overall pattern and steps of the opening up since 1979, China has adopted a step by step strategy promoted from the coastal to inland areas, from the west to east, from parts or sectors to the whole. It has achieved several important milestones with specific features in the following areas:

Poverty Reduction

China has made tremendous progress in poverty alleviation since the country adopted the reform and opening-up policy in 1978. According to FAO, the number of people living on one dollar per day decreased from 490 million in 1979 to about 90 million in 2002 in the rural areas. The giant stride in this aspect was recorded in the period from 1978 to 1984, during which the population living in poverty decreased by about 300 million. This was as a result of the successful agricultural reforms, which promoted family-based land contract management and increased the state purchasing price of grain, oil crops and pork. This also increased the country's agricultural output and income considerably. The total output of grains in China reached 434 million tons in 2006, up by 95 % from 222 million tons in 1977, and the per capital income increased by 90% from 1980 to 1985 in the rural areas.

Appeal for Overseas Studies

Since the first group of 30 Chinese schoolboys traveled to the US in 1872 to study science and technology, and learn about life in America, a steady stream of youngsters have headed overseas in search of a broader education. According to figures from the Ministry of Education, between 1978, when the country launched its policy of reform and opening-up and the end of last year (2008), more than 1.2 million Chinese students studied abroad, of whom 319,700 later returned home. Last year alone, almost

145,000 youngsters furthered their education on foreign soil, of which 44,000 returned home, 5 percent more than in 2006. In 1978, the later Chinese leader Deng Xiaoping said, "I support sending more students to study abroad, not a dozen but thousands, tens of thousands and more." That year, 860 government funded students traveled to study and the number has risen steadily ever since. Quoting figures from the MOE again, more than 62 percent of doctoral advisors, 77 percent of university presidents and 89 percent of members of China's academies of sciences and engineering have studied abroad. Chinese students are currently studying in more than 100 countries. The top three destinations are the US, Japan and the UK, each hosting more than 50,000 scholars.

Women Empowerment

In Chinese history, feudal ideology and an accumulation of many other factors meant that the position of women in the society was particularly bad. In the past few decades, however, women have the opportunity to receive education. Between 1931 and 1945, only 7.8 million women were enrolled in primary school, and only 0.46 percent received higher education. Despite their improved status after the foundation of the new China, women made up only 12.3 percent of deputies in the 2nd National people's congress. But the policy of reform and opening-up gave a new impetus to the progress of the Chinese women. Under the aegis of the China women's Federation, the first global women conference in which gender equality was at the front burner was held in Beijing, that added icing on the cake and also gave the Chinese woman a brand new look. At the 11th national people's Congress and the National committee of the 11th Chinese People's Political Consultative Conference, women deputies and women members made up 21.33 percent and 17.7 percent respectively, an increase of 1.09 and 1 percent over the 10th sessions. In urban residents committees and village committees, women account for 48.2 percent and 23.2 percent of representatives respectfully.

Further Opening-up in Science and Technology

The closed door situation in relation to science and technology in China has been transformed with the progress in the reform and opening-up. Foreign cooperation and exchanges in science and technology have been greatly expanded and an all round policy was initiated. By 1997, China had established scientific cooperation relations with 135 countries and regions in the World, signed 95 governmental agreements on scientific cooperation and joined 75 international academic organizations. A total of 283 research and development and higher learning institutions were granted the right to introduce foreign trade and management. The foreign

Participants having a lecture on the origin of Taiwan issue

technological trade grew steadily and rapidly, and the import and export of hi-tech products in 1997 reached 29.4 billion yuan in value.

Rise in Gross Domestic Product

In 1978, China's Gross Domestic Product (GDP) accounted for only one percent of world economy, whereas its share rise 5 percent in 2007, same year, China's share of global trade was less than 1 percent and share jumped to 8 percent. China's development has opened a huge market for international capital attracting about 780 billion dollars of net foreign investment over the last 3 decades. Direct overseas investment by Chinese companies had also grown substantially amounting to 21.16 billion US dollars in early 2006, in which, non financial investment was 17.63 billion USD (making up 83.3%), an increase of 43.3% over 2005. China's development has boosted growth of global economy and trade. With imports growing at an average annual rate of 16.7 percent since 1978, it has become the world's third largest import market and Asia's top import market. China now contributes to more than 10 percent of global economic growth and more than 12 percent of global trade expansion. By the end of 2006, over 5,000 entities had established nearly 10 thousand enterprises in 172 countries and regions. The direct foreign investment had then also grown to an accumulated 90.63 billion USD among which non-financial amounted to 75.02 billion USD and financial amounted to 15.61 billion USD making up 82.8% and 17.2% of the investment overseas respectfully. Its average volume is close to 560 billion US dollars, generating some 10 million jobs for its trading partners. President Hu Jintao said, "The past 3 decades of reform and opening-up have told us that China cannot develop itself in isolation from the world. And it is equally true that the world cannot enjoy prosperity or stability without China."

Challenges and Countermeasures

Despite the new-found wealth, prosperity comes at a price. One negative effect is the serious environmental damage. The outcome of a research conducted by the Chinese Academy of Sciences revealed that the exploitation of natural resources, ecological degradation and environmental pollution has outweighed China's economic benefits in recent years. Under the research program, the cost of environment damage was put at 2.75 trillion yuan (401.7 billion USD) in 2005, as against the growth in GDP for the same year of 2.24 trillion yaun. From this finding, it could be inferred that as China's growth pattern have changed a little over the last 2 years, it is likely the situation might not change if nothing drastically is done to arrest the abnormalities. This is particularly a worrisome development which the Chinese Vice Premier Wang Qishan reacted to as saying *"it is impossible for China, a country of 1.3 billion people to follow the old model of the developed countries by consuming large quantities of energy at the expense of the environment."*

Another challenge is the uneven distribution of wealth. Official data from 2007 showed the country's Gini Coefficient, which measures the inequality of income distribution has surpassed the warning mark of 0.4, with the per capital GDP of coastal Shanghai standing around 76,000 yuan (11,102 USD), more than 13 times that of the rural southwestern Guizhou Province. The growing income gap among the people could increase tension in the society and nourish wrong development in terms of crime. Regional disparity has also remained big. After 30 years of reform and opening-up, China's coastal areas have moved from the primary industrialized stage to high-grade industrialization, the western inland is still in the preliminary stages of big economic development, meanwhile, economic operation in China now face a series of challenges and problems.

Similarly, industrial output in the Pearl and Yangtze River Deltas, the nation's two most important growth engines, rose at a remarkable slow pace. Many small scale and medium sized companies particularly exporters of low end products are faced with increasing labor cost. Again at the coastal areas are feeling the pressure of inflation. The price of finished oil remains high, the transportation capacity of coal, electricity and oil is tight and prices of raw material keep rising. Furthermore companies also surfer from decreasing overseas consumer demand, a result of troubled world economy. The conclusion drawn by Chi Fulin, the Executive President of the China Institute of Reform and Development was that if this should continue "it shows that China is at the end of the reforms process."

Conclusion

The leaders of China conceptualized the concept of reform and opening-up which transformed the Chinese economy from a planned type to a market-oriented one. This was to bring changes in areas such as consumption, social and industrial structure as well as urbanization rate with a view to improving the livelihood of the citizenry. Consequently, the process was initiated and to be executed in 3 phases to start with the establishment of special economic zones, development of the coastal areas and gradually the inland areas. That was to be followed by introducing combined operations within the country and globally, while international cooperation is conducted in a multi-layered way and

Participants visiting College of Taiwan Studies, Beijing Union University

in extensive sectors as well. Finally, the implementation of the policy of one country, two systems was to be done in an innovative manner. So far, the practice has made some modest achievement in the areas of poverty reduction, education and women empowerment. Others are further opening up in science and technology as well as rise in GDP. These achievements however came with their attendant problems in environmental degradation, uneven wealth distribution and high labor cost in production among others.

Achievements and Challenges of China's Reform and Opening-up

Joseph Kapwani
Brig. Gen., Tanzanian Army

Background

The People's Republic of China was founded on October 1, 1949 by the Chairman of the CPC Mao Zedong. Through just 60 years of struggle, explore and reform, as the Party in power, the CPC has succeeded in bringing about China in a stable political situation, with steady economic prosperity and active diplomatic engagement as the world's most populous developing country.

The "Cultural Revolution" (1966-1976) was a period of turmoil in Chinese modern history. Erroneously initiated by Mao Zedong and exploited by the two counter-revolutionary groups headed by Lin Biao and Jiang Qing, respectively, it brought extensive damage to China and the Chinese people, and brought the economy to the verge of collapse.

After the downfall of the Lin Biao and Jiang Qing cliques, the Central Authorities led by Deng Xiaoping, restored order out of chaos and carried out policies of reform and opening-up, bringing China and the Chinese onto the road to modernization.

Decision on Reform and Opening-up

The Third Plenary Session of 11th CPC Central Committee, held at the end of 1978, brought in a new historic era for China. At this time, it was decided to make the reforms. Chinese Leader Deng Xiaoping vigorously promoted the policy of reform and opening-up directed to improve economic, political and cultural systems. Before the reforms China's economy was very underdeveloped. Deng's social and economic philosophy attempted to merge a market economic model with a socialist political system. Deng also stressed opening China to the outside world, the implementation of one country, two systems.

How the Major Sectors were Opened Up

Agriculture

The commune system was replaced by one where individual families lease land from the collectives, ensuring that almost all rural households have access to land. The reforms have received a sharp rise in agricultural production together with a dramatic fall in poverty and a significant improvement in the amount and quality of food available.

The introduction of the Household Production System where families lease land from the collectives, boosted production incentives, encouraged farmers to reduce costs, take risks, and enter new lines of production. At the beginning of the 1990s, when the economy grew very rapidly, consumers shifted their preferences from quantity to quality.

China has steadily increased grain yields and added variety to the supply of agricultural products, and has greatly improved rural incomes and made remarkable achievements in poverty alleviation. The year 2008 saw a marked increase in rural incomes, with per capita growth rate of 8%

in farmers' net income.

Industry

Before 1978, state-owned and collectively-owned enterprises represented 77.6% and 22.4% respectively of China's exclusively public-ownership economy. The policy of reform and opening-up has given extensive scope to the common development of various economic sectors. Individual and private industrial enterprises and enterprises with foreign, Hong Kong, Macau or Taiwan investments have mushroomed. The reforms in the industrial sector involved the following:

Responsibility system, under this system, families lease land for a period of up to 30 years, and must agree to supply the state an agreed quota of grain or industrial crops at a fixed low price in return. The remaining surplus can either be sold to the state or on the free market.

After being transformed into joint companies from the state-owned enterprises, the economic benefit of the state-owned enterprises increased steadily and their overall strength and quality were remarkably enhanced, gaining continuously in their control, influence and lead in the whole national economy.

Increased investment into capital construction programs and township and village enterprises was the government's solution to reviving the economy.

The collectively owned rural township and village enterprises as well as private and foreign joint-venture sectors.

The process of opening-up began with the establishment of the Shenzhen, Zhuhai, Shantou and Xiamen Specific Economic Zones in South and Southeast China in 1980. They were set to attract foreign investment and advanced technology with the specific purpose of developing the national economy. In 1984, a total of 14 coastal port cities were officially opened, including Dalia, Qinhuangdao, Tianjin, Yantai, Qingdao, Lianyungang, Nantong, Shanghai, Ningbo, Wenzhou, Fuzhou, Guangzhou, Zhanjiang, and Beihai. In 1985, the Yangtze River Delta, Pearl River Delta, Xiamen-Zhangzhou Triangular Area, as well as the Liaodong Peninsula and Jiaodong Peninsula were set up as coastal economic open areas. In 1988, Hainan Province was founded to become the largest economic special zone in China. Thus with such a move of establishing those special economic zones, led to the integration of China's development with the development of the rest of the world.

Military

Under the Political leadership of Deng Xiaoping the Military became disengaged from civilian politics. Deng reestablished civilian control over the Military by appointing his supporters to key military leadership positions.

As for the modernization of the military, reforms were made in the military organization, doctrine, education training, and personnel policies to improve combat effectiveness in combined-arms warfare.

Also another military modernization was the transformation of the defense establishment into a system capable of independently

Participants visiting Xiangtang cultural village in Changping District, Beijing

maintaining a modern military force.

Science and Technology

The great success of the four modernizations was the attention given to the development of Science and Technology. Without the development of science and technology it is very difficult to develop the national economy with the great changes taking place in the world. And therefore the Party Central Committee decided to call a conference in 1978 in order to encourage the policy of development of science and technology as the key role in China's journey towards the creation of a modern Socialist society by the year 2000. At present the number of professional technical people and scientific researchers in China is listed as number one in the world.

Achievements

The reform and opening-up policy has contributed in China's development in the following manner:

With the Reform and Opening-up China's market economy has made notable progress. There has been drastic improvement of living standards to the low and medium income earning people. This positive economic development is exemplified by the following: Annual GDP growth has reached about 10%.

The proportion of private enterprises is growing, while the proportion of state-owned enterprises is declining. This trend is testament to the emergence of the private sector in China.

Foreign trade and investment have brought about progress in science and technology. China's foreign direct investment also has increased to a large extent.

The development of the market economy has not only promoted the process of regional autonomy in China but has also raised the country's consumption rate. Moreover, its health care system, education system and legal system, including the establishment of property rights, are improving.

Transparency has improved greatly over the past 30 years. Chinese people are allowed to travel abroad and foreigners are largely allowed to travel freely in China. Briefly freedom has expanded since China transformed itself from a socialist planned economy to a socialist market economy.

China has followed the path of building socialism with Chinese characteristics and has formed a theoretical system of socialism with Chinese characteristics.

One important thing to note, why China managed to get through with reform and opening-up smoothly compared to other areas in the world like the Soviet Union? What we can say is that, despite the good leadership which initiated the reforms, China adopted a gradual approach to the reforms, sighting areas of interest first and then step by step to other areas. The reforms had the support of the people, therefore it was easy to mobilize the mass. As to the Soviet Union, the approach was a rapid one and the people were not educated enough to welcome the reforms known as "Perestoika Naglasnosti." So the reforms collapsed.

Challenges

Despite the great achievements as mentioned above China is faced with challenges which threaten the development of the country. And these are:

The huge population of about 1.3bn people that offers a good source of labor resources for the economic and social development, but also puts pressure on the economic, social progress, consumption of resources and environment. There is a serious pollution problem due to the extensive development of the economy.

China's ecological environment is deteriorating very fast and steps to combat this solution are not significant. With the high speed of economic development also energy consumption is high so soon China will face energy crisis.

There's an ever growing gap between the rich and the poor. There is also a big in balance in the development in the regions, the eastern areas being well developed followed by the central areas, those of the western areas lagging behind. This might cause serious social economic problems in the country where living in harmony is part of the doctrine.

The legal system also might be affected. Although China has established a legal system that covers private property, individual rights, the government as well as the division of power between the central government and local government, it does not have a comprehensive, effective department to enforce these laws.

Due to difficulties in law enforcements, the more developed China's economy becomes, the more complex its social, economic, legal and political relations. China needs good laws and effective enforcement; otherwise its economic growth may slow down or even come to a halt.

Conclusion

China's economic development and social progress in the past period of almost 30 years have directly benefited from the reform and opening-up, two great turning points of historical significance moving from the orthodox planned economy to a modern market economy and from a closed or semi-closed state to the decision to open up the country in an all-round way. Having entered into a new period and a new stage, and faced with new contradictions and problems, China depends on a process of all-round reform and innovation of its economic, political, social and cultural systems in order to realize its development goal—a moderately prosperous society in all aspects.

The contradictions and problems stemming from the growing pressures of development require the further improvement of the market economic system and the reform of the social system focusing on improving people's livelihood, as well as the changes and innovations in the political and cultural systems.

Under Deng Xiaoping's new policy of opening up China to the outside world, a large amount of new technology and many fresh approaches to economic organization, legal and social reform and foreign investment have been brought into China. Adherence to this policy is conducive to the further development of China's market economy.

In short, the pace of change was greatly speeded up in the formation of China's new open economy, while its investments actively and effectively also helped the Chinese to broaden their international perspectives and free themselves from antiquated ideas and concepts. On July 13, 2001, Beijing won the bid to host the 29th Olympic Games in 2008. The relationship between China and the outside world has entered a new stage in its development.

Recommendations

As we have seen the great economic development China has made in the past 30 years, there is need to have an equal income distribution especially, the income of farmers and residents in the west should be raised in the spirit of better addressing demographic migration.

The development of China's legal system should be deepened. The government should resolve not only problems in resource protection and environmental protection but also many economic problems (employment, currency, finance, fiscal stability and foreign trade) as well as problems concerning social equity.

China is advised to increase investment in environmental protection because the money spent in reducing pollution could create an impact on the growing economy of the country.

China is advised to stick to the path of socialism, adhere to the CPC leadership.

With the policy of reform and opening-up China has so far taken positive steps on education. Despite of good programs on education internally but so many students study or are sent abroad for exchange in education and activate cooperation. Chinese language is taught to foreigners widely. This puts China to be much more exposed to international affairs and cooperation.

Perception Management— a New Challenge for China

Ghulam Qamar

Brig. Gen., Pakistani Army

Prologue

China is projected to be a Superpower in the making by the first quarter of this century. Although China is paid attention in intellectual circles around the globe, it is felt that she needs much more attention than what is being talked and written in the media about China. The Chinese benign policies in world affairs may not be taken lightly, as she may be forced into a more proactive role in West, Central and East Asia. Despite US saber rattling in the Taiwan Strait she has displayed remarkable restraint and has followed a policy of "live and let live/peaceful development." China is vigorously following the policy of mutual respect of each other's sovereignty and territorial integrity, non aggression, non interference in each other's internal affairs, equality and mutual benefits and peaceful co-existence. This policy does not only augers well for China but is also an axiomatic for creation of a harmonious world, free of machinations by developed countries, economic exploitation and subjugative political order. However, some western countries continue to propagate against China to project its negative image for vested interests. This persistent propaganda affects the minds of common people and results in developing the negative perceptions about China, which the Chinese nation cannot afford in the media savvy global environment and needs to wrest the trend.

Spectrum of Misperceptions and Propaganda Themes about China

China's Political System: A growing western propaganda that

Communism does not afford opportunity to the masses to participate in Government functioning is gaining currency. They project that their styled democracy is the only system to ensure participation of common people in the state affairs. It also ensures formulation of policies according to common aspirations of the masses. Western nations also propagate that China is being ruled by a single party (CPC) without any opposition and democratic institutions, thus the suppressive rule does not afford a chance to commoners to have their say in the policy formulation.

China's Human Rights Index: The media and Human Rights Center working under the influence of western countries and US, publicize that a number of people were blacklisted and banned from the Beijing Olympic Games 2008, including the Dalai Lama. Numbers of online forums were shut down in the first half of 2006 for containing "subversive and sensitive content," part of an ongoing crackdown enforcing a government mandate that all media publish only news that has appeared already in a state-run publication. These forces also propagate that a number of school-age children, some as young as 12, are lured or kidnapped from rural Liangshan province to work in export zone factories desperate for cheap labour, notwithstanding China's minimum wage and child labour laws, to offset rising costs while maintaining low prices. The west led by US has used the question of human rights in sensitive areas like Sinkiang and Tibet; occasionally one listens to the western rhetoric about poor human rights record and bad plight of minority communities. Such concerns were even sounded during recent US President's visit to China.

China's Ethnic Grouping: The western media also highlights reports regarding discrimination of ethnic minorities, particularly in the field of employment, adequate standard of living, health, education and culture. It erroneously, by intent provides insufficient information regarding enjoyment of economic, social and cultural rights enshrined in ICESCR by populations in ethnic minority areas. It also spreads reports from anti China sources, other than the state party relating to right to free exercise of religion as right to take part in cultural activities, use and teaching of minority languages, history and culture of Xinjiang Uighur Autonomous

Region (XUAR) and Tibet Autonomous Region.

Chinese Religious Divide: The US and some other countries have particular concerns about religious freedom in China. Some western reports also assert that 1,500,000 approximate number of books, video tapes, and compact discs containing Falun Gong religious teachings were seized by the Chinese Government following a proclamation by President Jiang Zemin banning the Falun Gong in July 1999, and continuing to be banned ever since on the grounds that the Falun Gong is a cult and its practitioners consequently subject to arrest, detention, and imprisonment. The 2006 report on International Religious Freedom prepared by US also supports this assertion.

China's Economic Boom and Political Future: China's ascendance continues to attract international focus. While some pessimists point to the coming collapse of China, most nations appear deeply impressed with China's economic achievements and social progress. Few (western) analysts predict political upheaval in China in the foreseeable future. The signs in Pew's polling (available on internet) suggest that perceptions of China's increasing power—both military and economic—could boost anti-Chinese sentiment in years to come. In fact, there are some signs that this has already begun to occur in parts of Europe where worries about China's economic power are on the rise.

Imbalances in China's Development: Owing to its size and geographical realities, China has not been able to develop in a uniform manner. Without taking due cognizance of its development course, the western powers negatively project that Western China is not being developed by intent to keep these regions in a state of flux, thus endeavouring to create internal fissure.

Lack of Sophisticated Technology and Quality Control Issue: Few channels also undermine China's technological prowess and downgrade Chinese high-tech equipment on the quality control issue, thus creating hurdles in the product marketing.

Environmental Protection and Climate Change Syndromes: US in particular and many other developed nations in general speak aloud about the environmental issues related to Chinese industrial sector. The graphs exhibited by such opinion makers are often misleading and chaotic.

Population Growth and Related Issues: Population control policy of China is often blown out of proportion by those countries having negative growth rate. This policy is criticized under the garb of human rights and personal freedom, disregarding the fact that China is the most populous country in the world.

China's Military Power: In 32 of 46 countries surveyed, China's increasing military capability is viewed with alarm. These worries are most prevalent in two countries with a long and sometimes bitter historic connection to China: South Korea, where fully 89% view Chinese military might as a bad thing and Japan where 80% share that view. In neighboring India, a clear majority (59%) also expresses concern about China's military power as do 70% of Russians.

Why Misperceptions Persist?

The misperceptions about China are a legacy of the past gradually ascending owing to China's unprecedented rise. There are certain external and internal factors owing to which these misperceptions continue to persist, rather in some cases they are growing. Few factors are:

a. China's opening up and reforms have been introduced in the nineteen eighties, yet it is not completely accessible to the outside world. Owing to limited global exposure to the policies, misperceptions continue to grow. China's Defence Policy is a case in point.

b. Western media, specially of US is usually hostile towards China and projects negative propaganda about certain global issues like human rights, environmental protection, population control and western style of democracy.

c. China is seeking an increasingly important role in the global arena. Anti China forces have evolved a policy of containment of China in various dimensions covertly, though apparently engagement is trumpeted, the intentional creations of misperceptions about China is an essential element of their policies.

d. Western world has dominance over the powerful media. China does not have an effective media with global reach to checkmate such trends.

e. Some disloyal elements and dissident groups from within the country also mislead the foreign nations about Chinese policies and positive endeavours of the government to ameliorate their conditions.

f. Inadequate exposure of the Chinese think-tank and diplomats to address the global concerns and enhance positive image of China through global interactions.

My Opinion—the Realities and Situation on Ground

After having spent some time in China and interacted with intellectual class of the society, I have been able to crystallize my own perceptions about China. My analysis is based on my studies about China from the western sources, interaction with Chinese people, intellectuals and officials during visits and formal studies, curricular and extra-curricular activities. I am certain that the world so far, has not understood China in its entire spectrum of activities and dimensions. However, some western nations and anti China forces are purposefully involved in mudslinging on China for their vested interests. Their propaganda and "Defamation Campaign" against China can be viewed through the malfunctioned prism of their biased reporting; whereas, the reality is different.

While commenting on ethnic minorities, it should be noted that China has outlined an elaborate policy to assist ethnic minorities with economic, cultural, social and educational development. It has put poverty reduction and development of the ethnic minorities on top of the national poverty reduction agenda as gleaned through its long term policies. Today a new type of relationship characterized by equality, unity, and mutual assistance has been established between different ethnic groups in China. China continues to strive for a harmonious society at home and around the world.

China has implemented the policy of religious freedom in its entirety. A large number of religious structures have been restored and opened in recent years. Doctrines and varying cultures of different religions have been promoted and religious successors cultivated. In China, people enjoy freedom to practice their faith, conduct religious service and gatherings and maintain religious values. I have witnessed two events of such kind. China has some 85,000 venues for religious activities. However, some factions have indulged themselves in terrorist activities in the garb of religious freedom which need to be dealt with heavy hand. No country can tolerate such a nuisance to flourish on its soil.

It may be appreciated that Chinese economic miracle has largely addressed the question of human rights in China as well as given hope to the billion plus population. No one realizes the fact that keeping the billion plus population in good health by itself is a major achievement of the Chinese leadership. Some western countries employ double standards with regard to human rights, accusing others while turning a blind eye to their internal issues, as experienced by all. The west has always patronized anti China forces like Dalai Lama (stationed in India) and exiled Chinese intellectuals (working in the west) which have been taken by China with a pinch of salt. The Chinese government has included human rights amelioration in its development blueprint for 2006-10 and put the protection and promotion of citizens, civil and political rights on top of the nation's nine priority objectives for development in the coming years, the corresponding institutional guarantees will be established. All this marks a great progress in the human rights history of China, which the world needs to acknowledge.

Never seeking hegemony is China's established state strategy and the Chinese Government has promised to the international community that it will not be the first to use nuclear weapons. China's developing modern national defense and introducing new military equipment are intent to maintain active self-defense and ensure country's sovereignty and protect its interest on land, in air and at sea. It has no intent to invade or threaten any country, and follows the policy of active defence. China always supports peaceful resolution of all disputes.

China is both a big energy consumer and producer. Most of the energy consumed in China is supplied by domestic production, while a small portion comes from imports. The average per-capita consumption and energy import of China is lower than the world's average, and far below the average of developed countries. The Constitution of China clearly specifies: "The state protects and improves the environment in which people live. It prevents and controls pollution and other public hazards." Environment protection has been a basic national policy since the 1980s. The first Environment Protection Law was promulgated in 1989. So far, a number of laws have been promulgated at various tiers to address the issue. The State Environmental Protection Administration has been upgraded as the Ministry of Environmental Protection. Such steps have not been taken by any other country in the world so far. In the recently concluded Climate Change Summit at Copenhagen, China has committed to reduce CO_2 emissions up to 40% by 2020.

While commenting on China's development, one needs to understand various dimensions of China as a big country. It is not possible to affect development in the entire country at one pace in a uniform manner. However, China has outlined a balance development policy for all its citizens, irrespective of race and religion. The Western China is though relatively slow in progress, has a high priority for development in China's future development plans.

China's political system ensures democracy at the grass root level. The adopted "Socialism with Chinese characteristics" ensures participation of masses in the policy formulation process at all tiers of the government. However, in my views following the western style democracy is not a necessity for China. The Communist Party of China (CPC) is a consultative party and being the largest of all parties, it ensures respect to the opinions of others.

China's "One Child" policy is very flexible and realistic in its scope. This aspect should be viewed in the context of total population of China. The western nations with their negative growth rate have achieved developmental goals and are now projecting double standards about China.

The Way Forward—Recommended Strategy

Perception management is a challenge for China in the global village of today which is characterized by media charged environment and extensive information exchanges. As China is pursuing the policy of opening up to the world, it needs to develop its positive image abroad and eradicate wrong perceptions of the people about China and its policies. Therefore, there is a need to Chalk out a multipronged comprehensive "Perception Management Strategy" within the folds of Foreign Policy and Media Policy with clear objectives to be achieved on a well thought out time template. In the succeeding paragraphs, a possible and pragmatic strategy is suggested.

Foreign Policy Initiatives: A vigorous campaign through foreign office needs to be undertaken to address the misperceptions. All Chinese embassies, missions, and consulates around the globe should be explicitly tasked to undertake a Perception Management Drive. China should post a Media Attaché in every important embassy, if already not appointed or some senior diplomat may be assigned the task. His charter of duties may include the following:

a. Interaction with the foreign media to project positive policies of the Chinese Government, intermittently. He should support Chinese correct position on various issues with reference to facts and figures.

b. Educate masses of the host countries on China's peaceful history and culture. This can be done through frequent appearance on media and optimizing the opportunities of public interactions.

c. Accomplishments of Chinese Political System should be projected. It should also be highlighted that Chinese political system is not a typical socialist system, but it has Chinese characteristics built into it, is more flexible and ensures participation of masses at the grass root level.

d. Elaborate the Chinese Peaceful Development policy, Religious Policy, Policy of creation of Harmonious society and the World. China's principles of Peaceful co-existence must be highlighted at every forum.

e. Project the Chinese view point on conflicting global issues. China wants peaceful resolution of disputes which must be well projected.

f. Checkmate on required basis, any negative propaganda about China and initiate timely countermeasures through news papers and television interviews.

g. Chinese ambassadors in important countries should be picked up on merit and be mandated to enhance their public and media interactions with a specific purpose to eradicate ambiguities and project positive stand point of China.

h. Exploit the Community Centers' advantages to project the positive image. China Town exists almost in every major city of the world. Chinese community outside should be mobilized to project positive image of China and address misperceptions of the people through interpersonal interactions.

Media Policy: Media Initiatives to include:

Establishment of a strong TV Channel / network—CTN (Chinese TV

ISC participants and experts from Chinese Academy of Social Sciences

Network) or else with strategic reach, it should replace the name CCTV.

Establish credibility of the Channel through correct reporting. Develop media interest about China by intense publicity through news papers and established channels with the global repute.

Enroll foreign correspondents to project positive diverse opinion at international channels. The Chinese Policies can best be projected to alleviate any negative propaganda by other TV Channels.

Domestic channels may be regulated to address the audience at home on the lines of BBC and CNN.

National Day and other traditional festivals should be extensively projected to highlight the Chinese value system, peaceful culture and development focusing on the success of Political System. China may need to buy time on important channels to telecast programmes like "Dateline China" etc.

Selective lobbying in the existing global media may also be used to effectively encounter the negative propaganda.

Chinese news papers and periodicals in English language may be extensively circulated around the globe to enhance people's awareness about China.

Engage authentic writers in the foreign press to project positive image of China and its policies.

Establish "Alumni Associations": A large number of students from all over the world are studying in China. They are the ambassadors of China in their respective countries. A well chalked out policy should be formulated to establish Alumni Associations abroad. The Chinese National Defence University (NDU) should take a lead in this regard. CDS should create an "Alumni Forum Link" through a dedicated portal on its website. Such associations will be kept informed about the latest policies and developments through release of desired information and their members project the intended viewpoint in their respective circles of influence. The senior officers of friendly countries attending courses at NDU can effectively speak on behalf of China at very high level in their respective countries. This will help address misperceptions about

China on the one hand and checkmate the negative propaganda by a well informed cadre on the other. Other universities and colleges can follow the same model. UK and US are already following this precedence.

Tourism Policy: There is a need to re-align the mandate of Tourism Policy to focus on the "Image Projection" of China. A large number of tourists visiting China can well be educated in an effective manner by the professional tourist guides. A standard guideline can be printed for every tour operator and the guides can ensure that during their regular briefing to the tourists, important aspects like state of well being of the Chinese people, education standards, cultural aspects, peaceful development and progress of China are covered in essential details. The chain of tourists will positively enhance the positive image of China.

Opening-up Policy: The Opening up Policy should be pursued with heavy mandate. There is a dire need to regulate greater interaction of the people from all walks of life with Chinese society in this media savvy world. It should be projected through all intellectual forums that China is not following an air tight monolithic political system; rather it has an all participative and consultative political culture. It should be highlighted that Chinese socialism has distinct characteristics which suit the Chinese people.

Conclusion

China is developing with a fast pace, probably not exactly in line with the forecast by the developed world. There is an element of mistrust and jealously amongst various western nations which outline strategy of containment of China through all spheres of human activity. Their negative propaganda mars the positive peaceful development of China and its dream to create a Harmonious World. China needs to face this challenge squarely and undertake an effective "Perception Management Drive" to project its positive image and eradicate misperceptions harvesting the fruits of peaceful policies.

The Problems Facing China Today and Tomorrow

Benjapol Samruajbenjakul
Gp. Capt., Royal Thai Air Force

Introduction

Undeniably, China now has become a major player on the world stage. After the Communist Party of China (CPC) made a decision to launch a nation-wide reform and opening up campaign at the 3rd Plenary Session of the 11th CPC Central Committee in 1978, China's economy is the third largest economy in the world, behinds only the United States and Japan, respectively. With rapid industrialization, the country of 1.3 billion people has enjoyed an average annual GDP growth rate of 9 percent over the past three decades, turning China into an important engine of world economic growth. The life of the Chinese people has taken great changes dramatically; many difficulties have been solved. Shortages of food and clothing have been resolved and the housing shortage will be a thing of the past soon. Many isolated areas have been opened up. The education of the people has greatly improved; science has flourished, and the improved technology has speeded up the process of modernization. Foreign trade has such quantity and quality now that China is capable of competition on the international market. Advanced technology is imported and foreign capital is used to increase national economic growth. Trade with foreign countries has increased the foreign exchange reserve. Village Township Enterprises are an important pillar to rural economic development, and the Gross Domestic Product is increasing steadily. In the last three decades, per capita disposal income of urban residents and per capita net income of rural residents have increased by over 6 times respectively in real terms. Retirement and medical insurance has covered more than 200 million people, and population living under absolute poverty line in rural areas declined from 250 million to about 14.8 million. The success of the reform and opening-up since 1978 has encouraged the authorities so that many plans can now be carried out with better prospects.

Overpopulation

The most serious of all is overpopulation. Today Mainland China alone contributes to at least 20% of the world's population, which holds 1.3 billion of the world's total population. It is predicted to grow to 1.6 billion people by the year 2030. This problem will have a passive influence on the national economy, education and environment. It will be the main obstacle of economic development in China. The limited natural resources in China can hardly support the excessively large population. To deal with this problem, the one child policy that was first hinted by Deng Xiaoping in a 1979 speech and was later in place nationwide by 1981 is a good policy to solve this problem. However, I think that this has had a huge effect on Chinese culture. According to the Chinese tradition there must be a boy among the children in order to carry on the family's name and do the family's work. As a result of the one child policy, many infant females have been abandoned or killed in order to have another child, hopefully a boy.

However, the one child policy should be carried on to decrease the world population, but the Chinese government should pay more attention on the treatment of those rejected children living in the orphanages, the kids who are left to die because their parents wanted a boy. It would be an effective way to help those kids if the Chinese government would have less strict regulations or roles on foreign adoptions. There are thousands of couples in many countries in North America, Europe, and Asia who would give anything to have a child. They will provide the greatest chance for little Chinese kids. I think that Chinese children will be raised by healthy, economically with stable parents.

Social Uncertainty

China, as a country, seems to be experiencing dynamic changes, to be a nation in transition. China will be faced with an unstable society in the near future. The new rich policy and a large unstructured population will cause some problems. There are about 400 million people live in the towns on the coastal area, the modern China; there are more 900 million people still living in small village and countryside. The problem of unemployment remains serious as there were about 14 million laid-off workers and unemployed people in cities and towns, and approximately 10 million new urban residents are expected to enter the labor force. China's economic growth has benefited the south and eastern regions more than anywhere else. This has created a growing disparity between north and south. The agricultural north has, by contrast, been left behind. Many farmers struggle to make a living. Therefore, this has encouraged a migration of workers from north to south. There is a rush of poor peasants coming to the towns and engaging themselves as laborers. They have left their rural homes in search of work in cities. Building the community of new rich in some parts of China is rapidly increasing and making the inequalities between rich and poor people. China has struggled to deal with this regional inequality. Besides, in the long term China will be faced a demographic people because relative small number of young people will have to take care of a growing number of old people. So the issues of social security, retirement, and health care cost will become a grave challenges as China's population ages.

Economy Uncertainty

China's economic development has been hailed as miraculous. China currently has export surpluses around $275 billion dollars annually. Most of their surplus is due to the manufacturing of cheaper products. Much of China is engaged in the manufacturing industry and other countries are having difficulty competing against their low priced labor, high tech manufacturing equipment and strict economic policies. China has done so well in the last decade that they have national reserves around 1.3 trillion dollars. It is likely that they could supersede the US within ten years or less. However, the Chinese economy is at risk of instability and overheating. Inflation doesn't seem to be of a major concern but when the economy keeps soaring forward there is always a risk that inflation will raise. In the case of China the government is likely keeping its currency low so that it can continue to keep its products have low prices and export cheaper than everyone else in the world. Eventually the market forces are going to break through these government controls and force the economy into a recession.

Besides, the rising wages are also becoming a problem for Chinese manufacturers. Over the past few years Chinese wages have gone up as much as 40% in some sectors. One of the reasons these wages have gone up is because just about everyone is employed in many of the provinces. There is lots of competition between manufacturers and turnover rates in many industries are high. The higher the wages the more likely the cost of doing business will rise.

Ethnic Conflicts

The People's Republic of China is a multi-ethnic state consisting of 56 ethnic groups, identified and confirmed by the Central Government; only 8.04 percent of the population belongs to minority ethnic groups. Among of them, the Uyghur Muslims have seriously challenged China's political and strategic control. Currently, socially, and religiously distinct from the rest of the People's Republic of China, the Uyghur may present China with some security threats because of growing separatist violence, nationalist sentiment, and cross-border contacts with other extreme Muslims, especially the Taliban and Al-Qaeda Groups.

Another one is the Tibetan issue. China's Tibet problem is still no way out. Everyone has known Tibet has been a part of China since Yuan Dynasty (1206-1368); it was for about 1,000 years since the 13th century. However, the Dalai Lama clique has made repeated appeals and statements to impose pressure or punitive measures upon China.

Ethnic tension is something that is not easy to solve. Both sides, Chinese government and the ethnic groups, should realize that confrontation goes nowhere and should have a formal commitment to the dialogue as the first and necessary step toward the final solution to the problems.

Pollution Problems

China is choking on its own success. The economy is on a historic run, posting a succession of double-digit growth rates. But the growth derives, now more than at any time in the recent past, from a staggering expansion of heavy industry and urbanization that requires colossal inputs of energy, almost all from coal, the most readily available, and dirtiest, source.

The nation's move from an agricultural-based economy to an industrial one is causing enormous environmental problems. Pollution is a major problem in many industrialized cities. It is not too hard to imagine the impact upon the environment of over 1.3 billion people shifting from agrarianism to industrialism, and from eco-friendly transportation, walking and bicycling, to automobiles. There are many industrial centers in mainland China that make heavily pollution. In recent years, China already spews approximately 13 percent of the world's energy-related carbon dioxide emissions into the atmosphere, second only to the United States. The pollution is widespread, and takes many forms, especially the coal smoke. It is a severe ecological danger for China. The water pollution is another challenge for China as well. The polluted waters are utilized downstream for irrigation and household use. The use of polluted water by the citizens is causing significant health problems. Both polluted air and water are the current and future environmental disasters in China. The Chinese leaders must face these problems sooner than later. It is clear that Chinese officials and business leaders will need to work together with farmers and other citizens to resolve what is rapidly becoming the largest nationwide environmental crisis.

Taiwan Problem

China ceded the island of Taiwan to Japan at the end of the first Sino-Japanese War (1894-1895). In the Cairo Conference of 1943, the allied powers agreed to have Japan cede Taiwan to the Republic of China upon Japan's surrender. According to both the People's Republic of China and the Republic of China, this agreement was given legal force by the instrument of surrender of Japan in 1945.

Twentieth-century history has brought enormous tragedy to the Chinese people. Taiwan's people were spared some of that suffering because, as a colony for a half century, they were isolated from the China mainland. But Japanese colonialism and many decades of Nationalist government rule created a complex society with ethnic tensions. Expanding cooperation between the ROC and PRC regimes can heal ethnic rivalry in Taiwan and improve their economic and social integration, helping to preserve regional peace and prosperity. Despite the differences that now characterize these two Chinese societies, they share much in common. Prolonged and creative negotiations are the only way both regimes can build a cooperative framework to peacefully coexist in the future as equal partners of one China.

The thaw in cross-strait relations during the 1980s and early 1990s had promoted trust between the two regimes. Beijing's leaders had opened up the mainland market to Taiwanese merchants and investors, encouraged people exchanges between the two sides, and discussed how to resolve airplane hijacking, smuggling, and fishing jurisdiction disputes. By these actions, Beijing's leaders hoped to end China's civil war and resolve the Taiwan-Chinese sovereignty problem

If both Chinese regimes believe there is only one China, Taiwan can have ties with other states but not on a government-to-government basis. Taiwan should not try to develop government-to-government relations, enter international organizations of nation-states, or try to create "two Chinas" or "one China, one Taiwan." Both sides should negotiate to resolve the divided China problem according to this one-China principle. The PRC regime wants to resolve this issue peacefully but will use force if elements either within or outside Taiwan try to bring about an "independent Taiwan." Both sides should strive for peaceful unification because Chinese people should not fight Chinese people.

Conclusion

China is a sovereign state, and like all modern nations in the era of globalization faces tremendous challenges. Overpopulation has been a major problem in China. Chinese government adopted a "one-child policy" in order to help solve this problem. Actually, this policy will not show great results until the children who were born under this policy become older. China's recent rapid economic growth has come at a cost of environmental degradation. China has to find a model for how developing countries might achieve a proper balance between demands for economic development and environmental protection. For the Xinjiang, Tibet and Taiwan problems, it is clearly that China needs a new approach to resolve those tensions; purely the economic development strategies might not be enough.

However, I believe that China can achieve sustainability in the near future; although the country is facing many challenges. If China can take more steps to fix those challenges, China will become a better country to live in.

Challenges Facing China in Her Economic Development

Moloi Shdrack
Col., Botswana Army

This paper attempts to look at the challenges that are facing China in her economic development and also looks at the way in which China has tried to deal with these issues. The challenges facing China in this regard are many and varied, some of them needing urgent and immediate attention because if not given due consideration they may lead to serious social disharmony and disturbances. "For example, contradictions and problems are becoming more prominent daily, such as those relating to resources and the environment in the areas of sustainable development, a balanced urban and rural regional development, a fast and comprehensive growth of public needs and pressures brought on by the changes in public governance and social structure." I shall look at the following challenges and how the government is addressing them.

Income Disparity between the Various Regions

China took a deliberate step of opening up to the World in the early 1970s in order to achieve economic development which was clearly eluding them in the years that were characterized by a planned economy. Since it was an experiment to open up to the World, China decided to do so in stages and to open up only a few places so that a proper and focused analysis of the pros and cons could be done in an efficient and effective manner. This led to Eastern China been selected for this process. The economy was opened to private entrepreneurs and foreign investors. This led to rapid development of the East, leaving behind those areas that were not yet opened. Industries started coming up and businesses set up. The workers in these businesses were earning a salary which was by the then standards far much better than the people working in rural areas. The modern worker could afford to buy his basic needs and also afford to buy a few luxurious items, hitherto something never thought of happening in China.

The standard of living of these people improved tremendously compared to their rural counterparts who are earning far less than the modern worker in Eastern China. As industries and businesses have continued to reinvest their profits and expand; they have improved the salaries they offer to their workers making them better off. The rural people on the other hand have sort of stagnated as compared to people working in the cities and other urban areas. "In the new stage in which material wealth grows quickly, people also aspire for a more equitable and just distribution of wealth and equal access to basic public services." The income disparity between the urban and rural populations continues to be a major concern to the government.

The government has come up with a number of measures in order to address the income disparity between the people and the regions. The government has introduced the policy of cutting taxes for those companies that are setting up businesses in the Western region. This is a move aimed at encouraging both local and foreign investors to set up businesses here. The government has abolished the agricultural tax as a means of not only encouraging people to engage in agriculture but also a means to address the rural urban migration. The abolition of this tax means the farmers can now get more for their products, thereby further trying to reduce the income gap between both the people and the region. However the government has realized that the income gap between the people and the regions is continuing to escalate. The government must therefore speed up the reform of the income distribution system. The challenge here is to come up with an equitable income reform system that will ensure a fair method of sharing the benefits of reform and development. The government continues to provide education and basic social amenities such as health to these less developed regions. The government has made education not only compulsory but also free in the rural areas. The government continues to build hospitals in these areas as it is aware that the income in these areas will not attract business people to provide these services. Where the private sector cannot provide an essential service, then the government is duty bound to provide such a service. The Chinese government must be applauded for being proactive in this regard.

Energy Conservation, Renewable Energy and Environmental Issues

In the process of setting up industries, China did not come up with energy saving and conservation legislation at an appropriate time. It was only after realizing the effects of pollution on the environment that proper regulations were introduced. The government now has policies in place that will address this issue. The government is encouraging the use of clean and efficient energy to replace petroleum and coal in driving the economy. The government has taken deliberate steps to discourage old production methods which pollute the environment. One of the government emphases now lies in renewable energy and the application of new technology in production methods. The government is encouraging the use of hydro power, wind and nuclear energies. "… The government encourages the development and application of renewable energy, and meanwhile, exerts more efforts to eliminate technology and equipment that consume much energy and cause serious pollution." Corporations are encouraged to have the social responsibility of coming up with production methods that do not pollute the environment. They are to strike a balance between maximizing profit while at the same time protecting the environment. Enterprises are encouraged to effectively control the production cycle to ensure the use of safe raw material that will not pollute the environment to recycling most of their waste products. There is a shift from the traditional enterprise management of controlling workers and materials to a new dimension of a harmonious relationship between factories and nature.

More and more Chinese people are becoming aware of the dangers to the environment and they are therefore seeking a lifestyle that is healthy and encourages environmentally friendly consumption. More people are getting used to raveling on public transport there by reducing emissions. The use of bicycles is another way of reducing emissions while it also has health benefits. I have never seen so many bicycles anywhere else in the World except in China and I applaud the Chinese people's effort on reducing the use of petroleum fuel.

Since 2008 the government fiscal budget has included expenditure for environmental protection. The government has made a projection that it will spend 1.375 trillion Yuan between 2005 and 2010 on environmental protection projects. The government medium and long term plan is that by 2010 renewable energy should account for 10% of the total energy consumption in China, and that by 2020 it should account for 15%. Though this may be seen as a conservative figure, it nonetheless shows the government commitment to address the ênvironmental issues that are a result of rapid economic development.

Corruption in Government Beaurocracy

The reform and opening-up have brought rapid economic development to China. This development has being accompanied by one of the World's most elusive crimes, which is corruption by government officials. In their day to day dealings with the public or multinational corporations government officials have being corrupted by individuals and companies alike. These individuals and companies have offered officials huge sums of money as an inducement to help them win tenders or provide them with information which would provide them an edge over their competitors. Corruption by officials has therefore stifled competition and denied the government the value for money in the pricing system. Ordinary citizens have being appalled by the excessively rich officials when they themselves are finding it difficult to acquire any kind of wealth. They have found service delivery lacking when it comes to serving them because they cannot bribe the officials. The projects in their districts have being sub standard because officials are lax when inspecting these projects as a result of having being bribed. These public outcries of poor service delivery, sub standard projects and many other ills have forced the government to come up with measures that would address corruption.

As a response to this undesirable situation the government has set up the Central Commission for Discipline Inspection (CCDI). It is tasked with investigating corruption and bringing the culprits to face justice for their unlawful conduct. On the 14 January at a meeting of the CCDI, its leader Mr. He Guoqiang made the following statement: "The key to winning our war against official corruption is to put punishment and prevention on equal footing. We will place equal efforts in punishing crooked officials for their misconduct, as well as in establishing an anti-corruption system to get rid of corruption at its root."

As a means of trying to get as many people as possible in reporting corruption, CCDI is encouraging ordinary citizens to report cases of corruption through the internet. This is because about 350 million Chinese have access to the internet. This move has yielded encouraging results as ordinary people are reporting cases of corruption using the internet. It is easier because people who report need not reveal their identity for fear of revenge by these officials who in most cases are very powerful people because of their positions in government beaurocracy. One such case is the one involving Mr. Zhou Jiugeng, the former director of the real estate management bureau of Nanjing's Jiangning District. He was prosecuted and sentenced to eleven years in prison. He was investigated after people posted his photographs in the internet smoking expensive cigarettes and putting on Acheron Constantine watch which was worth about one hundred thousand yuan. Mr. Zhou Jiugeng was also driving a Cadillac.

There is a growing concern among ordinary Chinese that the Communist Party members are not being brought to justice even those known to be engaging in corrupt practices. This perception is seriously undermining government's efforts of trying to uproot corruption in official circles. At the 4th Plenum of the Communist Party of China, corruption was one of the major items for discussion. The Communist Party is aware that corruption is seriously undermining China's developments efforts, and that it is a source of social disturbances in many of the countries' civil unrests. "Each year there are outbreaks of civil unrest against abuses of power by local officials. They include the demanding of bribes, public revelations about mistresses and the forced sale of land to unscrupulous property developers."

In other countries there are independent trades and professional associations or bodies that help to limit corruption by their code of ethics. These are self regulating bodies which impose swift sanctions or penalties on erring members. These normally require very low burdens of proof that its member has transgressed a section of its self regulatory statutes. However a proper court requires proof beyond any shadow of doubt to convict an individual or an entity. Civil society as a whole also acts as a watchdog against improper behavior of the state, a group or an individual. However these bodies do not exist in China and the government is the only entity that is responsible for fighting corruption. Many observers think that corruption in China is not being adequately and systematically addressed. Official information for public consumption does not seem to show that corruption is not only growing in numbers but also in complexity.

Conclusions

Economic development has always brought with it challenges irrespective of whether such an economy is closely controlled or not. The industrialized countries of the West have experienced similar challenges and they have addressed them in a way that they felt would best suit their individual needs. The United States for example uses the taxation system as a means of trying to bridge the widening gap between its people and also amongst the corporations, such that those who earn more are taxed more than others. The accruing revenue is then used to pay for social amenities such as health care for those poor members of society who cannot afford the expensive private health care. This system has also brought about its own challenges as individuals and corporations continue to look for better and sophisticated means of evading taxes or giving false information in order to pay less tax.

It is my view that China is doing enough to address these challenges. Credit must also be given to China for recognizing these challenges and for putting measures in place to deal with them. However it is important to have mechanisms in place to review these measures to see if they are still relevant and bringing the desired goals. If they are not bringing the desired outcomes, then the strategy must be changed timeously. By attending to the economic challenges in time and using the correct strategies, China can balance her economic development with a good social democratic programme thereby continue to build a harmonious society. A society envisaged by the great Chinese philosophizer Confucius.

3 Foreign Policy of the People's Republic of China

China's Foreign Policy—Successes and Challenges

Ms Carmel Margaret Tamiloeni
Department of Defence, Papua New Guinea

Introduction

Since China adopted Deng Xiaoping's theory on Socialism with Chinese Characteristics and Reform and Opening-up Policy in 1978 the country has experienced phenomenal economic growth that is unprecedented anywhere in the world. China's transition from a centrally planned economy to a market economy in over the last thirty years has seen China go from a country deep in poverty at a rate of 53% to a reduced rate of 8% in 2001.

China's successful rise is attributed to its very practical foreign policy. This paper will therefore discuss China's Foreign Policy, its evolution, its successes and challenges.

China's Foreign Policy Evolution—Mao Zedong Era

When New China was founded by the Communist Party of China under Mao Zedong on October 1st, 1949 it was a country deeply humiliated, oppressed and victimized by Imperialist powers. Unequal treaties forced upon China's previous ruling dynasties had resulted in the loss of sovereign territories of Hong Kong, Macau and Taiwan to different imperial powers. Added to this the civil war between the Nationalist Party and Communist Party from 1945-1949 had left the country in extremely bad state of affairs. Emotionally the Chinese people emerged victorious and patriotic however social conditions were bad and the economy was shattered.

The country's urgent need then was to reconstruct and pursue industrial modernization to catch up with the rest of the world. A policy of self-reliance was adopted to develop the agriculture sector based on the concept of collectivism. Mao targeted industrial modernization as an important aspect of China's development particularly in the area of military however he required external assistance as the country lacked funds, technology and technical knowledge.

China's modernization was launched in an international unstable environment with revolutionary activities and wars occurring in other parts of the world such as Africa and Asia and Latin America relating to support for ideologies; Socialism, Capitalism and struggles from deliverance of colonialism.

Hence China's foreign policy reflected very much its internal development conditions and the external environment of that era. According to a lecture delivered by Dr. Liu Youfa of China Institute of International Studies on 21 August 2009 to participants of College of Defence and Strategic Studies, China's first foreign policy principles and objectives were stipulated in the 1949 provisional constitution, the Common Program for the Chinese People's Consultative Conference and were defined as follows: guarantee national independence, defend territorial integrity, support protracted world peace, carry out friendly cooperation with countries across the world, liberate Taiwan and oppose imperialist policies and war.

Against this background China's diplomacy was conducted along the strategy of "leaning to one side" which saw China forging formal relations with the former Soviet Union and countries that adopted socialism ideology such Bulgaria, Romania and Democratic Republic of Vietnam. In pursuing the policy of "One China" with Beijing as the only legitimate authority over the People's Republic of China and Taiwan an integral part of mainland China, additional countries switched recognition to Beijing. By the end of 1956 a total of 26 countries had established diplomatic relations with Beijing.

Under the Sino-Soviet Union Treaty of Friendship, Alliance and Mutual assistance, China received funding, technology and technical assistance to develop its industries and modernize its military. Unfortunately relations

Participants simulating multilateral talks

between the two deteriorated in 1961 over China's refusal to permit the Soviet Union to open up strategic basis on China's territory and differences in ideology concerning class struggles under Marxism there by affecting China's development plans.

China needed to seek alternative ways to continue to its development and industrial modernization by implementing the Great Leap Forward and the Cultural Revolution programs which resulted in huge economic and social losses to the country.

Foreign Policy under Deng Xiaoping

In 1976 after Mao's death the Communist Party relied on Deng Xiaoping as China's defector leader. Deng was committed to the Party's goals of developing China into a developed and prosperous modernized nation however mistakes made by the previous regime needed to be corrected.

He reflected on experiences of past policies and strategies as well as did assessments of China's internal conditions and the external environment and arrived at a number of conclusions that would go on to impact the country's path to development and subsequently its foreign policy. The main conclusions drawn then were:

- The Great Leap Forward and the Cultural Revolution had thrown the country backwards in development,

- the development strategies employed by the previous regime were wrong,

- socialist market economy should be the strategy for China to realize modernization and that peace and development were complementary to each other,

- the external environment was still very unstable with the United States and her capitalist block and the Soviet block and her socialist block in a cold war standoff and,

- China needed to continue with her development but for her to proceed the environment within which she developed must be peaceful.

Deng convinced and won support from the other leaders of the Communist Party to accept that "market forces are not the essential difference between socialism and capitalism and that a planned economy is not the definition of socialism as there is planning under capitalism and that both are ways of controlling economic activity." Therefore for China to modernise it should move to embrace both planning and the free market for economic development but maintain its socialist political system. From this came the birth of Socialism with Chinese characteristics and the four modernizations covering agriculture, industry, technology and military. The policy on reform and opening up became China's official policy when approved by the National Congress of the Communist Party of China.

Deng Xiaoping is now credited as the greatest architect of China's economic reform and opening-up as well as the country's greatest diplomat.

With the country's vision for development accepted by the leadership of the Communist Party, Deng proceeded to cultivate an environment for peaceful development by travelling abroad to establish friendly relations with other countries as early as 1979.

In the domestic front, production forces in the agriculture sector where freed up for the first time and diverted to more productive areas such as industry and services. Economic activity was allowed to go into the free market, trade and investment was encouraged by the government.

A revised foreign policy conforming to the new changes was adopted and as a result in the 1982 Constitution. Zhou Yihuang, in his book titled China's Diplomacy outlined China's revised foreign policy as "*China adheres to an independent foreign policy as well as the five principles of mutual respect for sovereignty and territorial integrity, mutual non aggression, non interference in each other's internal affairs, equality and mutual benefit, and peaceful coexistence in developing diplomatic relations and economic and cultural exchanges with other countries; China consistently opposes imperialism, hegemonism, and colonialism, works to strengthen unity with the people of other countries, supports the oppressed nations and the developing countries in their just struggle to win and preserve national independence and develop their national economies, and strives to safeguard world peace and promote the cause of human progress.*"

Well before this revised foreign policy was officially documented Deng Xiaoping began the task of paving a path for China's peaceful development by travelling abroad to establish friendly relations with western countries. He became the first Chinese leader ever to meet with a President of the United States when he met with President Jimmy Carter in 1979. He met with the British Prime Minister where both parties signed an agreement for Hong Kong to China at the end of Britain's 99 year lease period in 1997, met with India's Prime Minister where he discussed the common China-India land border issue. He met with the Japanese Prime Minister where he proposed that historical differences be put aside for the moment and for both countries to concentrate on areas of mutual interest for cooperation between the peoples of their two countries. A similar arrangement was reached with Portugal for Macau to be returned under an arrangement now known as "one country, two systems."

Foreign Policy under Hu Jintao

Under the leadership of President Hu Jintao the Chinese Government further revised the foreign policy and by 2009 when the book "China" was printed by the Foreign Languages Press it stated "China pursues an independent foreign policy of peace, promote common development, and contribute to the building of a harmonious world of lasting peace and common prosperity." Its main elements are as follows:
- Follow the path of peaceful development,
- Promotion of International and Regional Security Cooperation,
- Adhere to mutual beneficial and win-win strategy and,
- Develop friendship and cooperation with all other countries on the basis of the Five Principles of Peaceful Coexistence.

The concept of harmonious society is China's proposal for a new international order for interaction between states. It was first present by President Hu Jintao at Moscow's Institute of International Relations in 2003 then again before the United Nations in 2008.

Explanations on Elements of China's Current Foreign Policy

Follow the Path of Peaceful Development

The experiences of war, revolution and spill—over effects of cold war politics period and hegemonism by then Soviet Union and the United States restrained China developing its economy to levels of modernization that industrial countries in the West, United States and Japan had attained. Under Deng Xiaoping it became obvious that the only path to development for China was for development to take place in a peaceful environment. Peace does not come at its own free will rather it must be cultivated and therefore China placed great importance in promoting peace domestically and in its foreign relations. The core principle that China promotes and adheres to in its interaction with countries and organizations is that of peace. To demonstrate the significance of peace for the country China has established diplomatic relations with many countries. As of 2004 China has established diplomatic relations with 171 countries. Through this relations China is promoting friendship, development and peace through cooperation in the areas of economic and social development and cultural exchanges.

Promotion of International and Regional Security Cooperation

Another key element of China's foreign policy in the new era is the promotion of International and Regional Security Cooperation. China strongly opposes all forms of hegemony and will never engage in expansionism as it has been a victim of such policies in the past.

China strongly believes that the best approach to attaining peace and development is through cooperation at both the International and Regional levels. The belief is that there is an avenue for cooperation every state and nation has the opportunity to participate and contribute to the common goal of peace and development for all mankind. It follows than that where there is collective effort towards managing security issues conflict is minimized and nation states are free to rationally amass their national strengths towards development.

China is a member of the United Nations since 1971 and has concurrently held membership one of the five seats in the United Nations Security council. As one of five countries with veto power rights it has been known to underutilize that power in the past to influence decision making in the Security Council and hence failed affect outcomes on major security issues in the global arena. Since reform and opening up Chinese leaders and diplomats and citizens have had thirty years of exposure and experience in the workings of the international environment. The country has better understanding of the international system, the United Nations functional mechanisms and matured in diplomacy. It has since the late 1980s become more mature and decisive in addressing international security issues before the UN Security Council.

This maturity is seen in its change in position on participation in United Nations approved missions ranging from peacekeeping, arms control, counter terrorism, to fostering development, defending human rights and justice, and environmental protection including other activities of the United Nations specialized agencies.

In peacekeeping responsibilities China has reviewed its policy from one of non interference into other countries sovereign territories to one of participation but within the guidance of the principle of "independence." China has started taking up peacekeeping responsibilities as one of its key activities to satisfy its policy on international cooperation. According to Zhou Mingwei & others in the book "China," China has participated in 24 UN missions since 1989 and assigned more than 10,000 personnel for peacekeeping missions. Currently there are 2,150 Chinese peacekeeping personnel serving in peacekeeping operation regions.

China has matured in the role it plays in ensuring major international issues that threaten peace and stability is addressed. A good example is that of the significant role China is currently playing in mediating between the United States and North Korea to resume dialogue in the Six Party Talks on the issue of freeing the Korean Peninsula, Asia and the world of nuclear threats by North Korea. China is displaying self confidence in its independent style of addressing how other nuclear and terrorist issues. In the case of Iran while China stands for the principles of nuclear free world it does not agree that UN sanctions are the appropriate strategy to getting Iran to give up her nuclear development ambitions and has voted against the UN Security Council on this matter. In a statement released by the Chinese foreign ministry spokeswoman Jiang Yu told reporters "All parties should enhance diplomatic efforts and adhere to the right track of negotiations," confirming China's maturity in managing sensitive issues that impact on peace and stability. At the Un Climate Change conference in Copenhagen in December 2009 China displayed a highly degree of influence role in negotiating together with the BRICS developing country group more commitment by developed countries to commit to higher levels of carbon emission reductions and to contribute more to funding of programs and activities on cleaner energy use. This is a matter in which China received much international media publicity.

In the Asian region China is contributing to peace and stability through organizations such as the Shanghai Cooperation Organisation (SCO) and ASEAN. Through the SCO China, Russia and five former states of the Soviet Union are have come together to manage common international border issues in a collective and peaceful manner, cooperate in economic and security cooperation specifically in the area of counter terrorism. Through the ASEAN and SCO China contributes to regions security, peace and stability through confidence building measures in the area of security, cooperation in the areas of economics and trade, cultural exchanges and through regular ministerial and officials dialogue. China's contribution to a far safer and secure South East Asian region can be seen through the ASEAN-China Free Trade Area arrangement which came into effect in the beginning of 2010.

China is also a member of a number of numerous prestigious international organizations such as the World Health Organisation and World Trade Organisation and plays an active role in promoting the organizations objectives.

Adhere to Mutual Beneficial and Win-win Strategy

The objective of the mutual beneficial and win-win strategy is most visible in cooperation within the area of economics and trade when negotiating expected benefits from business activities that both parties engage in. Under this "China promotes common regional and international development by its own development, expanding the scope where interests of different sides meet. As China develops itself, reasonable concerns for other countries especially of developing countries will be taken into consideration. China will continue to expand market access in accordance with current international economy and trade rules, and protect the rights and interests of partners according to law."

On this policy objective, where economic and trade relations are the major area for cooperation China adheres to the strategy that exploitation of natural resources or any other economic activity should result in both China and its foreign partner seeing mutual and or win-win benefits from the economic activity. The strategy allows for both parties to negotiate for mutual end results rather than employ self interests.

Under this policy China has entered into relations with third world countries in regions of the developing world that Western powers have shunned interest from often quoting human rights violations, undemocratic governments, and high security risks as reasons for not engaging with them. In line with this policy China has established and strengthened relations with developing countries in African, Latin America, Asia, and the Middle East.

Develop Friendship and Cooperation with All Other Countries on the Basis of the Five Principles of Peaceful Coexistence

The Five Principles of Peaceful Coexistence are: mutual respect for sovereignty and territorial integrity, mutual non-aggression, non-interference in each other's internal affairs, equality and mutual benefit, and peaceful co-existence. These five principles are official norms that guide state to state relations regardless of political and social systems and development status of the guest state. The same principles are employed in managing issues of international concern at international forums and regional organizations. The principles reflect China's past experiences of humiliation, wars, and intimidation by hegemonic United States and former Soviet Union during the cold war era. By enforcing these principles China seeks to restore her integrity as a sovereign state, seek to resolve outstanding disputes with its neighbours, be a responsible member of the international community and contribute to a peaceful harmonious world.

Mutual Respect for sovereignty and territorial integrity is the most revered policy objective that China consistently seeks formal recognition for in every state to state relationship. While the People's Republic of China has been in existence for over 60 years and is now enjoying a rising superpower status its sovereignty over Taiwan remains outstanding. China argues its sovereignty is incomplete as long as Taiwan remains detached from the motherland.

Successes

Three main strengths are identified as successes of China's foreign policy. Firstly, constructive engagement and diplomacy with countries around the world has won Beijing recognition from the 170 countries as the sole legitimate government of the People's Republic of China.

Secondly the success of China's foreign policy reflects the visionary and collective leadership of all four generations of China's leaders beginning with Chairman Mao Zedong the founding father of the Republic, to the great architect of reform and opening-up, Deng Xiaoping, to Jiang Zemin and the now the very remarkable President Hu Jintao.

Thirdly and perhaps the most important and notable of all is the successes China has achieved in over thirty years rising from a poor nation to one that is economically prosperous today. Along with economic growth China has matured in diplomacy and won international respect as seen in the roles it plays in attending to international issues such as nuclear reduction, counter terrorism and environmental issues.

Challenges

Firstly, with maturity in diplomacy and China's phenomenal economic growth has come with it expectations by western and developing countries alike for China to be take up more active responsibilities in the international scene. China is still a developing country as compared to the United States and hence it cannot afford to divide its attention away from its own national priorities as yet. To do so will result in a negative effect on China's development.

Secondly, reform and opening-up has resulted in an increase in demand for energy and resources. In order to secure necessary requirements China is inevitably pushed into regions that Western powers consider their backyards resulting in unplanned competition and often unwarranted negative publicity.

Thirdly, the disparity between the developed east and the yet to catch up western part of China, the gap between the rich and the poor, the unresolved internal problems relating to Taiwan's reunification, Tibet and

Xinjiang is evidence that China needs to do more to develop and resolve these situations.

Conclusion

In conclusion, the last thirty years of China's diplomacy has had a profound impact on the country's economic development and elevated its status in the international community. China's foreign policy will continue to undergo more tests as Western developed nations continue to put up challenges. Hence China's leaders are expected to remain informed to protect the country's peaceful development.

China's Foreign Policy Featuring Peace, Development and Cooperation

Khamlek Sengphachanh
Wg. Cdr., Laos Air Force

Introduction

Foreign policy is a set of goals outlining how a country will interact with other countries economically, politically, socially and military. Foreign policies are designed to help protect a country's national interests, national security, ideological goals, and economic prosperity. This can occur as a result of peaceful cooperation with other nations, or through exploitation.

The foreign relations of the People's Republic of China draw upon traditions and culture extending back to imperial China in the Qing Dynasty (1616-1911) and the Opium Wars, despite Chinese society having undergone many radical upheavals over the past two and a half centuries, the goal of foreign policy was and is to create a strong, independent, powerful, and united China that is one of several great powers in the world, the Chinese foreign policy establishment maintains that in achieving this goal, they are not pursuing any hegemonic or warlike ambitions.

China's Foreign Policy

The Common Program of the Chinese People's Political Consultative Conference (CPPCC) served as a provisional constitution after it was adopted in September 1949. The document clearly stipulated that the basic principle of China's foreign policy was to guarantee independence, freedom and territorial integrity of the state, support protracted world peace and friendly cooperation among peoples of all countries in the world, and oppose imperialist policies of aggression and war. The Constitution of the People's Republic of China revised during the First

Participants visiting Poly Art Museum in Beijing

Plenary Session of the Eighth National People's Congress has the explicit stipulations concerning China's foreign policy: "China adheres to an independent foreign policy as well as to the five principles of mutual respect for sovereignty and territorial integrity, mutual non-aggression, non-interference in each other's internal affairs, equality and mutual benefit, and peaceful coexistence in developing diplomatic relations and economic and cultural exchanges with other countries; China consistently opposes imperialism, hegemonism and colonialism, works to strengthen unity with the people of other countries, supports the oppressed nations and the developing countries in their just struggle to win and preserve national independence and develop their national economies, and strives to safeguard world peace and promote the cause of human progress."

Following the above policies over the past 50 years, China has actively engaged in foreign activities, and in handling foreign affairs. China has made sustained efforts to developing friendly cooperative relations with all countries and in safeguarding world peace, and has made its contribution in these fields too.

Maintaining Independence and Safeguarding National Sovereignty

China had suffered imperialist aggression and oppression for over 100 years before the founding of the People's Republic in 1949. Therefore, China regards the hard-earned right of independence as the basic principle of foreign policy.

China maintains independence, does not allow any country to infringe upon its national sovereignty and interfere in its internal affairs. As to international affairs, China decide on our stand and policy according to whether the matter is right and wrong and in consideration of the basic interests of the Chinese people and the people of the world, and shall never yield to pressure and threat from other countries. China maintains independence, cherishes its own right and also respects for the right of independence of other countries. China upholds that any country, big or small, rich or poor, and strong or weak, should be equal. China maintains independence, will neither enter into alliance with any big power or group of countries, nor establish any military bloc, join in the arms race or seek military expansion.

Opposing Hegemonism and Safeguarding World Peace

The common aspiration of the Chinese people as well as the people of the world is to maintain peace and to eliminate wars.

After the World War II, the United States and the Soviet Union desperately engaged in arm races and regional domination in order to contend for world hegemonism. As a result, they caused severe threat to world peace. The Chinese government has constantly opposed arm races and regional domination, and actively stood for the complete prohibition and destruction of nuclear weapons and great reduction of conventional weapons and military troops. China decided in 1985 to reduce one million troops within two years and signed the Treaty on the Non-Proliferation of Nuclear Weapons in 1992. All these received favorable international comments.

Upholding the Five Principles of Peaceful Coexistence

The five principles of peaceful coexistence were put forward in line with the reality of a multipolar world. Respect to sovereignty is the most fundamental principle in a new type of international relations. Mutual non-aggression means to get rid of the threat of using arms and armed threat in the internal relations among countries. Non-interference in each other's international affairs is the most important principle in international relations to guarantee each country's right to take care of its own internal affairs and prevent any other country from interfering with any means. Equality and mutual benefit mean political equality, economic equality, cooperation, mutual benefit and supplement to each other's needs. Peaceful coexistence calls on all countries to seek common interests, reserve differences, respect each other, maintain friendly cooperation and live in harmony regardless of differences in their social systems and ideologies.

In the 1990s great changes have occurred in the world. Domination of two superpowers ended and the world is becoming more multipolar. On the basis of the five principles of peaceful coexistence, China stands for the establishment of a peaceful, stable, just and rational international order. China's stand conforms to the purposes and principles of the UN Charter, and reflects the trend of the times to seek peace and development.

Strengthening Solidarity of the Developing Countries, and Together Opposing Imperialism and Colonialism

It is a great cause of the people in the developing countries in Asia, Africa and Latin America that account for three-quarters of the total population of the world, to take the road of independence and development. China has constantly held that supporting the just demands of the developing countries and safeguarding solidarity and cooperation among the developing countries is its international duty. Whenever the developing countries suffer external aggression and interference, China is ready to give its support. Many leaders of the developing countries regard China as a "tested friend" and a "reliable friend."

China has become a formal observer of the nonalignment movement, and its cooperative relations with the Seventy-Seven Group and the South Pacific Forum has been steadily strengthened.

Improving Relations with Developed Countries to Promote Common Progress

On the basis of the principle of peaceful coexistence, China has constantly stood for establishing and developing relations with developed countries, and regarded improving the relations with developed countries and promoting development with them as an important task of China's foreign affairs.

The establishment of the diplomatic relations with France in 1964 broke the policy of Western countries to isolate China. In the 1970s the world situation experienced a great change, the United States had to readjust its policy on China, and China also readjusted its policy on the United

States. This resulted in a breakthrough of the long antagonism between China and the United State, and the normalization of diplomatic relations between the two countries through common efforts. Meanwhile, China established diplomatic relations and strengthened friendly cooperative ties with other Western countries successively. This further brought about a new situation in China's foreign affairs.

Removing External Interference, Promoting China's Reunification

Hong Kong and Macao have been inseparable parts of China since ancient times. China does not recognize unequal treaties imposed by imperialist powers. Regarding the issue of Hong Kong and Macao left over by history, China has constantly held the position of peaceful settlement through negotiations at a proper opportunity.

In order to accomplish China's reunification, Deng Xiaoping put forward the concept of "one country, two systems." The delegations of the Chinese and British governments finally reached an agreement after 22 rounds of talks, and formally signed the Joint Declaration on the Question of Hong Kong and three appendixes. Hong Kong returned to the embrace of the motherland on July 1, 1997. The Chinese and Portugal governments formally signed the Joint Declaration on the Question of Macao and two appendixes in 1984 after they reached an agreement through four-round talks. China will resume its exercise of sovereignty over Macao on December 20, 1999.

Taiwan is an inalienable part of Chinese territory. People of the two sides of the Taiwan Straits are looking forward to the realization of China's reunification. China resolutely opposes the "independence of Taiwan," the attempt to create "two Chinas" or "one China, one Taiwan." Chinese leaders call on Taiwan authorities to enter into political negotiations with the mainland at an early date. On the premise that there is only one China, the two sides of the Straits should end the state of hostility, and improve the relations between the two sides to accomplish the reunification of the motherland.

Main Characteristics and Features of China's Foreign Policy

Chinese foreign policy was formulated by Mao Zedong and Zhou Enlai, and lately by Deng Xiaoping who as a strategist and tactician combined the characteristics of Mao and Zhou and secured many useful pointers to current Chinese foreign policy. He emphasized that the fundamental goals Chinese foreign policy were to oppose hegemonism, safeguard world peace, and promote human progress; He said that socialist China belongs to the third world and will always stand by the third world, he always took strengthening unity and co-operation with developing countries as a basic part of China's foreign affairs, Deng also spelled out the strategic principle of keeping a level mind in observation, getting a firm foothold, having a sure hand, and accomplishing something. Deng's ideas on foreign affairs are an important part of his theory of building socialism with Chinese characteristics. And guided by Deng, Huang Hua as China's foreign minister and diplomatic oversaw the negotiations and signing of Sino-Japan agreements and Sino-US negotiations, though this senior diplomat paid special attention to making friends and coming to terms with people of different backgrounds and beliefs and especially with India.

The international community began to take note of China's "new diplomacy" in 2003; in that year the journal *foreign affair* spublished an article entitled *"China's new diplomacy"* by Evan Medres and Fravel Taylor. The basic principle of China's foreign policy is to guarantee independence, freedom and territorial integrity of the state, support protracted world peace and friendly cooperation among peoples of all countries in the world, and oppose imperialist policies of aggression and war. China adheres to an independent foreign policy as well as to the five principles of mutual respect for sovereignty and territorial integrity, mutual non-aggression, non-interference in each other's internal affairs, equality and mutual benefit, and peaceful coexistence in developing diplomatic relations and economic and cultural exchanges with other countries.

As to international affairs, it shall never yield to pressure and threat from other countries. it upholds that any country, big or small, rich or poor, and strong or weak, should be equal, it will neither enter into alliance with any big power or group of countries, nor establish any military bloc, or join in the arms race or seek military expansion, and actively stood for the complete prohibition and destruction of nuclear weapons and great reduction of conventional weapons and military troops.

China is firmly opposed to terrorism and the proliferation of weapons of mass destruction, and as for international treaties, it abides by all them in a faithful way, it respects the diversity of civilizations and advocates that different cultures make exchanges learn from each other, it is opposed to clashes and confrontations between civilizations, and does not link any particular ethnic group or religion with terrorism.

Conclusion

New China was founded in 1949 and that China has always, especially over the past 50 years, observed the diplomatic thinking initiated by late Chinese leaders Mao Zedong, Zhou Enlai and Deng Xiaoping, so that the nation has recorded monumental achievements in unswervingly implementing its independent foreign policy of peace. Deng Xiaoping, who directed China's diplomatic work for two decades, beginning 1978, had an excellent mastery of the domestic developments and of the changing international situation, as well a full grasp of the characteristics of the times. In other words Deng further developed and perfected China's foreign policy environment for China's socialist modernization drive.

Some analysts suggest that this priority is behind Beijing'sdecision in 2003 to tone down its anti-US rhetoric and criticism and instead to emphasize China's "peaceful rise" on the world. China is now in a delicate, sensitive and painful period of transition, the sheer size of China's huge population and China's growing power has already presented an enormous task to the new Chinese leadership, it will become an important player in the future in a multi-polarized world as

Participants experiencing China high speed railway

the nation's international status and prestige rise steadily and where it Wants and is calling for the establishment of a new world order that will ensure a long-term stable and peaceful international environment for development.

The efforts to promote the development of the world towards multipolarization are not targeted at any particular country, nor are they aimed at re-staging the old play of contention for hegemony in history. Rather, "these efforts are made to boost the democratization of international relations, help the various forces in the world, on the basis of equality and mutual benefit, enhance coordination and dialogue, refrain from confrontation and preserve jointly world peace, stability and development."

A country's affairs should be handled by its own people and international issues should be resolved through negotiations, and the United Nations, the organization that has the largest number of member nations should play a dominant role in international affairs, the common wish is for the establishment of a just and reasonable new political and economic order in the world, which helps in creating a long-term peaceful environment for the development of all countries in the world, but this road leading to a harmonious world characterized by sustained peace and common prosperity is a bumpy and challenging one, and reaching the goal demands long and unremitting efforts by the people throughout the world.

View on China's Foreign Policy

Sohail Ahmed
Commodore, Pakistani Air Force

View on China's Foreign Policy

The foreign policy of a country indicates that country's intentions in international relations. Similarly, the intentions can also be understood by the relations a country has with other key global players and these relations also indicate what would be the overall impact on stabilizing / destabilizing the world peace and security.

The PRC has proclaimed that its foreign policy is based on the "five principles of peaceful co-existence," which were put forward by Premier Zhou Enlai in 1950s. These principles are: mutual respect for sovereignty and territorial integrity, mutual non-aggression, non-interference in each other's internal affairs, equality and mutual benefit, and peaceful coexistence. Since 1950s, the central place of these principles in Chinese diplomacy has remained unchanged. President Jiang Zemin in 1995 said that China had consistently stood for the settlement of disputes through peaceful negotiations and opposed the threat or use of force in international relations. He said that the five principles are becoming even more vital and important in the modern world and that if all the nations abided by the five principles then a lasting peace could be achieved in international relations.

Disputes Resolution

The Chinese resolution of disputes with its neighbours indicates a more pragmatic and conciliatory attitude. Beijing has adopted a two-pronged approach for the resolution of these disputes. First, if the dispute is both trivial and marginal to China's larger interests, Beijing has resorted to solving it amicably to pursue its larger goals. For example, since 1991, China has settled border conflicts with Kazakhstan, Kyrgyzstan, Laos, Russia, Tajikistan, and Vietnam. A number of these conflicts have been resolved by China on less than advantageous terms. In most of these agreements, China received only 50% or less of the contested territory; for example in resolving the long-standing dispute over the Pamir Mountains with Tajikistan, China accepted only 1000 of the contested 28,000 square kilometres of area.

Second, if the dispute cannot be resolved quickly then China has advocated an indefinite postponement of the issue. This approach has been adopted in the disputes with India, Japan, and a number of ASEAN countries. The Chinese accommodative attitude is very evident from the language of the code, which included most of the draft language sought by ASEAN and little of what was offered by China. The dispute resolution policies followed by China give strength to the argument that China is not a revisionist power and is trying to create an environment conducive to its own development and the development of other nations in the region.

China's Peaceful Rise

Chinese foreign policy also indicates that China is not seeking a path of confrontation with other powers as China depends more on foreign investment for economic development and political legitimacy than rising powers before the two World Wars. China's political power has been dramatically increasing since 1978, when the economic reforms placed it on a course that led to a rapid transformation of its latent power potential into actual power. Consequently, China is becoming more integrated and an active participant in a wide variety of international diplomatic and economic institutions. Therefore, China would not do anything to disrupt the status quo because any disturbance would have a direct effect on the economic development and may cause domestic instability. China's "peaceful rise" will further open its economy so that its population can serve as a growing market for the rest of the world, thus providing increased opportunities for the international community rather than posing a threat to it. Some emerging powers in modern history have plundered other countries' resources through invasion, colonization, expansion, or even large scale wars of aggression. China's emergence thus far has been driven by capital, technology, and resources acquired through peaceful means.

Role of China in Global Security Issues

Chinese attitude in the global legal norms i.e. bilateral and multilateral treaties have changed considerably. Today China is a member of more than 220 multilateral treaties. The Chinese approach to bilateral relations, multilateral organizations, and security issues reflects a new flexibility and sophistication. Chinese officials now increasingly and explicitly talk about the need to share global responsibilities among major powers including China. The Chinese sponsorship of first the three party talks and then the six party talks on the Korean nuclear issue has improved the Chinese image immensely. In 2003, when the North Korean nuclear issue intensified, the world's eyes were focused on North Korea and the US. However, it was China, which played the most significant role in bringing Pyongyang and Washington to the negotiating table. The talks eased the situation in the Korean peninsula and initiated the process for a peaceful settlement of the issue. Chinese role in the Korean nuclear issue has brought about a realization in the international system that China is going to be a significant factor in the global political and diplomatic scene.

Chinese leaders and strategists have stressed on the international community that China does not seek hegemony or predominance in world affairs. It advocates a new international political and economic order, one that can be achieved through incremental reforms and democratisation of international relations. China's active participation in international institutions creates more chances to elicit cooperation on key issues. As the nation's stake in the international community expands, China is gradually becoming more involved in efforts to combat global security threats, both traditional and non-traditional. China has also increased its participation in UN Peacekeeping operations supporting contingents in East Timor, Congo, and elsewhere. Moreover, the new shift in Chinese foreign policy in anti piracy operations in off the coast of Somalia/Gulf of Aden is likely to enhance Chinese image as an emerging power.

China's Relations with Key Countries

Chinese relations and interactions with key countries / regions of the world, to a large extent determine the China's peaceful foreign policy.

China-Russia Relations

The "Treaty of Good-neighbourliness, Friendship and Cooperation" was signed between Russia and PRC on 16 July, 2001. According to Russian Deputy Foreign Minister, the treaty "creates favourable conditions for the strengthening of good-neighbourliness, friendship and cooperation both in political as well as in trade, economic, scientific, technological, humanitarian and other areas." The Russia and China conducted their first-ever bilateral large-scale war games called the "Peace Mission 2005" during August 18-25, 2005. The exercise was symbolic of the growing cooperation between the two countries against the US presence in Afghanistan and Central Asia.

Chinese relations with Russia is based on mutual cooperation in defence, economic and political fields, which meets the interests of the two countries as well as the interests of stability in Asia and in the world at large. The resolution of their disputes, the treaty of friendship, and the joint military exercises indicate that the two countries are heading towards a long lasting stable relationship. The growing stability in Sino-Russia relationship has the potential to have a positive effect on the regional and global stability as well.

China-EU Relations

China's relations with EU and its member states have also been growing in the recent past. The depth of China-Europe relations is impressive, and the global importance of the relationship ranks it as an emerging axis in world affairs. The growing trade relations between China and the EU have created an economic interdependence and are likely to grow even further. In the military and strategic domain, each side has designated the other as a "strategic partner."

Despite the rapidly growing relationship between EU and China, there is one issue, which is becoming an obstacle in further growth of relations and that is the arms embargo, which the EU forced on China after the Tian'anmen Square incident in 1989. The lifting of the embargo requires a unanimous vote in the EU and currently it is estimated that 16 out of the 25 EU nations favour lifting the embargo. However, some EU nations are forcefully opposing lifting of the embargo. All the EU nations appear to agree that the embargo is a major obstacle on the road to further growth in relations and strategic partnership but they are also sensitive to three concerns. First, the EU nations are concerned about the human rights situation in China. They agree that the HR situation in China has greatly improved; yet China needs to do more. Second, The EU nations are concerned that lifting the embargo would aggravate the Taiwan Strait situation. And third, the EU nations are concerned that lifting of the embargo would further aggravate the already strained transatlantic relationship with the US. Despite of all, Military exchanges between individual EU nations and China are already taking place, while EU level exchanges are being planned.

Nonetheless, there are a number of reasons for growth in China-EU partnership. The most important of these reasons is that China and EU have a convergence of views about the US, its foreign policy, and its global behaviour. Both China and the EU are seeking ways to constrain US power and hegemony through creation of a multi-polar world and multilateral institutional constraints on the US. Europeans see China as a great power with great and global responsibilities and wants to engage China as a responsible power in the management of global issues. Over time it has the potential to become a new axis in world affairs, and will serve as a Source of stability in a volatile world.

Participants visiting photo exhibition of Tibet

198

China-US Relations

The Sino-US relations indicate that both the countries have moved from a position of mistrust for each other to a position of increased cooperation in different fields. However, there are powerful lobbies within the US, which consider China as a challenge and future threat to American interests. India has sought to exploit the threat perceptions, presenting itself as a viable partner to promote US interests from the Persian Gulf to Central Asia and Afghanistan on the one hand, and regarding China, on the other. Initially, the US adopted the policy of containment of China. However, in the last decade or so, the US has realized that the policy of containment had potentials of creating tensions with China and thus moved to a policy of engagement as well. Both countries now realize that cooperation with each other is in their own national interests as well as the general interest of the stability of international security. Good relations between China and US and their economic interdependence are important for the stability in the international environment. However, Taiwan issue is very sensitive and very dear to China. On one hand, US supports the China's one China policy regarding Taiwan and on the other hand knowing the gravity of situation, US is planning to sell the arms to Taiwan which would definitely damage the China-US relation and cooperation. In fact, despite of all cooperation and good relation US would continue to consider China as a challenge and future threat to US interests and would continue to endeavour to keep China under trauma through a range of means.

Role of Media in Foreign Policy

The foreign policy of China is playing a great role in preserving global stability. However, media is one of the important aspects in projecting the image of the country and could be utilized effectively in attaining the objectives of foreign policy which China has not utilized efficiently despite having done a lot for world peace, security and non traditional threats. Media has emerged as a viable element of power.

Acceptance of this concept will allow the strategist to use information to its fullest extent. Modern technology has revolutionized the mass media especially the electronic media. While the improved communication and transportation systems accelerated the process of accessibility and verification of the stories for radio and press, the television made media men sufficiently powerful to considerably influence the policy formation, campaign processes, issue developments etc.

China needs to have a strong worldwide Media to guard the interest of China's Foreign Policy which is at present dominated by the Western powers. President Hu Jintao while addressing the World Media Summit at the Great Hall on Oct. 9, 2009, highlighted the important role played by foreign media in telling the world about the changes in China. Having heard the address of Hu Jintao, I need not to emphasize more regarding the role of media in all polices especially the foreign policy. In my view, China needs to do a lot about media. Chinese's media can play effective role in the foreign policy provided if the Chinese media is well-matched to the world powerful channels, credible enough to magnetize the people outside China and technically vigorous enough to project all what China needs.

Conclusion

The decision to open up the Chinese economy was perhaps the most important decision of the 20th century for Chinese people. Since 1978, China has progressed at a breathtaking pace and now boasts one of the largest economies of the world, with attendant enhancement in its political stature.

The increase in economic, political and military strength of China has had a major impact on the international system. The China has become a major player on the international scene. The China is following the path of peace and stability in the world. The development and growth of Chinese economy depends on a peaceful international environment, The Chinese foreign policy and their actions in the international fora indicate that indeed the Chinese intentions are peaceful. Chinese relations with their neighbours and other major power centres are growing and will prove to be a source of stability in the world. There are some irritants in Chinese relations with other powers, but these are minor in nature and may be resolved with sincere efforts. The only issue that could destabilize the international peace is the Taiwan issue. However, there too, Chinese pragmatism and the US support to the Chinese stance, may resolve the issue with the passage of time. Thus, the foreign policy of China indicates the intentions are peaceful and good for global stability. However, China needs to set up a strong worldwide Media to guard the interest of China's Foreign Policy.

China's Foreign Policy Featuring Harmony

Ali Abdulla S M AL-Subaiei
Col., Qatar Army

Introduction

The foreign relations of the People's Republic of China draw upon traditions extending back to imperial China in the Qing Dynasty and the Opium Wars, despite Chinese society having undergone many radical upheavals over the past two and a half centuries. The goal of Chinese foreign policy is to create a strong, independent, powerful, and united China that is one of several great powers in the world. The Chinese foreign policy establishment maintains that in achieving this goal, they are not pursuing any hegemonic or warlike ambitions.

Recent Chinese foreign policy makers may be seen to adhere to the realist rather than the liberal school of international relations theory. Thus, in sharp contrast to the former Soviet Union and the United States, China has not been devoted to advancing any higher international ideological interests such as world communism or world democracy since the Cold War; that is, ideology has been secondary to advancing its national interest.

Main Characteristics and Features of China's Foreign Policy

First we will highlight on the Institutions of foreign policy, like most other nations, China's foreign policy is carried out by the Ministry of Foreign Affairs. However, the Foreign Affairs Ministry is subordinate to the Foreign Affairs Leading Small Group of the Communist Party of China, which decides on policy-making unlike most other nations, much of Chinese foreign policy is formulated in think tanks sponsored and supervised by, but formally outside of the government. China is also distinctive for having a separate body of Chinese strategic thought and theory of international relations which is distinct from Western theory.

China made its policy of peace in foreign relations clear when Deng Xiaoping said that its fundamental goals were to oppose hegemonism, safeguard world peace, and promote human progress. He tied the principle of independence closely to that of peaceful foreign relations. Also Deng emphasized that socialist China belongs to the third world and will always stand by the third world. He always took strengthening unity and co-operation with developing countries as a basic part of China's foreign affairs, Deng also spelled out the strategic principle of keeping a level mind in observation, getting a firm foothold, having a sure hand, and accomplishing something.

Deng's ideas on foreign affairs are an important part of his theory of building socialism with Chinese characteristics and a creative development of the foreign policy of peace formulated by Mao Zedong and Zhou Enlai, also an important strategy for China's foreign affairs policy is a multi layer framework around China with a good, rich, and comfortable neigherhood, including the theory of regional integration.

The basic principle of China's foreign policy was to guarantee independence, freedom and territorial integrity of the state, support protracted world peace and friendly cooperation among peoples of all countries in the world, and oppose imperialist policies of aggression and war. China adheres to an independent foreign policy as well as to the five principles of mutual respect for sovereignty and territorial integrity, mutual non-aggression, non-interference in each other's internal affairs, equality and mutual benefit, and peaceful coexistence in developing diplomatic relations and economic and cultural exchanges with other countries.

China consistently opposes imperialism, hegemonies and colonialism, works to strengthen unity with the people of other countries, supports the oppressed nations and the developing countries in their just struggle to win and preserve national independence and develop their national economies, and strives to safeguard world peace and promote the cause of human progress.

China maintains independence, does not allow any country to infringe upon its national sovereignty and interfere in its internal affairs. As to international affairs, China decide its policy according to whether the matter is right and wrong and in consideration of the basic interests of the Chinese people and the people of the world, and shall never yield to pressure and threat from other countries.

China maintains independence, cherishes its own right and also respects for the right of independence of other countries. China upholds that any country, big or small, rich or poor, and strong or weak, should be equal. China will neither enter into alliance with any big power or group of countries, nor establish any military bloc, or join in the arms race or seek military expansion, and actively stood for the complete prohibition and destruction of nuclear weapons and great reduction of conventional weapons and military troops. China signed the Treaty on the Non-Proliferation of Nuclear Weapons in 1992.

China is upholding the Five Principles of Peaceful Coexistence, with the reality of creating a multipolar world, where the respect to sovereignty is the most fundamental principle in international relations, and the Mutual non-aggression means to get rid of the threat of using arms and armed threat in the internal relations among countries. Also the non interference in each other's affairs is an important principle in international relations.

The Equality and mutual benefit mean political equality, economic equality, cooperation, mutual benefit and supplement to each other's needs, where the Peaceful coexistence calls on all countries to seek common interests, reserve differences, respect each other, maintain friendly cooperation and live in harmony regardless of differences in their social systems and ideologies, and Strengthening Solidarity of the Developing Countries.

China has constantly held that supporting the just demands of the developing countries and safeguarding solidarity and cooperation among the developing countries is its international duty. Whenever the developing countries suffer external aggression and interference, China is ready to give its support .China has become a formal observer of the nonalignment movement, and its cooperative relations with the Seventy-Seven Group and the South Pacific Forum has been steadily strengthened.

China maintains that all countries, big or small, should be treated equally and respects each other. All affairs should be consulted and resolved by all countries on the basis of equal participation. No country should bully others on the basis of strength. And will make judgment on each case in international affairs, each matter on the merit of the matter itself and it will not have double standards. China will not have two policies: one for itself and one for others. And it believes that it cannot do unto others what they do not wish others do unto them.

China is firmly opposed to terrorism and the proliferation of weapons of mass destruction. China is a member of the international community, and as for international treaties, China abides by all them in a faithful way. China respects the diversity of civilizations and advocates that different cultures make exchanges learn from each other, China is opposed to clashes and confrontations between civilizations, and does not link any particular ethnic group or religion with terrorism.

China calls for Removing External Interference, Promoting China's

Reunification, and In order to accomplish China's reunification, Deng Xiaoping put forward the concept of "one country, different systems." Hong Kong and Macao returned to the embrace of the motherland and at same time Taiwan is an inalienable part of Chinese territory. The two sides of the Straits should end the state of hostility, and improve the relations between the two sides to accomplish the reunification with the motherland.

China's Foreign Policy Achievements in Diplomacy, and Challenges

It resumed the exercise of sovereignty over Hong, and Macao pushing forward its great cause of peaceful reunification of Taiwan with the motherland, and It has promoted good-neighborly friendships, and developed friendship and co-operation with its neighboring countries; and strengthened unity and co-operation with most other developing countries.

On the basis of the Five Principles of Peaceful Co-Existence, it has developed relations with Eastern Europe and the Commonwealth of Independent States, and improved its relations with Western countries, and created a good international environment for continuing its reform, opening-up, and modernization drive by expanding economic, trade, and technology exchanges and co-operation, and cultural and other exchanges with other countries; and also initiated negotiations on such free trade areas as the China-Southern African Development Community, China-Gulf Cooperation Council, and China-New Zealand, China-Chile, China-Australia and China-Pakistan, and signed relevant agreements with its partners,. 23-China is also an active and pragmatic participant in the activities of the Asia-Pacific Economic Cooperation, Forum on China-Africa Cooperation, Sino-Arab Cooperation Forum, Asia-Europe Meeting and Greater Mekong Sub region Economic Cooperation Program, China sticks to the principle of mutual benefit and win-win cooperation, tries to find proper settlement of trade conflicts and promotes common development with other countries.

As for the challenges we can mark the sea change in the international situation since Deng's and even Jiang's times, so it must readjust its relations with other major powers. European countries headed by Germany and France are striving for a bigger say in international affairs and are criticizing the United States for its unilateralism, Russia is trying hard at finding a bigger role in world affairs, China must work with all potential major powers and have a say in international institutions and in the world order.

China has to balance domestic factors and foreign policy goals. And do its best to preserve stability at home, by satisfying an increasingly diverse society with multiple demands. China faces pressure from an entire spectrum of forces. It must put its own house in order first and then devote more attention to its foreign policy agenda. However, domestic and external developments do not always follow people's will. The SARS crisis is a case in point. China has to move up its agenda and meet squarely the new challenge of an increasingly blurred division between domestic and foreign affairs.

China is now in a delicate, sensitive and painful period of transition. The sheer size of China's huge population and China's growing power has already presented an enormous task to the new Chinese leadership. The new leadership had planned to put domestic issues such economic growth and narrowing the gap between the wealthy coast and poor inland areas at the top of it priorities.

The 16th Party Congress presented a blueprint for China's external strategy and foreign policy that the new leadership will keep to. In the short- and mid-term, China will pay special attention to improving its relations with developed countries, particularly the United States, and with its neighboring countries. And will strive to enhance high level visits, especially promoting personal summits so as to enhance mutual understanding and continue strategic dialogues with other of the world's major powers for nurturing a favorable external condition for its modernization program and building a well-off society in an all round way by 2020.

Conclusion

A country's affairs should be handled by its own people and international issues should be resolved through negotiations, and the United Nations, the organization that has the largest number of member nations should play a dominant role in international affairs. The common wish is for the establishment of a just and reasonable new political and economic order in the world, which helps in creating a long-term peaceful environment for the development of all countries in the world.

Understanding of China's Independent Foreign Policy of Peace

Paseuth Thiengtham
Lt. Col., Laos Army

Introduction

During around two months, I have studied module of China studies, the College of Defense Studies has given us a lot of theoretical and practical exposures about China, the Chinese people and especially about China's foreign policy. So, on the basic of my understanding, I would like to share some points on China's foreign policy independence and peace.

As we known, *foreign policies are designed to help protect a country's national interests, national security, ideological goals and economic prosperity....* China's foreign policy and strategic thinking is unswervingly pursues an independent foreign policy of peace. The fundamental goals of this policy are to preserve China's independence, sovereignty and territorial integrity, create a favorable international environment for China's reform and opening up and modernization construction, maintain world peace and propel common development.

Charactersitscs of China's Foreign Policy

China's foreign policy has three striking characteristics as follows:

Firstly, uphold the principle of self-independence and absolutely safeguard China's national sovereignty and national dignity. In international affairs, China determines its position and policies by proceeding from the fundamental interests of the people of China and other countries and judging each case on its own merits. China does not yield to any outside pressure or enter into an alliance with any big power or group of countries.

Secondly, establish and develop normal relations with other countries according to the Five Principles of Peaceful Co-existence. That is to say, China carries out the principles of mutual respect for sovereignty and territorial integrity, mutual non-aggression, non-interference in each

Participants voicing their views at the seminar

other's internal affairs, equality and mutual benefit, and peaceful co-existence in dealing with international relations with all other countries, whether or not they have the same social system with China. The five principles conform to the principles of the United Nations Charter and reflect the trend of the times to seek peace and development, and are the basis to formulate a fair and rational international political and economic new order.

And thirdly, strengthen solidarity and cooperation with the developing countries, oppose hegemonism and safeguard world peace. China maintains that disputes between nations should be settled peacefully through consultations instead of resorting to force or the threat of force. China opposes imposing one's social system and ideology upon others. No country should interfere in the internal affairs of another country under any pretext, still less bully the weak, invade or subvert other countries.

Principles Governing the Establishment of Diplomatic Relations with Other Countries

With the inauguration of the People's Republic of China on October 1, 1949, the Chinese government declared solemnly: "This government is the sole legal government representing the Chinese people. It is ready to establish diplomatic relations with all foreign governments which are willing to observe the principles of equality, mutual benefit and respect for each other's territorial integrity and sovereignty." There is only one China in the world. Taiwan Province is an integral part of the territory of the PRC. Any country seeking to establish diplomatic relations with China must show its readiness to sever all diplomatic relations with the Taiwan authorities and recognize the government of the PRC as the sole legal government of China. The Chinese government will never tolerate any country scheming to create "two Chinas" or "one China, one Taiwan;" nor will it tolerate any moves on the part of countries having formal diplomatic relations with China to establish any form of official relations with the Taiwan authorities.

China's Foreign Policy of Independent and Peace

Over the past 60 years since the establishment of the People's Republic of China, the country's foreign affairs have gone through two general stages: The 30 years before, and the 30 years after, the reform and opening up program which was introduced in 1978. During these periods, China has been always pursuing a foreign policy of independence and peace.

This basic foreign policy principle was worked out by Mao Zedong and Zhou Enlai. Since the introduction of the reform and opening up policy, some important readjustments concerning some aspects in international strategy and foreign policy have been made under the guidance of Deng Xiaoping Theory. This is the current foreign policy that continues to be carried out by the generation to the generation of collective leadership with Jiang Zemin and then Hu Jintao at the core. The main content of this policy includes:

China has all along adhered to the principle of independence. With regard to all the international affairs, China will, proceeding from the fundamental interests of the Chinese people and the people of the world, determine its stand and policy in the light of the merits and demerits of the matter, without yielding to any outside pressure. China does not form an alliance with any big power or group of big powers. Nor does China establish military groups with other countries, or engage in arms race and military expansion.

China opposes hegemonism and preserves world peace. China believes that all countries, big or small, strong or weak, rich or poor, are equal members of the international community. Countries should resolve their disputes and conflicts peacefully through consultations and not resort to the use or threat of force. Nor should they interfere in others' internal affairs under any pretext. China never imposes its social system and ideology on others, nor allows other countries to impose theirs on it.

China actively facilitates the establishment of a new international political and economic order that is fair and rational. China holds that the new order should give expression to the demands of the development of history and progress of the times and reflect the universal aspirations and common interests of the peoples of all the countries in the world. The Five Principles of Peaceful Coexistence and the universally recognized norms governing international relations should serve as the basis for setting up the new international political and economic order.

China is ready to establish and develop friendly relations of cooperation with all the countries on the basis of mutual respect for sovereignty and territorial integrity, mutual non-aggression, mutual non-interference in each other's internal affairs, equality and mutual benefit, and peaceful coexistence. It is an important component of China's foreign policy to actively develop good-neighborly relations of friendship with the surrounding countries. China has resolved problems left over by history with the overwhelming majority of neighboring countries. And China's mutually beneficial cooperation with its neighbors has witnessed a vigorous development. It is the fundamental standing point of China's foreign policy to strengthen its solidarity and cooperation with numerous developing countries. China and these countries share common historic experiences and are faced with the common tasks of preserving national independence and achieving economic development. Therefore, their cooperation has a solid foundation and a broad prospect. China sets store by improving and developing its relations with developed countries. It advocates that countries should surmount their differences in social system and ideology, respect one another, seek common ground and shelve differences and enhance their mutually beneficial cooperation. Their disputes should be appropriately solved through dialogue on the basis of equality and mutual respect.

China pursues a policy of all-dimensional opening up to the outside. It is ready to develop, on the basis of equality and mutual benefit, extensive trade relations, economic and technological cooperation and scientific and cultural exchanges with countries and regions of the world so as to promote common prosperity. At the end of 2001, China approved 390,000 overseas-funded enterprises with 745.9 billion dollars of contractual capital and 395.5 billion dollars of used capital. In 2001,

China's import and export volume amounted to 509.8 billion dollars, ranking the sixth in the world. After 15 years' talks, China finally acceded to the World Trade Organization (WTO) on December 11, 2001. While enjoying the relevant rights, China has begun earnestly honoring its obligations within the framework of the WTO and its commitments. China remains ready to play a positive role, together with other countries, in improving world multilateral trade system and promoting prosperity and progress in the world. The world economy is an inter-connected and inter-dependent whole. Economic globalization has brought both opportunities and big risks for the economies of various countries. It is a common challenge confronting the governments of all the countries to preserve financial stability, prevent financial crisis and ensure economic security.

China takes an active part in multilateral diplomatic activities and is a staunch force in preserving world peace and facilitating common development. As a permanent member of the Security Council of the United Nations, China actively participates in the political solution of the problems of regional hot spots. China's peace-keepers have joined United Nations peace-keeping operations. China supports the reform of the United Nations and a continued important role of the United Nations and other multilateral organs in international affairs. China is firmly opposed to all forms of terrorism and has made important contributions to international anti-terrorism cooperation. China devotes itself actively to pushing forward the cause of international arms control, disarmament and non-proliferation. To date, China has joined all the treaties related to international arms control and non-proliferation. With regard to non-proliferation, China has all along scrupulously abided by its international obligations and, thanks to its active efforts in enacting laws on non-proliferation, set up a relatively perfect export control system for non-proliferation. The Chinese government has attached importance to human rights and made unremitting efforts in this regard. China has joined 18 human rights conventions, including the International Covenant on Economic, Social and Cultural Rights, and signed the International

Covenant on Civil and Political Rights. China remains ready, together with the international community, to enhance cooperation to address the global problems facing mankind including worsening environment, resources scarcity, unemployment, population explosion, narcotics spreading, and rampant transnational crimes.

Achivements of China's Foreign Policy Independent and Peace

The past 60 years, in upholding its foreign policy of independence and peace China has the main achievements as follows:

On the basis of the Five Principles of Peaceful Co-Existence, China has set up and developed friendly cooperative relations with 168 countries, conducted exchanges and cooperation activities with 220 countries and regions in terms of economy, trade, science and technology and culture. China has consolidated and strengthened solidarity and cooperation with developing countries, and set up good-neighborly mutual trust, friendly relations and cooperation with almost all neighboring countries. Relations with developed countries and major powers have also continuously improved.

As the largest developing country, China actively takes part in multi-lateral foreign affairs, and plays a unique, constructive role in international affairs. China has always firmly opposed any form of hegemonism and power politics, safeguarded the legitimate rights and interests of developing countries, and actively promoted the establishment of a fair and rational international political and economic new order. As an important member of the Asia-Pacific Economic Cooperation (APEC) and the Asia-Europe Meeting (ASEM), China has striven to promote the healthy development of regional cooperation. Following the Asian financial crises, the Chinese government adopted a series of internal and external policies and measures to contribute to the steady restoration of the regional, or even the world finance and economic system to stability, establishing itself an image of a big responsible country.

China, one of the permanent members of the United Nations Security

Council, upholds the principle of resolving international disputes through peaceful methods. China took part in, and actively promoted the international disarmament process. China, on its own initiative, launched two large-scale rounds of disarmament in 1985 and 1997, with the size of army cut by 1 million and then by a further 500,000 personnel. The move was highly appraised by the international community.

China absolutely safeguarded State sovereignty and territorial integrity, with the reunification of the motherland advancing greatly. Through Sino-British and Sino-Portuguese negotiations, China resumed the exercise of sovereignty over Hong Kong on July 1, 1997, and will resume control of Macao on December 20, 1999. China will still hold to the principles of "peaceful reunification" and "one country, two systems" in dealing with the Taiwan issue. China has firmly fought the splitting activities toward "two Chinas," or "one China, one Taiwan." As a result, China has, for six straight years, frustrated Taiwan authorities' attempt to "return to the United Nations," thus, safeguarding the national independence, sovereignty and dignity.

Moreover, in recent years, Chinese leaders have been regular travelers to all parts of the globe, and China has sought a higher profile in the UN through its permanent seat on the United Nations Security Council and other multilateral organizations. Closer to home, China has made efforts to reduce tensions in Asia, hosting the Six-Party Talks on North Korea's nuclear weapons program, China has also taken steps to improve relations with countries in South Asia, including India. Following Premier Wen's 2005 visit to India, the two sides moved to increase commercial and cultural ties, as well as to resolve longstanding border disputes. The November 2006 visit of President Hu Jintao was the first state visit by a Chinese head of state to India in 10 years. China has likewise improved ties with Russia, with Presidents Putin and Hu exchanging visits to Beijing and Moscow in April 2006 and March 2007. A second round of Russia-China joint military exercises was scheduled for fall 2007. Relations with Japan improved following Japanese Prime Minister Shinzo Abe's October 2006 visit to Beijing, and continued to improve under

Prime Minister Yasuo Fukuda until his resignation in September 2008.

Some Challenges of China's Foreign Policy

China still faces some challenges, especially peripheral Security Environment as follows:

China's periphery incorporates two major military powers (Russia and India), two economic giants (Japan and South Korea), and emerging markets for which all major Powers would compete (India, ASEAN etc.) .

China is hemmed in by United States military alliances and American forward military presence in Japan, South Korea, Taiwan and Philippines.

Regional conflict flash-points exist on China's periphery in the Korean Peninsula, Kashmir and Afghanistan.

China faces pro-independence movements in Taiwan, Tibet and East Turkistan.

With these challenges, China has been actively engaging in its foreign affairs, exerting its sustained efforts to develop cooperative relations with all the countries and institutions on the bases of Five Principles of Peaceful Coexistence.

Conclusion

Over the past 60 years, observed the diplomatic thinking initiated by collective Chinese leaders from Mao Zedong, Deng Xiaoping, Jiang Zemin to Hu Jintao, so that the nation has recorded monumental achievements in unswervingly implementing its independent foreign policy of peace.

The international situation is experiencing a great change, and peace and development have become the mainstream of the time. China needs to maintain stable foreign relations with developed countries, and with its neighboring countries. It takes strategic visions of the Chinese leaders and government to continue to implement the independent and peaceful foreign policy and to make greater contribution to the cause of safeguarding world peace and promoting human progress, and to building socialism with Chinese characteristics.

China's Rise as Soft Power and Challenges

Khan Tahir Javed Khan
Brig Gen., Pakistani Army

The use of word "soft power" came to prominence following a writing by Professor Joseph Nye of Harvard University in a 1990 book named "Bound to Lead: The Changing Nature of American Power" and another book in 2004 named "Soft Power: The Means to Success in World Politics" in which, he used the term soft power and gave its interplay in the international arena. According to him, *"Soft power is the ability to obtain what you want through co-option and attraction rather than the hard power of coercion and payment."* The indirect way to get what you want has sometimes been called "the second face of power." A country may obtain the outcomes it wants in world politics because other countries admire its values, emulate its example, aspire to its level of prosperity and openness.

China in the last three decades is constantly on a rise both, politically as well as economically. China's much-noted economic progress has been accompanied by a steady expansion in its cultural and diplomatic influence globally especially in the developing world. While, it may not be easy to compete with a sole super power in many fields, yet many scholars believe that China's soft power status is growing fast. In this paper, an effort will be made to indentify China's soft power status along with challenges it faces while offering few recommendations.

Elements of Soft Power

There are different views on the development of a soft power in China. Most of the scholars in China go along parameters laid down by professor Nye i.e. culture, political values and foreign policy. However, there are other opinions. Few scholars consider Chinese model of development as a source of the nation's soft power. Su Changhe argues that soft power is evident in a state's international institution-building, agenda-setting, mobilization of coalitions and ability to fulfill commitments. Another study suggests that China's soft power includes cultural diplomacy and multilateral diplomacy. There is yet another school of thought that lays importance on mass media. According to them, the capability and effectiveness in mass communications are important aspects of a state's soft power. Yan Xuetong believes that soft power lies in the political power of political institutions, norms and credibility, rather than in culture while Zhu Feng argues that soft power has little to do with sources of power, but rather whether or not the international community accepts a nation's policies and strategic choices, and to what extent these choices accord with other nations' interests. Few Chinese scholars take the soft power development in a different context. They lay more emphasis on the domestic orientation i.e. national cohesion, domestic political institution-building, social justice, social morality and educational quality.

From the above debate, one can conclude that soft power rests on wholesome strength and behavior of a nation where, resources and their application, attitudes and values of masses as well as of the government are all important. All these elements can be reflected in a country's foreign policy, defence policy, media policy, economic policy in such a way that influence the other states in one's favour. Not that they listen to you because of your authority but cooperate on the basis of good. Not that they follow your culture because it is superior but rather on the basis of its values and so on. The measure of one's soft power is the extent to which these primary elements of soft power are able to attract or repel other actors to "want what you want."

China's Rise as Soft Power

Chinese leaders pay a close attention to its rise as soft power and there have been number of debates at various forums on ways and means of projecting it both domestically and internationally. While addressing Central Foreign Affairs Leadership Group meeting on January 4, 2006,

President Hu Jintao said: "The increase in our nation's international status and influence will have to be demonstrated in hard power such as the economy, science and technology and defence, as well as in soft power such as culture." The President again highlighted soft power in his political report to the 17th Party Congress of October 2007, stressing the urgency of building China's cultural soft power sufficiently to meet domestic needs and increase international competitiveness. With a clear vision, Chinese leadership and its scholars are laying a strong foundation of Chinese soft power. Today, China is projecting its soft power in many fields which are discussed below.

Cultural Aspect of Soft Power

Traditional Chinese culture is singled out as the most valuable source of Chinese soft power, on the premise that it boasts a long history, and a wide range of traditions. Chinese culture takes its main character from Confucianism and Taoism with values like winning respect through virtue (yi de fu ren), peace and harmony (he), and harmony without suppressing differences (he er bu tong). The Chinese government has done much in recent years to promote cultural exchanges with the outside world including establishment of over 295 Confucius Institutes in 78 countries to teach Chinese language and promote Chinese culture. The Chinese Diaspora throughout the world is a good platform for promoting Chinese culture.

Foreign Policy

China's foreign policy has changed fundamentally in last three decades. Since 1978, China has expanded the number and depth of its bilateral relationships, joined various trade and security accords, deepened its participation in key multilateral organizations, and helped address global security issues. Foreign policy decision-making has become less personalized and more institutionalized and Chinese diplomats have become more sophisticated in their articulation of the country's goals. More broadly, the Chinese foreign policy establishment has come to see the country as an emerging great power with varied interests and responsibilities. China's current promotion of concepts such as "peaceful development," "harmonious world," "win-win solutions," and "strategic partnerships" has a greater appeal to the developing world as against United States' hegemonic and policing attitude. Chinese foreign policy based on fundamental principles of co-existence for maintaining world peace through friendly relations and cooperation has a wide recognition today than before, enhancing the foundation of China's soft power development over time.

Fostering Bilateral and Multilateral Initiatives

On a bilateral basis, China has established Strategic Partnership, Friendship and Cooperative Partnership and Free Trade Agreements throughout Latin America, Asia, and Africa. In addition to bilateral initiatives, China increasingly has grown more active in international multilateral organizations. China also has successfully sought entry in one form or another to existing regional groupings in Asia, Africa, Latin America and the Caribbean. These include Asia Pacific Economic Cooperation (APEC) Forum, ASEAN Regional Forum (ARF), Forum for East Asia and Latin American Cooperation (FOCALAE), Organization of American States (OAS). China in the last one decade has also sought to devise new multilateral organizations to support its interests and expand its international influence like East Asia Summit (EAS). Shanghai Cooperation Organization (SCO) and Forum on China-Africa Cooperation (FOCAC). Chinese active engagement allows her to occupy a space that was once denied to it by Western Powers. These organizations allow China to exert its influence in the outcome of international issues through its soft power.

Sustainable Economic Growth

This rapid and sustained economic growth has served as powerful driver of China's international trade and investment agreements. China steadily and successfully has sought trade agreements, oil and gas contracts, scientific and technological cooperation, and de-facto multilateral security arrangements with countries both around its periphery and around the world. The strength of Chinese economy actually came to realization once it acted as a stabilizing factor during the Asian financial crisis in 1997 and has proved its fundamental strength in the sub-prime crisis of 2007. The interdependence of developed nations with China and growing influence of Chinese economy around the globe has aroused suspicions and sense of insecurity amongst the hegemonic states but at the same time, it has enhanced China's soft power influence.

China's Soft Power Influence in Different Regions

Latin America: Of the 33 independent countries in the Latin America and Caribbean region, China currently has official diplomatic relations with 21, while the remaining 12 nations maintain relations with Taiwan. Over the years, China has signed strategic partnership agreements with Brazil (1993), Venezuela (2001), Mexico (2003) and Argentina (2004). Friendly and cooperative partnership agreements have been signed with Bolivia, Chile, Colombia, Cuba, Ecuador, Jamaica and Peru. Total trade between China and the Latin America and Caribbean region rose from $8.2 billion in 1999 to almost $140 billion in 2008. The Chinese government has negotiated more than 400 trade and investment deals with Latin American countries in the last few years. China is also increasingly supporting cultural and educational programs in the region. China's assistance to Grenada in the aftermath of Hurricane Ivan in 2004, its support to Peru in the aftermath of a devastating earthquake in 2007, writing off $15 million Chinese debt owed by Guyana, provision of soft loans to Jamaica, Suriname, Venezuela, Trinidad and Tobago, establishment of $6 billion joint development fund between China and Venezuela in 2007 has enhanced China's soft power influence in the region.

Africa: In Africa, as elsewhere, China advocates international norms of political neutrality and state sovereignty, particularly with respect to non-interference with respect to countries' internal affairs that increases its acceptance level amongst the African communities. Strong bilateral and economic ties with Africa has allowed a greater space for China to isolate Taiwan and influence African votes within UN and other international forums in order to achieve diverse policy goals. Among the most notable of China's efforts to foster closer ties with Africa, both bilaterally and at the continental level, is the Forum on China-Africa Cooperation (FOCAC) to build mutually beneficial economic development, trade cooperation and political relations with Africa and is rooted in principles of "South-South Cooperation." China's practice of building roads, hospitals and bridges in countries where it has made substantial energy investments like Sudan, Angola, and Equatorial Guinea has drawn public praise. Winning Africa to its side is a good reflection of Chinese soft power.

Southeast Asia: China's growing influence or soft power in Southeast Asia is largely economic, stemming from its rapidly expanding role as a major source of foreign aid, trade, and investment. The PRC has also wielded power in the region through diplomacy, admiration of China as a model for development, ancient culture and an emphasis on "shared Asian values." Over the past decade, China's trade with ASEAN has expanded sharply in terms of trade volume, percentage increase, and size relative to US trade levels. From 1997-2007, its exports to, and imports from, ASEAN countries grew by 642% and 777% respectively. These trends are expected to continue in the years ahead as economic ties continue to deepen as a result of the implementation of the China-ASEAN Free Trade Agreement (FTA) and other cooperative initiatives. China's soft power in the region is expected to grow as Southeast Asian economies become more dependent upon or integrated with the PRC. China's changed bilateral relations with Australia are an interesting parallel to recent dynamics in Southeast Asia and demonstrate how the economic aspect of soft power can transform a bilateral relationship with a state that is a close ally of the United States.

Central Asia: Central Asia occupies a significant place in China's stability owing to number of factors. Central Asian states act as a buffer between China and Russia. Being Muslim states, have a natural Xinjiang connection and being rich in energy resources, can address China's energy requirements, being immediate neighbours can provide economic opportunities for China's Xinjiang Uighur Autonomous Region and can reinstate Central Asia as a transit corridor ("Silk Road") between China and Europe and between China and the Middle East. China's relations with Central Asia slowly evolved during the 1990s have now developed into strong bilateral ties with each Central Asian state as well as multilateral ties through the Shanghai Cooperation Organization (SCO). China has concluded Friendship and Cooperation Treaties with Kazakhstan, Kyrgyzstan, Tajikistan, and Uzbekistan that provide a framework for enhancing bilateral relations. Among multilateral ties, China cooperates in the Central Asia Regional Economic Cooperation program (CAREC) whose members are China, Afghanistan, Azerbaijan, Mongolia, and all the Central Asian states except Turkmenistan. Trade turnover between China and Central Asia has increased from negligible amounts during the Soviet period to almost $22 billion in 2008. China has secured rail and road links with Kazakhstan and has also secured energy supply through recently inaugurated pipeline. China has very successfully engaged Central Asian states to contain Xinjiang problem. Its border demarcation agreement with Tajikistan in May 2002 enhanced its soft power image as a good neighbor and this also resulted in stepped up bilateral cooperation.

Southwest Pacific: South Pacific countries are increasingly important for China because, Of the 23 countries with which Taiwan has diplomatic ties, six are in the Pacific. Greater cooperation and engagement with these countries afford more space to China to isolate Taiwan. By some accounts, the PRC has become the third-largest source of foreign aid to the South Pacific. China has become a growing political and economic force in the Southwest Pacific. There reportedly are more than 3,000 Chinese state-owned and private enterprises in the Pacific, with a total value estimated at around $1 billion. The governments of the largest Pacific Island countries like Papua New Guinea (PNG), Fiji and the Solomon Islands have welcomed investment from China as part of their "look north" foreign policies.

Japan and South Korea: In Northeast Asia, China's rise and its soft power are causing fundamental changes in its relations with Japan and South Korea. These countries have entered into a new era in which the economic benefits of trade, tourism, investment, and cultural flows are gradually overcoming the inertia of long harbored feelings of enmity. The grown economic ties of China with these countries can be judged from the fact that in 1995 Japan's imports from the United States were twice those from China, by 2006 nearly the opposite was the case. In the cultural and social area, China also is drawing closer to Japan and South Korea. There were about 3.5 million tourist visits to China by both Japanese and South Korean in 2008. China's success to establish ASEAN+3 (China, Japan and South Korea) block in regional trade can be seen as a success story with more Chinese influence in the region.

Organization of World Level Events

The organization of 2008 Summer Olympics in Beijing attracted a record 4.7 billion television viewers worldwide and brought a wide appreciation for China. Thousands of tourists were able to see a different China to what they had perceived through Western Media. The planned Shanghai Expo 2010 and hosting of Asian Games in Guangzhou are a full display of a developing nation's transformation into a developed world.

Challenges to China's Soft Power

Image Building: The first and foremost challenge to China's soft power is western propaganda on the system of government, non democratization of the country and human right issues. Being a communist country following one party system of government, China faces severe criticism from the western countries. The world at large continue to perceive China in the same prism of communist regimes that once existed in Stalinist era in former USSR whereas, the things have changed a lot in actual reality. In my view, the system followed by China is much different to that of former communism. Chinese run the country with a mix blend of communism and democracy which can be called a democracy with Chinese character a little different way to that of Western style. However, the Western media tells a different story to the world which to some extent tarnishes its political image with resultant effect on its soft power.

Language: The colonization of the world by the Western countries from 17th to 20th century resulted in expansion of Western culture and languages in Latin America, Pacific islands, Africa, Middle East, South and South East Asia. Even after the independence of colonial countries, the Western legacy has stayed in these countries in which language is one main component. On the other hand, Chinese language has remained confined within China. Utilizing the power of language, literature and institutions of higher learning, West has made itself more appealing to the outside world. Resultantly, people from all spheres of life tend to orientate themselves towards the West for their higher learning. They find more literature and technical knowledge in the languages which they easily understand. What China should do, is a major dilemma. Should it orientate it's educational and literature towards the Western languages like English and Spanish, it would have serious effect on their own language, on the other hand expansion of Chinese language in other regions is a difficult task. China has to find out a strategy to sell itself to the world in the language which the world understands. Something more than just the opening up of Confucius institutes.

Chinese Culture: Just like language, the peculiar Chinese culture is mainly confined to China though its cultural values have an appeal for the outside world. China's cultural soft power is presently marginalized by predominant position of the West in general and United States in particular with regards cultural literature, movies, popular music, television programmes, fast food and fashion etc. As per one of the research conducted in China, the country imported 4,068 book titles from the United States but exported only 14; it imported 2,030 titles from Britain but exported only 16; and imported 694 titles from Japan but exported only 22. This alarming import: export ratio of 4,000:24 should be a serious concern of Chinese government as well as intellectuals. The continuation of this process would continue to affect China's soft power image in the near future.

Development of Comprehensive National Power: While soft power is a tool to influence the behaviours without use or threat of use of force, the proportionate hard power provide leverage for its full play. As per Li Mingjiang (a Chinese Scholar), "A great power needs material or hard power as well as soft power to enjoy flexibility within international politics and maintain advantageous positions in international competition." In other words, soft power is just a component of State's comprehensive power which flows from range of other factors. Notwithstanding the significance of other factors, the technologically advanced armed forces and their reaction capability in various parts of the globe figures out as one singular important factor in which China is lagging behind.

Human Resource Development: A nation can only influence the other nations if it has a something special to offer in terms of intellect, ideas and values. If the populace of a country projects itself as a role model, the others would be morally influenced from the conduct and behavior. As of now, there remains a serious gap between economic and human resource development. The Chinese society is passing through a transitional phase which is formative in nature but quite slow. Education sector, social institutions and development of civil society remains a challenging task.

Media Challenge: A strong Western media poses a major challenge to China's soft power. As per a survey report, currently, the four major new agencies; Associated Press, United Press International, Reuters, and Agency France-Presse producing four-fifths of the total news stories in the world belong to the West. The 50 top Western transnational media corporations hold 90 percent of the world communication market. The United States alone controls 75 percent of the TV programs in the world. In many developing nations, 60 to 80 percent of the content in TV programs comes from the US. Western dominance in media and mass communications has resulted in their "cultural hegemony" or "media imperialism." Chinese leaders I believe also realize the fact.

Li Changchun, one of China's top leaders (the politburo standing committee member in charge of ideology), on the commemoration of the 50th anniversary of CCTV in December 2008 said: "Enhancing our communication capacity domestically and internationally is of direct consequence to our nation's international influence and international position."

China's International Influence: The basic philosophy of soft power is to influence the behavior of others through means other than the hard power. One of such means is the strength of a country which it can wield in international institutions. While China holds a veto power at Security Council and is also a member of all important multilateral organizations, its influence so far, has remained under shadow due to its weak position in world financial institutions like world bank and IMF and its tacit win-win policy at international forums in general and united nations in particular. Despite its clear position on various issues, it sometimes, failed to influence the decisions of Western powers with regard to the developing countries, the world climate conference notwithstanding.

China Threat Thesis: In the course of recorded history, various nations came to dominate the world using different strategies. Greeks had a superior cultural, philosophy and political institutions. Romans had strong land forces, Ottomans drew strength from Islamic Ideology, Western Powers after long internal conflicts started expanding using superior naval forces, United States surpassed everyone in technological advancements and now China is emerging a strong economic power. The superiority of nations in any field ultimately led them to expand their influence in other field as well once they attained a distinct position. On the similar model, China's rise as a leading economic power is being propagated as a future threat. The "Chinese threat" thesis is an easily saleable philosophy owing to its long animosity with Japan, Russia, and unresolved issue in South China Sea and Taiwan factor. China threat thesis is figuring out frequently in intellectual discussions and Western media propaganda which has consequences for its soft power.

Harmonious World and Win-Win Policy Concept: Although, the world at large, appreciates China's concept of harmonious world but many critiques particularly in the developing countries question its win-win policy. There are serious issues in the world where, countries have different positions on their resolution. Win-win policy means, not annoying any side and that would not be possible in many cases. The option then left is to close one's eyes on those issues which do not have a direct impact on the Chinese national interests. In the overall interest of China, this may be a good option but it has negative implications in the projection of soft power.

Piracy and Product Quality Issues: China has been a serious subject of piracy and copy right issues that has and is constantly damaging its image in general in the developed world. In the competitive economic environment, Western countries might initiate collective actions which may affect Chinese trade with certain countries. Another issue that is impacting on China's image is wrong business practices where, certain enterprises produce and export low quality products. Although number of steps has been taken to formulate and implement piracy and copyright laws, yet, a lot is required. On the production side too, there has been an improvement, however, image building requires further efforts.

Recommendations

In last two decades, China has emerged as a major economic power. Its role in Asian Financial Crisis, Sub Prime crisis, World Climate Conference has enhanced her soft power image, however, there are challenges discussed earlier which actually indicate a great weakness as well. Few recommendations are proffered to further enhance it soft power.

(1) China's domestic reforms, attention to civilian rights and domestic institution building are steps in right direction. Its reformed communist system with Chinese character with fair democratic touch might have more appeal if the NPC sessions are convened with more frequent intervals. Such sessions may be covered by international media. The tiered process of electing deputies to the People's Congress and National People's Congress is fairly democratic, notwithstanding the secret

ballot. A change from secret to open ballot alone would enhance public confidence and improve international image of the CPC.

(2) The language barrier issue is a difficult question. China might consider a middle ground by adopting a prominent foreign language for selective adoption in its education system. China may also like to offer English curriculum to foreign students, doctors, engineers and people interested to adopt higher studies in China. China also needs to build a capacity and policy to absorb intellectuals from the foreign countries on the lines of United States.

(3) While China has taken concrete steps for promotion of its culture abroad, two areas need to be brought under focus: Extensive translation of Chinese literature in foreign languages and development of Hollywood style movie industry in English for international audience.

(4) Modernization of armed forces, development of blue water navy, strategic air force and raising of quick reaction force is fundamental to comprehensive power and complementary to soft power. In the longer run, China might consider some bases in the friendly countries to extend its strategic outreach to safeguard its interests in different regions. (US, at present has troops in 30 countries around the globe)

(5) Educational reforms, establishment of social institutions, development of civil society require special attention for better human resource development.

(6) China must develop more effective strategies for dealing with Western media; and second, China must enlarge its media capacity within international communications.

(7) The outcome of World Climate Conference exhibits China's soft power and its influence on the outcome of major decision on the international issues. While, it is playing a significance role in Iran-West and North Korea-West confrontation, it needs to enhance its say in the international financial institutions and acceptance of its currency for international trade.

(8) China's role in stabilizing Asian Financial situation in 1997 played a significant role in reducing the hidden fears of "China Threat" in the

South East Asian Region. Its enhanced bilateral economic cooperation with Japan, South Korea, Australia, Taiwan and resolution of border disputes with number of neighbouring countries provide it a moral high ground and more strategic space to down play "China Threat" thesis. Early resolution of issues at South China Sea and joint exploration projects would further reduce "China Threat" thesis propaganda.

(9) In the international diplomacy, while avoiding a confrontational approach, China needs to play more proactive role on issues like war on terrorism, resolution of Palestine issue and restoration of sovereignty of nations like Afghanistan and Iraq. China can also play a leading role in African stability owing to its neutrality and more acceptances by African nations.

(10) PRC is currently in a position to invest more in the developing world and it is doing that well. However, to change their orientation from West to East, developing and poor countries need to be brought out of Western shackles through provision of soft term loans, initiation of social assistance programmes and provision of special grants.

(11) China's tarnished image on piracy and copy right issues need to be revived and the government will have to adopt more strict laws to attain a moral authority in the international community. It also needs to curb wrong business practices to ensure product quality. As long as this image is not improved, it would be hard to sell the idea of "made by China" instead of "made in China."

Conclusion

China is a country with an age-old history, a brilliant civilization, and magnificent landscapes. China gave the world remarkable inventions, most noticeably gunpowder, paper making, printing and the sundial. However, it never enjoyed a dominant position in the international politics owing to number of factors; the most prominent of which was probably the unfounded fears to preserve its culture and social values from outside. The rebirth of China in 1949, although provided it new opportunities, at a time once new world order was being established, however, its international isolation and number of other challenges forced its continuation of inward looking policies. While, it successfully thwarted all external threats, it slowly started moving forward in a difficult international situation. Its re-orientation in 1979, with a concept of "opening up" has led it to a respectable place today, in the comity of nations. Not only that it has restored its historical dignity and honour but is also emerging as economic super power in the foreseeable future. China in the last three decades is constantly on a rise both, politically as well as economically. China's much-noted economic progress has been accompanied by a steady expansion in its cultural and diplomatic influence globally, especially in the developing world. The history once again is presenting an opportunity for it to rise which China must capitalize on.

The Role of the Chinese Media in China's Foreign Policy

Musallam Smail Musallam Al-Zeidi
Col., Oman Army

"The MEDIA's the most powerful entity on earth. They have the power to make the innocent guilty and to make the guilty innocent, and that's power, because they control the minds of the masses."

—Malcolm X (American black leader)

Introduction

The rapid growth of China's peaceful Foreign Policy and national strength has drawn attention from the entire world by major media in Europe and the

US. They looked at China's economic performance and opening to the world as of interest and concern. However, during module one of the NDU English course number 24, the participants of any countries were able to hear from Chinese side the development and opening of the country to the world peacefully.

China's peaceful approach to the world was felt more during the China's foreign policy lectures and discussions. Truly, all that information and teaching from module one has had profound effect on my understanding of peaceful China and it is absolutely different than that broadcasted on foreign media, especially the Western media.

The Chinese media is playing brilliant role inside China. However, still not reaching far outside China in order to promote the principles of China's foreign policy and economic opening, which was tailored to guarantee independence, freedom and territorial integrity of the state, support protracted world peace and friendly cooperation among peoples of all countries in the world, and oppose imperialist policies of aggression and war.

Therefore, one could ask many questions about the Chinese international media, is it really supporting China's peaceful foreign policy? Is the media reaching the world in their language? Is the name of China Central TV (CCTV) is clear to people around the world from which country is broadcasting? And can the Chinese media be more open to the world in order to support China's Foreign policy?

Meaning of the Media in This Paper

MEDIA, like *data,* is the plural form of a word borrowed directly from Latin. The singular, MEDIUM, early developed the meaning "an intervening agency, means, or instrument" and was first applied to newspapers two centuries ago. In the 1920s MEDIA began to appear as a singular collective noun, sometimes with the plural MEDIAs.

This singular use is now common in the fields of mass communication and advertising. The form MEDIA is often used as a singular to refer to a particular means of communication, as in *"The Internet is the most exciting new MEDIA since television."* People also use MEDIA with the definite article as a collective term to refer not to the forms of communication themselves so much as the communities and institutions behind them. In communication, MEDIA (singular medium) are the storage and transmission channels or tools used to store and deliver information or data. It is often referred to as synonymous with mass MEDIA or news MEDIA, but may refer to a single medium used to communicate any data for any purpose.

There are many meanings to the MEDIA. However, in this paper MEDIA is the means of communication that reaches and influence people around the world, such as radio, television, newspapers, magazines, and nowadays internet.

Chinese Media Development

Media of the People's Republic of China primarily consists of television, newspapers, radio, and magazines. Since 2000, the Internet has also emerged as an important communications medium. Since the founding of the People's Republic in 1949 and until the 1980s, almost all media in China were state-run. Independent media began to emerge at the onset of Economic Reforms, but the development within the media sector takes a slower course than in other branches. The International interest in the Chinese media appears to be rising with high expectations that the China's media will soon reform to the world standard and expectations.

Therefore, the rate of Chinese media has increased locally but internationally still need to be reformed and developed further. However, this paper does not suggest that commercialization of mass media gain political independence from the state control, especially the internet, but it should be compatible to the world powerful channels and technically robust enough to project all what China needs.

China's Foreign Policy with Strong Media

China needs to have a strong worldwide media, as strong as its booming economy in order to promote China's peaceful foreign policy. This approach was confirmed by His Excellency the Assistant Foreign Minister Mr. Zhai Jun during his discussion with me in Beijing. It is very important for the Chinese media to present the name of China and guard the interest of China's foreign policy, by reaching other nations at all levels and in all continents with major languages.

During the opening ceremony of the World Media Summit at the Great Hall of the People in Beijing, on Oct. 9, 2009 the Chinese President Hu Jintao said that the foreign media coverage had played an "important role" in telling the world about the changes in China.

The Chinese foreign policy was supported by China's national defense policy, which is based on defense that renders the so called "China threat" groundless. However, China's foreign policy in my opinion is not effectively supported by the current Chinese media policy, regardless the size of the Chinese local and national media. Therefore, a media reform is essential in order of producing a strong media that can support the foreign policy.

The Media Support to China's Intelnal Issues

The peaceful China's foreign policy need to be backed and supported by clear media goals in order to build a coherent grand strategy to support the continued building of China into a wealthy and powerful state nationally and internationally, a media that can help in further promoting the foreign policy strategy worldwide, that is able to reach the people's heart and mind promote the internal sensitive issues to the world that is seen by the foreign media as a point of debate or concern.

During the environmental protection policy lecture on 28 Sep. 2009 given by lecturer Yang Chaofei and translated by Shen Zhixiong in the NDU, I emphasized to the lecturer the importance and the role of the Chinese media in promoting the Chinese environmental awareness and efforts locally and internationally, and I gave one example that happened only a day before the lecture that "a foreign TV reporter in Beijing was interviewing Chinese citizens and other nationalities on the concerns on the environment if the Chinese people start to use air-conditioning in their houses."

Also during the lecture on East Turkistan given by Lecturer Yu Zidong and translated by Kang Jianwu had profound effect on the foreign pParticipants, especially after watching the pictures of the torture of innocent people during July 2009 disturbance in the Xinjiang province, these events and torture was hardly covered by the Chinese media for the international community through any medium, therefore, the Chinese media need to be able to tell the world about the Chinese view of the problem and to show pictures of killed people, burnt cars and shops.

The Role of China TV in China's Foreign Policy

China has one of the world's oldest civilizations and the oldest continuous civilization. It has archaeological evidence dating back over 5,000 years. It also has one of the world's oldest written language systems and is viewed as the source of many major inventions. Historically, China's name and cultural sphere has extended across East Asia and the world.

The Chinese TV had been able to reach many countries in different languages to spread the culture and values of the country. However, there are many people who know very little about China Central TV (CCTV), also CCTV means Close Circuit TV. During one of my visits to Beijing, I asked a Foreigner if he watches China TV, he said, "No, I watch CCTV sometimes!" Although nowadays the China's TV is reaching many countries but the name of "China's TV" is not there. Therefore, China need to reform the TV name and programs in order to promote the country's name and culture and support the foreign policy of China.

The Role of Newspapers in China's Foreign Policy

Soon on my arrival to Beijing on 24 August 2009, I saw a Chinese English news paper called "China Today" and without hesitation I bought it from the shop, for me as a foreigner this is great; I will get more news from the Country source. One could say that the Chinese news papers and magazines published in English are excellent way of supporting the foreign policy.

The Xinhua News Agency has done a great job in covering the country news and supporting other agencies. Xinhua is a publisher as well as a news agency, it owns more than 20 newspapers and a dozen magazines, and it prints in all six official languages of the United Nations (Chinese, English, Spanish, French, Russian, and Arabic).

Also China News Service is playing a noticeable role in China's foreign policy. It serves mainly overseas Chinese and residents of Hong Kong, Macau, Taiwan and with news offices in foreign countries, including the United States, Japan, France, and Australia. Therefore, China has strong presence in the world by its Xinhua News Agency and China News Service.

However, the global media pattern is undergoing unprecedented reforms and cooperation to meet the increasing diversity of the audience's demands. Therefore, China has to work vigorously to promote exchanges and cooperation with its worldwide colleagues and news agencies and open its news media to the private sector with special supervision. Also China needs to offer foreign media an access to useful links in order to promote own policies to the world.

The Role of Internet in China's Foreign Policy

There are now over 137 million estimated users of Internet in China, and that the number has been growing up. At the current rate of growth in China, the number of Chinese web surfers will surpass the number of Western Countries in the coming future. Therefore, the internet can be another good tool to boost the country's foreign policy and opening to the world, if it is used correctly by the content filtering firewall that the government maintains to control information and discussion of topics the government deems unworthy. In addition, active engagement in cracking down people who post negative opinions about the government and the internal issue is need to be further enhanced with a clear internet policy.

The control of internet will require China to corporate with other governments in fighting widespread piracy of movies, music, and software, especially since so many corporations are involved with companies outside China. One can say that Internet is the correct tool to reach the world and shape the international opinion if it reformed correctly and given some flexibilities.

Conclusion

According to the above the Chinese international media has developed steadily to meet the country's demand for effective role in China's foreign policy and its peaceful opening to the world. The Chinese media has supported China's foreign policy, which developed from 1949 until today and tailored to maintain a strong, independent, powerful, and united China. The China's foreign policy maintains a peaceful approach as the Chinese are not pursuing any hegemonic or warlike ambition.

China's foreign policy is supported by a peaceful defense policy that serves only to safeguard national sovereignty and territorial integrity and protect the country against aggression and separatism, China also employs comprehensive media network, however, the Chinese foreign media is still not as strong as the Country's foreign policy and not as strong as the foreign media of Western powers with view that China is becoming a superpower.

Therefore, China needs to reform the media policy in order to support the foreign policy in line with defense policy. China's improved relations with other major powers can be extended to media sector after the economic sector in the same precedence order. Finally, the Chinese media need to have a greater role to play by reforming and developing in the coming future.

Recommendations

In light of the above discussion the following is recommended:

a. It is recommended that the name of China Central TV (CCTV) be changed to "China TV," so no more "CCTV" which is also the common abbreviation for the term "Close Circuit TV" used for security purposes. Only one name "China TV" for all local and international languages. It is also suggested that each channel is identified by a numerical number such as "China TV 1, 2 etc." This recommendation will definitely export China's values and name to every corner of the world. It will establish "China" as a brand name.

b. It is recommended that more international languages are added to "China TV." More authentic anchors with fluent English expression should be added.

c. It is recommended that "China TV" is merged to ensure collaboration with popular and respected international TV Channels such as BBC, CNN and other worldwide TV channels to share important news that concern China.

d. It is recommended that "China TV" and news agencies employs experience reporters and give chance to foreign known reporters who are loyal to their job, due to their ability to win the heart and mind of the viewers, especially on sensitive issues like Taiwan, Tibet and Xinjiang.

e. It is recommended that China's media should be given more freedom to be able to present the world with facts and issues that supports China's foreign policy.

f. It is recommended that the English news paper "China Today" is widely published in different languages and circulated around the world in cooperation with other international agencies in order to reach a wider circulation and reader population around the world. For this, China will need to offer opening to the world's recognised news papers and periodical as a reciprocal gesture.

g. It is recommended that more flexibility is given to the internet users, with special supervision on the sensitive issues.

h. It is recommended that China popularize her own web sites on the net through Google and other recognized search engines to promote own view point.

i. It is recommended that China create favourable media environment through positive lobbies.

j. It is recommended that China acquire latest state of the art technology to create media effects.

4 Life in China

Culture of China

L. K. J. C. Perera
Major Gen., Sri Lankan Army

Preface

Being a most renowned and ancient civilization over 5,000 years of history in the world, China possess a great culture which undoubtedly nonparallel and unique. The Chinese culture is diverse yet a unified one which supports its present stature as a giant and becoming a super power in the globe with its cultural strength behind. Therefore it is of vital importance that who studies about China to pay attention to the culture with carefully. The aim of this research is to create an awareness to achieve this purpose.

Introduction

A land spreading over 9.6 million square kilometers in area, from the heights Qinghai-Tibet Plateau in the west, up to the Pacific Ocean in the east including vast number of towns, cities and provinces—this is China, mother of fifty six different ethnic groups and the cradle of Chinese culture. The Culture of China is one of the world's oldest, most complex cultures and multicultural cultures existing. The area in which the culture is dominant covers a large geographical region in eastern Asia with customs and traditions varying greatly. Chinese culture embodies philosophy of holism. Ancient Chinese philosophers believed that all the things of the universe exist in the state of interrelatedness, and that Heaven, Earth, and Humanity from a unified whole. This holistic philosophy influences every aspect of Chinese culture, including language, literature, art, medicine and education, as well as the daily lives of the Chinese people. Chinese culture upholds the central position of the human beings within the unity of Heaven and Earth. Imbued with a deep sense of humanism, Chinese culture attaches great importance to personal ethics and self-cultivation and thus to the pursuit of moral perfection. Advocating moderation, it seeks balance and harmony among all things. Chinese culture has persisted from its birth at the dawn of civilization until the present, in large part because of its indomitable spirit of self-improvements. According to the traditional Chinese philosophy, the universe is actively evolving, and human beings should struggle to improve themselves as well. Of course, self-improvement does not mean self-isolation. China is a nation composed of many different ethnic groups. Throughout the great sweep of history, the people of China have joined together to labor and produce, to resist foreign invaders, and to protect the unity of their country and people. Respecting other way and civilization, they have learned from their differences to create a multi-faceted, inclusive culture. From antiquity to the present, Chinese culture has embraced peace and diversity, becoming ever more prosperous and advance.

Cultural Identity

At present 56 distinct ethnic groups are identified in China. The majority amongst all these, the pre-eminent ethnic group is the Han Chinese. Throughout history, many groups have been assimilated into neighboring ethnicities or disappeared without a trace. At the same time, many within the Han identity have maintained distinct linguistic and regional cultural traditions as a deciding factor of the cultural development with linguistic development. The term *Zhonghua Minzu* has been used to describe the notion of Chinese nationalism in general. Much of the traditional cultural identity within the community has to do with distinguishing the family name.

Regional Identity

Traditional Chinese Culture covers large geographical territories with each region is usually divided into distinct sub-cultures without affecting the feelings and emotions of any identified ethnicities. Each region is often represented by three ancestral items. For example Guangdong is represented by chenpi, aged ginger and hay. Others include ancient cities like Lin'an (Hangzhou), which includes tea leaf, bamboo shoot trunk and hickory nut.

Basis of Social Structure

Historical evidence suggests that the Three Sovereigns and Five Emperors period, some form of Chinese monarch has been the main ruler. Different periods of history have different names for the various positions within society. In each imperial or feudal period similarities are evident, with the government and military officials ranking high in the hierarchy, and the rest of the population under regular Chinese law. Since the late Zhou Dynasty (1046-256 BC), traditional Chinese society was organized into a hierarchic system of socio-economic classes known as the four occupations. However, this system did not cover all social groups while the distinctions between all groups became blurred ever since the commercialization of Chinese culture in the Song Dynasty (960-1279 AD). Ancient Chinese education also has a long history; ever since the Sui Dynasty (581-618 AD) educated candidates prepared for the Imperial examinations that drafted exam graduates into government as scholar-bureaucrats. Trades and crafts were usually taught by a *shifu*. The female historian Ban Zhao designed the curriculum for the Lessons for Women in the Han Dynasty (206 BC-220 AD) and outlined the four virtues women must abide to and the scholars of the caliber of Zhu Xi and Cheng Yi expanded these. Chinese marriage and Taoist sexual practices are some of the customs and rituals found in society.

Values

The base for the existing social values is either derived from Confucianism or Taoism. The subject of which school was the most influential is always debated as many concepts such as Neo-Confucianism, Buddhism and many others have come about. Reincarnation and other rebirth concept is a reminder of the connection between real-life and the after-life. In Chinese business culture, the concept of guanxi, indicating the primacy of relations over rules, has been well documented.

Mythology and Spirituality

Chinese religion was originally oriented to worshipping the supreme God (*Shang Di*) during the Xia and Shang Dynasties, with the king and diviners acting as priests and using oracle bones. The Zhou Dynasty oriented it to worshipping the broader concept of heaven. A large part of Chinese culture is based on the notion that a spiritual world exists. Countless methods of divination have helped answer questions, even serving as an alternate to medicine. Folklores have helped fill the gap for things that cannot be explained. There is often a blurred line between myth, religion and unexplained phenomenon. While many deities are part of the tradition, some of the most recognized holy figures include *Guan Yin*, Jade Emperor and Buddha. Many of the stories have since evolved into traditional Chinese holidays. Other concepts have extended

Participants visiting China Radio International

to outside of mythology into spiritual symbols such as Door God and the Imperial guardian lions. Along with the belief of the holy, there is also the evil. Practices such as Taoist exorcism fighting mogwai and *jiang shi* with peach wood swords are just some of the concepts passed down from generations. A few Chinese fortune telling rituals are still in use today after thousands of years of refinement.

Language, Literature and Art

The development of Spoken Chinese in the first 4,000 years included both Old and Middle periods of the Chinese, after which it began to split into various dialects and languages about 1,000 years ago. In the Ming Dynasty (1368-1644) standard Mandarin was nationalized. Even so, it wasn't until the Republic of China era in the 1910s when there was any noticeable result in promoting a common unified language in China.

The ancient written standard was Classical Chinese. It was used for thousands of years by scholars and intellectuals. Until the 20th century millions of citizens especially those outside the imperial court were illiterate. Only after the May 4th Movement did the push for Vernacular Chinese begin. This allowed common citizens to read since it was modeled after the linguistics and phonology of a spoken language.

Chinese literature began with record keeping and divination on Oracle Bones. The extensive collection of books that have been preserved since the Zhou Dynasty demonstrate just how advanced the intellectuals were at one time. The era of the Zhou Dynasty is often considered as the touchstone of Chinese cultural development. The Five Cardinal Points are the foundation for almost all major studies. Concepts covered within the Chinese classic texts present a wide range of subjects including poetry, astrology, astronomy, calendar, constellations and many others. Some of the most important early texts include *I Ching* and *Shujing* within the Four Books and Five Classics. Many Chinese concepts such as *Yin* and *Yang*, *Qi*, Four Pillars of Destiny in relation to heaven and earth were all theorized in the dynastic periods.

Notable Confucianists, Taoists and scholars of all classes have made significant contributions to and from documenting history to authoring saintly concepts that seem hundred of years ahead of time. Many novels such as Four Great Classical Novels spawned countless fictional stories. By the end of the Qing Dynasty, Chinese culture would embark on a new era with Vernacular Chinese for the common citizens. Hu Shih and Lu Xun would be pioneers in modern literature.

The music of China dates back to the dawn of Chinese civilization with documents and artifacts providing evidence of a well-developed musical culture as early as the Zhou Dynasty. Some of the oldest written music dates back to Confucius's time. The first major well-documented flowering of Chinese music was for the *qin* during the Tang Dynasty, though it is known to have played a major part before the Han Dynasty.

Different forms of art have swayed under the influence of great philosophers, teachers, religious figures and even political figures. Chinese art encompasses all facets of fine art, folk art and performance art. Porcelain pottery was one of the first forms of art in the Palaeolithic period. Early Chinese music and poetry was influenced by the Book of Songs, Confucius and the Chinese poet and statesman Qu Yuan. Chinese painting became a highly appreciated art in court circles encompassing a wide variety of *Shan shui* with specialized styles such as Ming Dynasty painting. Early Chinese music was based on percussion instruments, which later gave away to string and reed instruments. By the Han Dynasty paper cutting became a new art form after the invention of paper. Chinese opera would also be introduced and branched regionally in additional to other performance formats such as variety arts.

Martial Arts

The historical background of China as one of the main birth places of Eastern martial arts. The names of martial arts were called Kung Fu or its first name *Wushu*. China also includes the home to the well-respected Shaolin Monastery and Wudang Mountains. The first generation of art started more for the purpose of survival and warfare than art. Over time, some art forms have branched off, while others have retained a distinct

Chinese flavor. Nevertheless, China has produced some of the most renowned martial artists including Wong Fei Hung and many others. The arts have also co-existed with a variety of weapons including the more standard 18 arms. Legendary and controversial moves like Dim Mak are also praised and talked about within the culture over a period of time connected to martial arts.

Fashion

Different social classes in different eras boast different fashion trends. China's fashion history covers hundreds of years with some of the most colorful and diverse arrangements. Fashionable but questionable practices such as foot binding have also been part of the culture. Many symbols such as phoenix have been used for decorative as well as economic purposes.

Architecture and Construction

The history of Chinese architecture dates back over 2,000 years and has long been a hallmark of the culture. There are certain features common to Chinese architecture, regardless of specific region or use. The most important is its emphasis on width, as the wide halls of the Forbidden City serve as an example. In contrast, Western architecture emphasize on height, though there are exceptions such as pagodas.

Another important feature is symmetry, which connotes a sense of grandeur as it applies to everything from palaces to farmhouses. One notable exception is in the design of gardens, which tends to be as asymmetrical as possible. Like Chinese scroll paintings, the principle underlying the garden's composition is to create enduring flow, to let the patron wander and enjoy the garden without prescription, as in nature herself. *Feng shui* has played an important part in structural development.

Food

The overwhelmingly large variety mainly comes from the emperors hosting a banquet of 100 dishes each meal. A countless number of imperial kitchen staff and concubines were involved in the food preparation process. Over time, many dishes became part of the everyday-citizen culture. Some of the highest quality restaurants with recipes close to the dynastic periods include Fangshan Restaurant in Beihai Park, Beijing and the Oriole Pavilion. Arguably all branches of Hong Kong eastern style or even American Chinese food are in some ways rooted from the original dynastic cuisines.

Leisure Activities

There are many games and pastimes are popular within Chinese culture. The most common game is Mah Jong. The same pieces are used for other styled games such as Shanghai Solitaire. Others include Pai Gow, Pai gow poker and other bone domino games. *Weiqi* and *Xiangqi* are some other popular games to name. Ethnic games like Chinese yo-yo are stay in as a part of the culture.

Cultural Development

The river of China culture has flowed without a break for several thousand years, Not only Chinese culture blended and integrated the culture of China's many ethnic groups, it has also maintained its vitality through contact with the outside world. Since ancient times, China has assimilated many outstanding achievements from around the world, drawing from the nomadic cultures of Central Asia, as well as the culture of Persia, India, the Arab world, Europe and Africa. At the same time, these foreign cultures were nourished and stimulated by their extensive contact with China. Cultural exchange between China and foreign counties is mutually illuminating and mutually beneficial, and has no end in sight.

The modern era has seen an influx of progressive Western culture into China, giving rise to major changes in Chinese society. At the same time, the Chinese people have demonstrated their spirit of self-reliance, diligence and practicality, drawing from the full range of modern culture to rapidly improve and develop their country.

With the growth of the Chinese economy and tourist industry, the number of Chinese citizen engaging in international travel has increased rapidly. In 1999 alone, there were over 9 million border exits from China, and over 72 million border entries. The people of China are emerging into the world, seeing other countries with their own eye, and personally experiencing foreign cultures. An even greater number of foreign tourist are visiting China, where they are able to experience first hand the fascinating culture of this ancient land, as it comes to life in the warm welcome and hospitality extended by the Chinese people.

Conclusion

The Chinese culture is consisted of intellectual pursuits, such as philosophy, politic, religious, culture and art. It also is an integral part of the everyday life of the Chinese people, expressed in areas including food, celebrations, marriage, funeral and sport. Chinese culture

Participants visiting Central University for Nationalities

stresses the harmony and respects the differences between culture and civilizations, embodying the traditional philosophy of "seeking unity in diversity." While maintaining its own foundation and centre, Chinese culture seeks to learn from other cultures, giving full play to creativity and constantly striving for betterment. Like the Changjiang and Yellow rivers, originating on the heights of the Qinghai-Tibet Plateau, Chinese culture has flowed through many twists and turns and overcome many obstacles over the years, while always maintaining its own course. It is this indomitable spirit, the ongoing quest for self-improvement that is the driving force behind China's continuing advance into the future challenging super powers of the world as an emerging global giant.

China Knew and China Seen: An Overview

Shamsul Alam
Capt., Bangladesh Navy

Introduction

Since my childhood, especially from the age my brain got little adopted to assimilate something more than as usual, I can remember that China being one of the very close neighbors has always been in my learning list. In our teachings, China very often was to be cited as a good example. Some of those I still remember and value them in my personal life. This is how, China and Chinese people initially got birth in my curious mind and subsequently with the wave of time passed, interest in myself increased to know more about the country covering its social life, culture, values, education, politics, economy, military etc.

I being a naval officer second significant chance came in my life to learn about China after joining the Navy. As Bangladesh Navy has good number of Chinese origin war ships in her inventory, therefore, I automatically got chance to command and serve in many of them during my service career. This in turn gave me an added opportunity to enjoy the first flavor of Chinese technology and their workmanship practically. More importantly, in those days, many Chinese experts used to visit my Navy with numerous training missions and I was one of the few fortunate who was lucky to get training being very near to them. During those interactions I could really observe them from close, meet with them familiarly and avail the chance to learn many aspects of their emotion, sentiments, culture, language, food habit and customs.

But I was still very thirsty to learn even more about this country and wishing a chance to visit China. My dream appeared to be true when I got selected for the "Strategic Studies Course" under the National Defense University (NDU). And the dream came into reality when I on 29 August 2009 stepped into Beijing to attend the course. Consequently, in the last few months, I have received fine opportunity to learn this country theoretically and to some extent see it practically. This added experience has encouraged me to write something about China relating the old impressions that I carried from the home and the China that I have practically seen here.

China Learnt in Bangladesh Perspective

Full Blown Relationship

Before coming to NDU, I knew China mostly from Bangladesh perspectives. The country is Bangladesh's near neighbor and its border is 100 kilometers in the north over the Himalayas. China recognized Bangladesh on 31st August, 1975. Since then China and Bangladesh had developed sound relations. The progress of the state of bilateral relationship was dramatic and China entered in a big way as a development partner in Bangladesh. The all-round and multi-faceted exchanges and cooperation in the fields of politics, economy, trade, culture, science and technology have yielded outstanding results.

Pragmatic Cooperation in All-around Way

For many commonalities and also for other political and strategic realities, China has become one of the much liked neighbors of Bangladesh. Since the establishment of diplomatic ties nearly 34 years ago between China and Bangladesh, bilateral relations have been growing smoothly on the basis of the Five Principle of Peaceful Coexistence. The head of the successive governments in Bangladesh visited China and met the Chinese leaders to strengthen the bilateral relations in every possible direction. As an example, one of the Head of the States named Hussain Muhammad Ershad alone visited China six times in 1982-1990. Similarly, Chinese Foreign Minister visited Bangladesh in 1994. And China's Premier visited Bangladesh in January 2002.

Bilateral trade has been growing steadily and experiencing impressive leap over the last few years. Following import and export data from Bangladesh justify this argument.

Year	Import (I)	Export (E)	Trade Gap	I & E
2000	18,844,712	899,587,155	880,742,443	-
2001	16,701,625	955,166,593	938,464,968	971,868,218
2002	32,358,560	1,066,368,880	1,034,010,320	1,098,727,440
2003	33,387,770	1,334,625,397	1,301,237,627	1,368,013,167
2004	57,006,736	1,906,151,212	1,849,144,476	1,963,157,948
2005	78,603,114	2,402,739,328	2,324,136,214	2,481,342,442
2006	98,838,319	3,090,250,341	2,991,412,022	3,890,886,660
2007	114,098,597	3,325,672,402	3,211,573,805	3,439,770,999
2008	132,000,000	4,548,000,000	4,416,000,000	4,680,000,000

Source: Collected from Bangladesh Embassy, Beijing (data given in US$)

China and Bangladesh have always have had an amiable relationship in the defense sector as well. A defense co-operation agreement was signed between Bangladesh and China during the visit of Bangladesh Prime Minister, Begum Khaleda Zia's visit to China from December 23 to 27, 2002. This new agreement was signed to help institutionalize the existing accords in defense sector and also to rationalize the existing piecemeal agreements to enhance cooperation in training, maintenance and some areas in production.

China Seen with a Comprehensive View

China's Culture: Past to Present

Ancient Culture. China is one of the oldest civilizations in the world. Chinese people had unique and glorious culture with very magnificent and delightful arts and customs. The family set-up was patriarchal, with emphasis on filial duty, respect to elders and dispute settlement by them. The society was basically hierarchical, like all ancient societies, with the mandarins or learned men at the peak, followed by farmers, artisans, merchants, traders, bankers, soldiers and lastly servants. It is seen that the Confucian philosophy stressing the harmony, respect, and education had mostly embraced the Chinese culture and way of life. Although, over the centuries many other philosophies came into being but ultimately Confucian's outlook mostly made its way. China's scientific glory was also reckonable. The world was benefited by many great inventions that originated from ancient China. Compass, printing machinery and gunpowder were few of the significant inventions for which Chinese are still credited.

Modern Culture: A New Outlook

Modern China is being ornamented by modern apartment complexes and towering high-rise buildings as well as modern style homes. However, tradition still lingers in all Chinese households and societies all over the world. In older neighborhoods, rural mud and straw houses can still be seen, and in rural areas the traditional way of life are still very alive. And although the way of life now is much modernized, traditional values of family importance and reputation still is felt by all families.

Today, the Chinese live in smaller family units, usually only with parents and children, and sometimes grandparents. Almost all adults have a job, male or female. Today, girls as well as boys are valued. Women now do many kinds of work outside the home. Many young households share in the shopping, housecleaning, cooking, and caring for the children to show that they believe the sexes are equal. Relationships have become more democratic as parents no longer expect their children to show unquestioning obedience. As for marriage, young people today generally choose their own marriage partners on the basis of shared interests and mutual attraction. However, parents still play a role in arranging some marriages, especially in rural areas.

In the last century, the Chinese have adopted Western ideas and philosophies. After the British defeated the Chinese in 1842, the Chinese questioned whether they were better than the Westerners. As the European Countries began to establish their spheres of influence in China, many of the Chinese people realized the need to adopt Western techniques and ideas. Sun Yat-Sen wanted to turn China's government into a democracy pointing out that some of the ideas of Western democracy were similar to ideas of Confucianism. In 1912, the Republic of China was established, and the Chinese elected Sun Yat-sen as President. Due to civil war, the Republic fell apart. When the Chinese Communists took over in 1949, the Chinese philosophy changed drastically. The Chinese masses looked upon economic equality with great favor. Between 1949 and 1952, there was a virtual role reversal in Chinese society. The roots of this phenomenon lie in the rise of Mao Zedong and his communism ideology. Communist ideology embedded with Chinese characteristics being practiced in politics and social life until now.

China's Historical Legacy and Standing up

Painful Past: China had painful past. Traditionally we find that throughout much of the country's history some sort of monarchic rule had prevailed over the masses. The country had been ruled by many different dynasties throughout the course of time. Particularly an important element in the formation of China's modern identity has been the legacy of the country's "humiliation" at the hands of foreigners. Out of those, China's defeat in the Opium Wars in the mid-nineteenth century is most significant.

Standing Up: During the past hundred years, the citizens of the entire country, suffering under the oppression of foreigners were unanimous in their demand that the national humiliation should be retaliated, and the state be made stronger. Dr. Sun Yat-sen who was titled as "China's George Washington" could make the first breakthrough and save the country from the feudal rules. And finally when the People's Republic of China was founded in 1949, China took his first wobbly steps to firmly stand up, as Mao Zedong famously declared, "Ours will no longer be a nation subject to insult and humiliation. We...have stood up."

China's Economic Rise: a Chronological Portrayal

The Great Leap Forward: After the communist assumed the power, the first attempt to improve the economic condition of PRC started with the plan the "Great Leap Forward." This name was given to the Second Five-year Plan from 1958-1962. It was an economic and social plan to use China's vast population in transforming China into a modern, industrialized communist society. The plan did not work as per expectation resulting in gruesome consequences, including mass starvation. It caused millions of deaths and widespread economic dislocation. Later Chinese called this plan the "Great Leap Backward."

Economic Reforms: The economic reforms that were introduced by the great leader Deng Xiaoping in the late seventies have transformed the Chinese economy and produced a period of spectacular growth. The magnitude of economic growth is quite unprecedented in the world history. China's Gross Domestic Product (GDP) has grown at a rate of at least nine per cent per year for more than 25 years, the fastest growth rate for a major economy in recorded history. In 2005, China became the fourth largest economy in the world in terms of nominal value ranking after United States of America (USA), Japan and Germany and the second largest when measured by purchasing power parity with a GDP of US$ 8.8 trillion in 2006. In the same period of time it has moved three hundred million people out of poverty and raised the average Chinese person's income by eight times.

Economic Stride: Few nations have changed as fast or as dramatically as China since the 1970s. In 2008, China's GDP is estimated to exceed 24 trillion yuan, up 11 percent over 2007. According to an economic survey published by the Organization for Economic Cooperation and Development (OECD) in 2005, Chinese exports grew at an average rate of 6% since the mid-1980s. Although China's export growth was affected by a global slowdown, the country overtook the US to become the world's second largest exporter by end-2007. The OECD had predicted that China would become the world's largest exporter by 2010. In the 1970s, the Chinese government started reforming its economic policies and

Group photo of the participant with Hui people

adopted market socialism. This led to an upsurge in the growth of the country's private sector, resulting in China becoming a major player in the international market. The impact of the liberalization of Chinese trade and economic policies is exhibited in the subsequent statistics:

Measured using Purchasing Power Parity (PPP), China's GDP reached $7.8 trillion in 2008, making it the third largest economy after US and Japan. China is a strong emerging economy, with 11.4% GDP growth in 2007 and 9% in 2008. The country's global trade surged past $2.4 trillion in 2008. The increase of GDP from 1990 to 2007 is shown in the graph below:

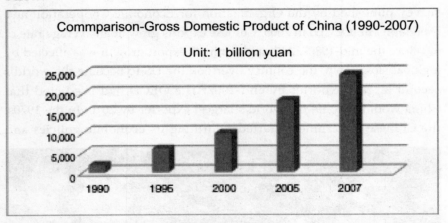

Source: http://www.stats.gov.cn/tjsj/ndsj/2007

China's Foreign Relations—a New Approach

Mao and Deng Era: In recent years, China has begun to take a less confrontational, more sophisticated, more confident and at times more constructive approach towards regional and global affairs. In contrast to a decade ago, the world's most populous country now largely works within the international system. It has embraced much of the current constellation of international institutions, rules and norms as a means to promote its national interests. In a sense, the evolution of China's foreign policy begun under Deng, who, as supreme leader initiated China's first major diplomatic transformation by launching the "reform and opening" movement in the late 1970s. Prior to Deng, Mao's foreign policy was noted for its language, strong opposition to the super powers (the USA and the USSR) and close association with developing countries, relating isolation from international or organizations, and economic autarky.

Deng took China in the right direction. To facilitate economic modernization at home, he promoted engagement with the international community. China expanded its international profile by significantly increasing its participation in inter-governmental and non-governmental organization, especially, financial ones, and China gradually begun to come out from isolation from international community. Deng's transformation was only partial, however, and Chinese participation in the international community remained thin during his tenure. The processes of forging foreign policy under Deng also remain highly centralized and China's diplomatic corps remained under trained and inexperienced.

Relation with Other Countries: In recent years, China's leaders have been regular travellers to all parts of the globe, and it has sought a higher profile in the UN through its permanent seat on the United Nations Security Council and other multilateral organizations. Closer to home China has made efforts to reduce tensions in Asia; its relations with its Asian neighbours have become stable during the last decades of the twentieth century. It has contributed to stability on the Korean Peninsula, cultivated a more cooperative relationship with members of the Association of Southeast Asian Nations (ASEAN) and participated in the ASEAN Regional Forum. In 2005 the "ASEAN Plus Three" countries together with India, Australia and New Zealand held the inaugural East Asia Summit (EAS). Relations have improved with Vietnam since a border war was fought with one-time close ally Vietnam in 1979. A territorial dispute with its Southeast Asian neighbours over islands in the South China Sea remains unresolved, as does another dispute in the East China Sea with Japan. Taiwan's merger with Mainland China is a question that seems to have no immediate answer.

China's Sense of Equality and Building up Harmonious World: As per the foreign policy mentioned above as well as relation with other countries China does not display any hegemonic attitude towards other countries. Its foreign policy expresses, "China opposes hegemonic posture and in favour of preserving world peace." China believes that all countries, big or small, strong or weak, rich or poor, are equal members of the international community. Countries should resolve their disputes and conflicts peacefully through consultations and not resort to the use or threat of force. Nor should they interfere in others' internal affairs under any pretext. China never imposes its social system and ideology on others, nor allows other countries to impose theirs on it." In this connotation hegemonic behaviour is unlikely from China in any form.

Enormous Domestic Progress

Spirited modern China has now reached to a stage of mature walking. The country has emerged as a great economic power in Asia-Pacific. It has enjoyed in average 9.8% annual economic growth over last many years. According to some estimates, the proportion of the population living in rural poverty has fallen from 75% to 4% in the last two decades. Infrastructural development around whole country is going on in a very appreciable pace. China recently has taken up a policy which is praised as unique in the history of mainland reforms. This policy has appeared in two parts: one is called a "New Socialist Countryside" and the other is the scheme to increase infrastructure spending in poor rural areas. The new initiative signifies the effort of the Hu Jintao administration to re-chart the course of development from urban areas to the rural. In addition, China is taking efforts to minimize toxic gasses to ensure its sustainable development. Authority is also trying to give due attention to make development in the disturbed provinces so as to earn the hearts of minorities thereby, mitigate further troubles.

China's Military Reforms with Defensive Posture

The People's Liberation Army (PLA) the largest force in the world with more than 2.3 million active duty troops. The PLA also encompasses the Chinese navy, air force and strategic missile forces commonly known as the Second Artillery Corps. China is undergoing a massive effort to improve and modernize its military technology, equipments and power projection capabilities. With a rapidly growing defense budget over the years, China is poised to have an organized, well-trained and well-equipped military power by 2020. But, all these forces have been developed with an "Active Defense Posture" to safe guard sovereignty and territorial integrity only.

China's Future: a Rational Analysis

China will Continue to Develop. From 1949, a significant part of China's effort has been to create a new national identity basing on the dream of restoring the country's territorial integrity and development. China's development has been commented by one of the western analysts as, "Good-bye Chinese humiliation, hello China Number One: at the Games and in technology, manufacturing and art and science and everything the West is good at." Since starting to open up and reform its economy in 1978, China has averaged 9.4 percent annual GDP growth, one of the highest growth rates in the world. It accounts for four per cent of the world economy and has foreign trade worth $851 billion—the third-largest national total in the world. 12 years ago, China barely had mobile telecommunications services. Now it has more than 300 million mobile-phone subscribers, more than any other nation. As end of 2009, nearly 348 million people there had access to the Internet. China's economy is expected to be double the size of Germany's by 2010 and to overtake Japan's, currently the world's second largest, by 2020.

Good Foreign Policy will Pay Dividend. China has unswervingly pursued an independent foreign policy of peace. The basic objectives of the policy centre on safeguarding national independence and state sovereignty, and creating an international environment favourable to its reform, opening and modernization efforts, as well as maintaining world peace and promoting common development. The collective changes in the content, character and execution of China's foreign policy over the years represent an important evolution from her narrow and reactive approach to global affairs in the 1980s or before. China's new diplomacy is sure to continue which will present US and Asian policy makers with both opportunities and challenges. Taking the advantage of spectacular economic rise, China will try to go ahead with her economic diplomacy to influence the nations keeping the military aspirations aside.

Non Hegemonic Posture will be the Bridge of Mutual Trust. China is economically rising. It is said that when nations are weak, they cite principles, when they are strong, they invoke artillery. Will this dictum be true of economically prosperous and militarily powerful China? Therefore, a major question would be "Will, a strong and powerful China, be tempted to project its military power outside its borders and overseas?" To answer this question it can be said that history is the mirror to measure China's attitude. Throughout the history, China was never hegemonic and even until now the country is displaying itself as a peaceful nation. So, such kind of anticipation can be termed as a kind of wrongly perceived appreciation that does not have any basis.

Conclusion

A unique nation endowed with long civilization, had suffered a lot, and now has set out a goal to build a prosperous country to present happy life for the people. The economic resurgence of China has resulted from clearly defined goals and pragmatic policies laid down by the government. The economy started growing only after the adoption of the policy of Reform and Opening-up. Highest values of Chinese civilization, lessons learned from the history and the prestige of the state have brought the Chinese people to the present state.

China's peaceful posture is now quite evident in the world stage. Her effort to build a happy home through domestic development is quite appreciable. Simultaneously, she is also seeking stability in the international environment. "With the cooperation oriented foreign policy Beijing is endeavoring to improve its relationship with all its neighbors.

Her military ambition is maintaining defensive profile too. China's foreign policy approach is also aimed at achieving a "harmonious world" embodying four points like, "first is to uphold common security; second, persist in mutually beneficial cooperation to realize common prosperity; third, uphold the spirit of inclusiveness for a harmonious world; fourth, uphold a policy to promote the reform of the United Nations."

China's effort towards building a harmonious world characterized by sustained peace and common prosperity is also appreciable. This is going to be a glorious example for the mankind if can be accomplished successfully. Of course, in this hegemony world, this is not going to be an easy task. However, as the tranquility and harmony accords with the fundamental interests of the mankind, it is expected that all peace loving nations of the world, under the umbrella of China will work hand in hand with unremitting efforts to shape the world's common future.

How is the Chinese Culture Seen in Some Latin American Countries?

Manuel Mendible
Col., Venezuelan Army

Introduction

In many countries in latin america when they are hearing the name "China" immediately located in our minds people thin, white, with eyes almost closed, very friendly, always smiling, with many children, owners of small restaurants, warehouses, etc.

But really they do not know the true from Chinese that in almost all countries have their ambassadors of the world, so who are very humble and honest living with us.

Below, I offer a brief narration, very personal, that was what it meant for me to understand a Chinese, before come and discover this great and beautiful country.

How is the Chinese Culture Seen in Some Latin American Countries?

For many of us, when we heard the word "China," once a person we imagined short, thin, pale, her eyes almost closed, hard-working, always smiling, with many children, who in our case for example (Venezuela), on sunday (in small towns) many stores, do not offer its services to the community because is Sunday and so not work, but if any store, small market or supermarket, if the owner is Chinese, probably that store is open.

At Christmas and New Year celebration (December), or when we have some important activities where we want to use fireworks, there is no better option for us to go where the Chinese to acquire the best and the lowest price.

If we want to buy some electronic equipment, whether PC, CD player, some TVs, etc., there is no better consultant to us than a Chinese, as happens when these damaged, there is not better option than Chinese technicians.

But not the same thought or defining the personality of a Chinese, being in our country, that coming to China and met in person, is that what I want to reflect continued across these very humble and sincere words of what he learned from China that I did not know in details.

The biggest impression that took me to get to China, the plane was landing and when I arrive at terminal number 3, at the Beijing airport, was the organization, neatness, order and speed with which I did the process of immigration to the country, it was something very nice, only with the failure to answer a questionnaire, seek views with rejection, abuse, etc., as is well known in other countries in America, quite the contrary, smiling faces, good manners, very helpful, care, I felt the time of arrival in China. When I left the airport, my perspectives were different, believed to see many cycles, few vehicles, nor was it, what we saw was huge highways, cleanliness everywhere, excellent care of vegetation, as well as the great state of the highways, huge buildings, many people and vehicles, but all this coupled, much order and organization.

China, the second largest nation, is second only to Russia in terms of size and is larger than all Europe and Oceania; it takes a quarter of the territorial extent of Asia and approximately one twelfth of the area from around the world.

Another important factor that distinguishes our dialect or language is the Chinese calligraphy, a rare and exotic flower in the history of civilization and the same without a jewel in eastern culture. From the visual perspective, it can be compared to the painting for its ability to arouse emotions through the rich variety of forms and traits. Abstract art as manifests itself in all its purity, rhythm and musical harmony. All added to a practical part.

A visit to the China's pharmacy comes to become like entering into a museum of natural science in miniature. Ready in strict order of little box rows, we can find the most variety of animal products, vegetable and mineral, each with a particular purpose.

The preparation of a recipe for a Chinese doctor is a process to behold. The pharmaceutical selects few of the hundreds of ingredient that keeps on his shelves. The patient takes to the house, the cook up transformed into a kind of soup and drinks it.

The Chinese have their own system of classification of diseases which differ widely from occidental. It supports the philosophical doctrine that Chinese medicine is that man lives between heaven and earth, and is itself a miniature universe.

Aside from the medicines, another form of treatment often used in Chinese medicine is acupuncture. Its history goes back to times before the appearance of Chinese writing but did not reach its full development until after the Han Dynasty. Its theoretical basis is in the regulation of qi—

flow of vital energy. *Qi* flows by the body through the system of main and secondary channels (Jing luo). At certain points of these channels, can be placed acupuncture needles or artemisa burn china (ai cao) moxibustion through, for the purpose of resolving the imbalance in the flow and concentrate *qi* self cure capacity of the body in the places adequate. In 1980, the World Health Organization issued a list of 43 kinds of pathology on be effective acupuncture treatment. Long ago the use of acupuncture as anesthesia or surgical process for labor without pain stopped being a novelty.

As to the architecture, China is characterized by distribute space unit rectangular coming together to form a whole. The rectangular shape was also used in Greek temples, but the effect was of austerity. Chinese style, on the contrary, rectangles of different sizes combine in different positions and agree to the importance of the organization of the set. Stand out clearly different levels and elements. The result is an impressive exterior appearance, but at the same time dynamic and mysterious, very interesting all these comments.

In the traditional houses, for example, the rooms are assigned according to the position of each person in the family hierarchy. Head of household occupy the bedroom, older members of this family living in the back and the youngest in the left and right wings, the oldest at the left and in the right the youngest.

Chinese architecture is also characterized by use of structure of wood beams and columns and a wall that surrounds adobe three sides of the building. The gate and main window is located on the front. Using the Chinese take the wood as one of its main building materials from thousands of years ago. Wood is the life and this is the main idea that Chinese culture, in its many manifestations, trying to communicate. This feature has survived to this day.

In the Chinese temples find a wide range of architectural styles. Religions to which is enshrined these temples are mainly Buddhism, Taoism and ancestral religion and traditional but they all share a common structure.

Participants visiting Capital Museum

The New Year holidays and other traditional Chinese festivals are moments of joy and celebration. Many of these traditional customs and shows part of competition and acts made in connection with the Chinese New Year festivals and other, and have been passed from generation to generation. The most common may be dragon dance and lion dance.

The dragon inspires a deep respect for the Chinese, as it is symbol of power, dignity and good luck. The mask of the dragon and the body to be employed in the dance can be golden color, green, jasper or red fire. The dance can be interpreted both day and night. In the latter case, it often is preceded by a person with a torch to light the procession. A giant dragon may be 120 feet long, total weight of the head and body is more than 100 kg. The body is golden and brilliant and need them more than 100 men to take good fornos.

Lion dance also has a long history. Dance is accurate fewer participants. Head and body of leon are easier to prepare and the time required for its performance is small. All this makes that you can contemplate virtually anywhere during Chinese New Year and other parties. It usually takes two people to control the lion: one for the other for head and tail. Sometimes a third person involved takes some silk flowers or will cover with a mask representing and smiling Buddha holding a fan of banana leaf. This causes the lion character, adding more and a note of joy to the festive atmosphere.

Among the oldest party of China are the Spring Festival and the Lantern Festival, the first is called before the New Year festivities because it corresponds to first day of the lunar calendar that followed the Chinese. As the solar calendar, this feast falls between late January and early February.

In ancient times, China had a highly developed agriculture and such party concerned, obviously, to their agricultural producers. To start the year, people made offerings to the divinities of the heaven and earth and ancestors, praying for a rich harvest of grains and wish that made all doing well.

During the party, the nicely people likes decorate their homes with engravings representing New Year and congratulations festive scene. People also love distic paste spring to both sides of the door he hoped for a happy life, write them are greeting with brush phrases red paper strip.

The night before the spring, the night that is old is the most important moment of the family reunion in the middle of tasted delicious dinner. Then, sit down and talk family or hit to break the dawn, this is called "ensuring during New Year Eve." The next morning exchange visits are among friends or relatives to wish happy New Year.

National character other party to be held in China is the Lantern Festival, the conclusion of the first month day 15 of lunar and matching first full moon night after the first party. In this party there many folklore programs such as parades of stilt walking and dragon dances.

A typical meal at this event is the ball of sticky rice with sweet filling or meat. As they are compact and round, they represent the solid family union.

Night of this festival, organized in many cities, lamps displays and riddles enjoy complimentary evening. Written on paper, they will hang on the da lights and place your solution to grant awards. In the field is celebrated with fireworks, parades of strides, swing sets and yangge (a folk dance popular in the north China).

Culinary art in China has a long history and worldwide fame; styles vary by their differences of area, climate, products, and customs. Testing in China Chinese delicacies is an unforgettable experience, is totally different than what I used to see in our country.

The table: a time to eat is available 3 glasses on the table, one great for beer or water medium for one white or red wine and liquor for the small one, being the most popular of the mao-tai China factory is based on sorghum. The wang chao is the traditional drink that is drunk before a meal, typically, is based shark fin soup, ganz in soy sauce, chicken noodle dishes special.

In Latin America we used to eat Chinese food, which is mixed with some food ingredients that we use for the preparation of our traditional food, however, here in China, is the real Chinese food, where there are many varieties of plants, vegetables, and meat. But one of the most exquisite dishes I've ever tasted in my life is the famous duck rotisserie.

There is a wide variety of sandwiches here in China, have different shapes and flavors and taste, the most popular are prepared in the south with rice and wheat flour, in the north, in Beijing, preferred sweet taste in Guangzhou, the western flavor and in Suzhou, diversity, the best sandwiches are north: *shaomai* dumplings, cone *aiwowo*, cream of bean, *goubuli* pie, etc. And the south: crab ovarian dumplings, cake with seeds, soup chicken oil dumplings, dumplings of five seeds, ravioli crab meat, rice balls, etc.

In regard to the marriage, traditionally, Chinese people avoid marrying people with the same family name, but this has changed a bit, with the pa-tzu (eight Chinese characters). For traditionally minded, eight characters indicating the support by year, month, day and time of birth. Far as I know, if the marriage by the storm surge shaping are sons can only have up to two children. But in Latin America we can see clearly that the Chinese have up to six children or more in some cases.

In the past, here in China for delivering a groom's parents empower the woman he wanted to marry, consisted usually expensive gifts or money. But today many families simply accept the more abstract benefits of the future son that have a good education or own strong employment prospects. In Latin America, we can see Chinese people getting marriages with Latins, but does not exist in any part.

Chinese today use equals clothing that is used in America, Europe or any other part of the West. The respect for the elderly people is the same or maybe here is a little remarkable that in our countries.

In Venezuela we are used to greet men women with a kiss on the cheek, so do the women with other women, parents to their children, grandchildren and vice versa here in China, the greeting is conducted by shaking hands, not be used kisses on the cheek, or lean the bodies how we see in some other Asian cultures.

Here are some of the most common characteristics of Chinese culture, totally different than we thought there was being in our country, just enough to come and see.

Conclusions

To know a country, it is not enough just read in a book about their history, culture and customs, today, despite that many methods exist to meet a country without travel or be present at the same, but it must be done and be in person to learn and discover it directly and effectively throughout its history, people and customs.

Very personally, what you can learn in detail of a country is not written in books or can be watched on TV programme, you must be there and experience it.